"One of Ron Cassie's vignettes in *If You Love Baltimore, It Will Love You Back* is titled 'The Polaroid Guy,' and that's exactly who Cassie is. Only instead of film, Cassie uses the page. His empathetic approach, concern for justice, and keen journalist's eye have been honed over years on the Baltimore beat. As Cassie crisscrosses the city, what develops is an image of an urban landscape and its people in a constant state of rehab—in every sense of the word—that's emblematic of American cities today."

> — Gregg Wilhelm, founder and director emeritus, Baltimore's CityLit Project, director of Creative Writing, George Mason University

"Nicolás Ramos, writes Ron Cassie in this anthology of survival in Crabtown, arrived in the U.S. as a teenager to pick broccoli on a farm in Texas before winding his way to Baltimore. Cassie, a reporter with literary instincts worthy of Nelson Algren—eye, ear, and heart full of soul—didn't begin writing about Charm City until he was 42. But oh, the harvest he has gleaned since in this most improbable of cities. It's all here, 171 stories worth in what I trust will be the first of many books Cassie will deliver as his roots sink deeper into the hard red clay along the shores of the Patapsco."

> — Rafael Alvarez, former city desk reporter at *The Baltimore Sun*, short story writer, staff writer for the first three seasons of *The Wire*, author of *Basilio Boullosa Stars in the Fountain of Highlandtown*

"An expansive and yet microscopically detailed portrait of a city—painted with love. Cassie's intimate portrayal of Baltimore's residents, their triumphs and tragedies and work-a-day lives serves as a gorgeous rebuttal to President Donald Trump's tweeted dismissal of Baltimore City as a "disgusting," "very dangerous and filthy place." As Studs Terkel investigated the wage-earner in *Working* through scrupulous listening, Cassie similarly attends to the tenor of residents' experiences;

the composite result is a paean to a rust-belt city . . . in all its quirky glory."

— Karen Houppert, former *Village Voice* and *Baltimore City Paper* editor, author of *Chasing Gideon: The Elusive Quest for Poor People's Justice*, associate director, Master of Arts in Writing Program, at Johns Hopkins University

"When local papers, politicians, police officers, and other people who frequent Baltimore collectively decided to demonize 'squeegee kids'— Ron Cassie stepped up and delivered a dose of humanity, humanity that many other outlets ignored. Cassie could've taken the easy route and sided with most publications, but instead he did what was right. He met the kids, brilliantly documented their reality, and crafted a beautiful story that the mainstream desperately needed. Cassie is a gem. His writing is extremely urgent, necessary, and we need more writers like him."

— D. Watkins, *New York Times* bestselling author of *The Cook Up* and *We Speak for Ourselves*, editor at large at *Salon*, University of Baltimore writing professor

"An essential addition to your Baltimore bookshelf, Ron Cassie's collected vignettes of city life provide a master class in the art of feature writing. In *If You Love Baltimore, It Will Love You Back*, Cassie gifts the reader with vivid sketches of the region's hidden heroes, snubbed landmarks, and unheeded history. From the father and son duo who taught generations of city kids to swim in their backyard pool to the ex-drug dealer persuading a new generation to turn away from violence, from mourners looking to salvage a piece of the defunct Sparrows Point steel works to kids trying to make a buck washing car windows at city intersections, Cassie reveals both the richness and pathos of life in our town."

— Deborah Rudacille, author of *Roots of Steel: Boom and Bust in an American Mill Town* and Professor of the Practice, UMBC

IF YOU LOVE BALTIMORE, IT WILL LOVE YOU BACK

171 Short But True Stories

IF YOU LOVE BALTIMORE, IT WILL LOVE YOU BACK

171 Short But True Stories

Ron Cassie

Apprentice
House Press
Loyola University Maryland

First Edition

Casebound ISBN: 978-1-62720-308-1
Paperback ISBN: 978-1-62720-309-8
Ebook ISBN: 978-1-62720-310-4

Printed in the United States of America

Design by Courtney Kenny
Editorial development by Sofia Barr
Promotion plan by Jacqueline Kohaut
Cover photographs by John Patterson, Ron Cassie, Mike Morgan, Erin Douglas, Jonathan Dimes
Back cover author photo by Sarah Cassie

Apprentice House Press
Loyola University Maryland

Apprentice House Press
Loyola University Maryland
4501 N. Charles Street
Baltimore, MD 21210
410.617.5265
www.ApprenticeHouse.com
info@ApprenticeHouse.com

*For my mother, the daughter of two immigrants, who loved people,
simple pleasures, and good stories.*

Contents

Introduction

A few weeks after reading that the former Bethlehem Steel mill at Sparrows Point would be scrapped for parts, I learned Hilco Trading, the liquidator who had purchased the massive ghost town in a bankruptcy sale, was offering bus tours for prospective buyers. Diligent, curious reporter that I am, I signed up and went on the first available date, which turned out to be a frigid, January Monday morning.

I didn't intend to buy anything. Generally, I have little need for cranes, industrial machinery, and 200-ton transport trucks. I didn't tell Hilco or anyone I was writing a story. Did not know that I would, but since I'm a senior editor at *Baltimore* magazine, I stuck a notebook in my back pocket. I only knew that I wanted to roam around the grounds of the once-greatest steel mill in the world and try to get a feel for the place—what it had been and what it had meant to those who made the steel that built the Empire State Building, Golden Gate Bridge, our own Bay Bridge, and a thousand other iconic American structures. I hoped—a hunch, I guess—that I might come across an old union guy who'd spent his working life alongside the legendary, 32-story L Blast Furnace and wanted one last look at the place. Representatives from a small Colorado steel manufacturer were on the bus when I got there. So was an executive from a Japanese steelmaker.

I was grateful there was coffee, and that the corporate buses were well-heated. A retired local steelworker named Lawrence Knachel was also on board, staring out a window. Knowing the whole place was being sold off and shuttered for good, he told me that he couldn't stay away. "I came here in 1962, right out of Kenwood High School, into an apprentice program," he said. "We had 27 softball teams. Shipping side used to play the steel side after work."

1

Later, inside a drafty repair shop, another former steelworker, who labored inside the hot tin mill for 39 years, manned a security post, earning a few last, non-union wages before the place was completely barren. A Midwestern manufacturing rep asked him what had caused the plant's closure. The ex-steelworker gave the question some thought and shook his head inside a yellow hard hat. "Everyone has a different reason," he said finally. "I'll tell you, though, the other day I got home, and my wife was crying: 'My grandfather worked there all those years,' she says. 'My dad worked there all those years, you worked there all those years, and now you're [there] shutting it all down.'"

I can't speak for anyone else, but there was nowhere on the Earth I'd have rather been that morning.

Same thing when I grabbed a stool at the counter for the last shift at the Bel-Loc Diner in Parkville, whose regular customers over the years had included Colts and Orioles legends like Johnny Unitas and Luis Aparicio. "We're like a lot of the waitresses," said one longtime patron, sharing a booth and final breakfast with his wife and sister-in-law, both of whom grew up down the street from the Bel-Loc. "We don't know where we are going to go now."

I felt that way when I ventured to the legendary East Baltimore basketball court known as The Dome to catch a summer high school tournament. The annual event had recently been renamed after the promising 6-foot-8 forward John Crowder, who should've been playing, but had been fatally shot three years earlier. One of his childhood friends won the tourney MVP. And I felt that way, too—nowhere on Earth I'd rather have been—when I met a real-life Rosie the Riveter who'd moved up from a North Carolina farm at 19 to make planes for the war and then never left Baltimore. And when I rode along with a 50-something-year-old cyclist who delivered Meals on Wheels lunches and dinners by bike, and the time I hung out for an afternoon with Vander Pearson, the decades-long owner of Pearson's Florist at the corner of North Charles Street and North Avenue, which earned its 15 minutes of fame on *The Wire*. (Baltimore native, former rowhouse neighbor, and CityLit founder Gregg Wilhelm described my pursuits here as a kind of "narrative archaeology" and I like that concept.)

On and on. For a decade now, I've observed this city, its past and present, up close. From the inside out. It's been my beat, and my not-so-secret-indulgence. As I've continued, somehow I still find these stories, or they find me, every few weeks. I'm often burned out, over-whelmed with deadlines, teaching, and my own life, and then someone shares the ordinary, yet intimate details of their life, and my internal pilot light flickers on again. Suddenly, there comes the need to under-stand their story more fully, deeply, and then synthesize and translate it for others. For me, too. And maybe them. In the process, each time, I learn more about this city, which I call my spiritual home, myself, and my life as well. How do you express gratitude for people who open up themselves and their lives to you like that? (For the record, I grew up in Allentown, Pennsylvania, next door to the original Bethlehem Steel mill, and coming to Baltimore in my early 20s, there was an immediate sense I belonged.)

In this collection are short, personal encounters with the likes of U.S. Rep. Elijah Cummings, U.S. Senator Barbara Mikulski, and Hall-of-Fame pitcher Jim Palmer. My favorite vignettes, however, take place around people and places few have probably ever heard of, like the graffiti artist Nether working on a desolate street like North Bruce in West Baltimore; city native James Reid, who created the statue of Billie Holiday in Upton, and Marvin Thorpe II, who, along with his father, since deceased, taught an estimated 15,000 kids, nearly all Black (and therefore six times more likely to drown), to swim at their backyard pool in Windsor Mill.

Each story was published in some form over a 10-year period in *Baltimore* magazine. Some have been expanded. Others were culled from longer stories. Many have been reworked and updated. Nearly all are told in a real time, fly-on-the-wall reporting style. None are tied to any kind of breaking news. None of the stories were assigned to me. All began with feeling that there might be something fun or unexpected—or simply someone interesting—where I was headed. These adventures, and that's what they usually felt like, were my chances to explore the cracks and crannies of Baltimore and the people who live here and have lived here.

Most of the stories began as part of a regular monthly series I took over when I came to *Baltimore* magazine after *Urbanite* magazine, where I'd served as editor, folded. At the time, there was a section in *Baltimore* magazine called The Chatter, which generally included a couple of short pieces each month, largely built around popular happenings in the city—the opening of a casino or a celebrity appearance. I saw The Chatter as an opportunity to go a bit off the grid. Spend time with a pigeon racer from Linthicum, for example. A taxidermist, a sign painter, and the squeegee kids. And sure, every once in a while, an Elvis impersonator, former Pimlico jockey, ex-Playboy bunny, and Miss Hon contestant. Along the way I got to see "the Duchess" in action—Hoehn Bakery's 1927-built brick-oven hearth—watch a group of Black girls from Baltimore meet Michelle Obama, witness the Orioles play a game before an empty stadium, march 10 miles with anti-violence protestors from one end of North Avenue to the other, and run 26.2 miles around the city as part of the Baltimore Marathon.

Together, these vignettes became something akin to a jigsaw puzzle, each new piece making the picture of Baltimore and its inhabitants a little clearer and a little more complex at the same time. They are about the intrinsic character of the city, its sense of place, and the meaning people give to it.

After about five years in the original Chatter format, I'd begun to feel like it was time to break out into something new. Initially, we added a photo and an extra column. Later, we changed the format to its current form—from three very short vignettes to a single, longer piece, which allowed me to go deeper into stories. We also moved it to the back page of the magazine. We changed the name, too, from The Chatter to You Are Here, a nod to the in-the-moment feel of these vignettes.

To me, these stories are more akin to micro-nonfiction than anything in traditional journalism. Although, unlike micro-nonfiction, these are not memoirs or essays but simply short stories about other people's lives, people deeply connected to this city like I am.

My friend and former *Baltimore Sun* reporter and author Rafael Alvarez once said, "No matter what they put up in this town, it was built upon something that makes for a better story: Burke's beneath the chicken fat of a Royal Farms at Light and Lombard; orthodox synagogues and the bones of organ grinder monkeys beneath the new restaurants of Little Italy, heavy metals in the soil beneath Harbor East."

Mary Rizzo, an American Studies Ph.D. and past co-editor of *The Public Historian* journal, once told me that while every city claims to be a "city of neighborhoods," Baltimore actually is. Partly, that's because it remains a largely an insular place, and out of such insular places come eccentric characters, Billie Holiday and William Donald Schaeffer to name two, and particular culture obsessions, such as duckpin bowling, painted screens, and roller skating at the Shake & Bake recreation center.

If nothing else, I think this collection proves both Alvarez's and Rizzo's words ring as true as ever.

"[A single story] makes recognition of our equal humanity difficult. It emphasizes how we are different, rather than how we are similar . . . I've often thought it is impossible to engage properly with a place or a person, without engaging with all of the stories of that place or that person."

— Chimamanda Ngozi Adichie, Nigerian author

1. The Polaroid Guy

Jim Lucio opens a shoe box, searches, and then pulls out a photo he took nearly two decades ago. It's a Polaroid of a teenage girl wearing an orange bikini, floating atop a blue swimming pool, her white legs and arms splaying casually as she looks up at the camera.

At a glimpse, it's simply a youthful summer snapshot. Hold the picture a second longer and it becomes evident it's also a terrific portrait, an expressive subject framed at a quirky angle, compellingly composed, saturated with color. Time has not faded the image—the sunlight still glimmers in the water around the girl—or the memory. "That's my cousin Lisa from 1990 at a country club in Carmel Valley we used to sneak into to go swimming on hot days," says Lucio, 39, with a smile in his Lauraville home studio. "I do like the fact that you can tell it's mine, that the same qualities in my pictures today are there early on."

Last spring, Lucio, a former *City Paper* graphic designer and the co-owner of Flux Studios gallery, assembled a bunch of his Baltimore portraits in a self-published coffee-table collection called *MONDO DEFEKTO: The Polaroid Photography of Jim Lucio*. (Defekto is a moniker he uses on Flickr, the popular photo-sharing website.)

"Basically, [the self-published book] has been a marketing tool to get a 'real' book deal," he explains. "I made a hundred, numbered them and sold them for $50." And he actually sold a few, too. "It did help add to my non-existent income," he laughs, "and paid a couple months of the mortgage."

Getting a "real" book deal is becoming more urgent for one simple reason: The film that's made pictures magically appear for 60 years is about to disappear itself.

Lucio was initially drawn to Polaroid film as a teenager because he was impatient—he didn't want to wait a week for his film to develop (this, of course, was before the dawn of digital cameras). Later, he became attached to the rich quality of the color and the unique intimacy between subject and artist that Polaroids encourage.

Embraced over the years by artists such as Andy Warhol, Robert Rauschenberg, Robert Mapplethorpe, David Hockney, and Chuck Close, Polaroid stopped manufacturing cameras two years ago. When the company announced in February it was shuttering film production as well, websites such as SavePolaroid.com popped up, organizing online petitions and letter-writing campaigns, trying to convince another company to buy the rights to the patented chemical-emulsion process.

Twenty years after he started taking his instant portraits, Lucio's recognized as "the Polaroid guy" around Baltimore for his cool, yet intimate close-ups of pals, hipsters, curious strangers, Jesus freaks, tattooed superheroes, punks, addicts (including a friend who has since died of an overdose), naked wrestlers, masked misfits, musicians, magicians, Roller Girls, bartenders, bike messengers, trapeze artists, and transvestites.

"Jim relates to everybody. He spends time with them, and they open up to him," says photographer Josh Sisk, a friend who has been published in *Rolling Stone*, among other magazines. "Even those people who are more theatrical seem to reveal themselves underneath whatever they are wearing. When you see his photographs, you might think, 'This person looks a little crazy,' but you also think that this is someone I'd enjoy talking to. I just know I can't do what he does."

When he first heard that Polaroid was discontinuing film production, Lucio bought all the spare film he could find, got on a waiting list at a New York camera store, and began stockpiling film in his refrigerator in Lauraville. "I might have to get another one for food eventually," he says, noting the instant film comes with an expiration date and lasts longer in cold storage.

Eventually, Lucio will have to forge on without his trusty 1980s-era Spectra camera. He promises the loss of Polaroid film won't deter him forever. He has other interests, including writing and painting—and taking digital photos "like everyone else," he adds.

"But yeah, I'm upset over it," he sighs. "I've taken probably 2,000 portraits in Baltimore over the past six years." He estimates he has maybe 700 exposures left and says he's trying to let go gracefully. To that end, he started chronicling his final several hundred shots in a photo blog, "The Last Days of Polaroid."

"I love the nostalgia aspect of Polaroid and his style, but really his stuff is about the community of Baltimore," says G-Spot co-founder Jill Sell. Her gallery/performance space hosted Lucio's "In Your Face" show—where he took one portrait every single day for a year—back in 2006. "Baltimore is a small village, and his work makes you feel connected to that, to the neighborhood people you might know in his photographs, and also to the strangers because you can check them out, too."

This month, Lucio's exhibiting new work at his Flux Gallery at Station North alongside digital portrait artist Chase Lisbon. And in November, Metro Gallery owner Sarah Williams has scheduled him for a solo exhibition. "One thing that's funny is that now when people see Jim with his camera, they'll purposely try to get in front of him to see if he'll take their picture," Williams says.

Lucio's philosophy can be boiled down to this: everyone deserves a portrait.

"I think there is something interesting and of value in everyone," Lucio says. "I don't think that I have actually ever put this into words before, but maybe what I've wanted all along is for everyone else to realize that, too."

2. Old Heads

At dusk in the 3100 block of McElderry Street in East Baltimore, Dante Barksdale grabs a bullhorn. In baggie shorts and work boots, a hoodie pulled over his shaved head, Barksdale, whose very name is associated with violence in the city (courtesy of the HBO series *The Wire*), strides into the intersection of McElderry and North Robinson streets, stopping traffic.

Forty-eight hours earlier, a young man was shot on this corner.

Barksdale addresses everyone within earshot: the women looking on from their front stoops, a group of older men standing near a car, store owners peeking outside, and his target audience—the teenagers and twenty-somethings in white T-shirts milling about. His demeanor is deadly serious; his voice is filled with urgency. "Life is precious," Barksdale shouts. "Let's not make funerals a part of our lives. Everybody has a purpose. We want the streets to be safe."

The cadence of his speech becomes rhythmic, almost poetic: *This is not a jungle, this is our home/ We have to live in harmony, not carry guns/ Stop the shooting, stop the killing.*

Now in his mid-30s, Barksdale bounced around dock and construction jobs after serving a 10-year prison sentence for heroin and cocaine distribution. For the past 18 months, he's been a full-time outreach worker with Safe Streets, an innovative two-year-old City Health

11

Department initiative aimed at reducing the leading cause of death among males aged 15 to 34 in Baltimore City: homicide.

Barksdale leads a march around the block, with a gathering group of community activists, outreach workers, neighbors, and youngsters in tow. "Put away the guns," he implores. "Put away the guns."

Modeled after Chicago's CeaseFire, a program credited with substantially reducing shootings and homicides in the roughest Windy City neighborhoods, Safe Streets hires ex-offenders who are turning their lives around and trains them as mediators and outreach workers. They work in the same streets they once ran, establishing relationships with men and women considered at high risk of getting shot—or shooting others.

"We cut through all the bull crap and put the light on all the bad stuff," says Barksdale. "[We] tell them the truth. Like prison: no air conditioning, no girls, and you're under a whole lot of pressure in jail, dog. I tell them, 'They steal your peace of mind in there.'"

He goes on: "They're thinking, 'I can get a pack [of coke], get rid of that in five days, then I can get me some clothes.' The only thing is, you might not be alive when that pack is done. Seven grams of cocaine, maybe you make $500 or $600, but before you finish it, you might have a bail of $50,000. I wake them up."

Barksdale says many of the friends he grew up with are dead or in prison. Both facts haunt him, as that cycle continues. "I don't like it when I see the same things happening," he says. "I didn't like it even when I was a part of it. But this is still my neighborhood, and that's my motivation. I want to make my mother proud today, allow her to hold her head up. Maybe I can help save someone."

His first night canvassing, Barksdale spotted about 16 young men standing in the middle of a street, blocking a Lincoln Town Car. In what was a potentially violent standoff, two guys had stepped outside the car and one remained inside. Barksdale recognized a few of the participants.

"I'm thinking, 'This doesn't look right,'" he recalls. "But I keep walking up. I keep walking and I'm smiling—I am not afraid of nothing—I mean, I grew up on these same streets. And I'm handing out Safe Streets literature, telling everyone I'm from Safe Streets and asking, 'What's going on here?'"

One of the two guys standing by the car told him it was about "what this girl said."

"What this girl said?" Barksdale asked. Then, he laughed at the absurdity of it all and laid out a likely scenario.

"Murder in cold blood, that's what is going to happen," Barksdale told the teenagers. "People are going to get arrested. Two or three are going to snitch. One person is going to be a gunshot victim. One person is not going to survive. And someone is going to go to jail and not have anyone send him any money in there.

"And you're telling me this is over some girl who isn't even here, not even to look her in the eye and find out if she is telling the truth? Somebody is going to get shot over this? Oh, no. No, no, no."

Postscript: As of March 2020, the Safe Streets initiative, Barksdale included, remains active in McElderry Park and has expanded to other neighborhoods including, Cherry Hill, Park Heights, Sandtown-Winchester, Penn-North, Brooklyn, and Franklin Square.

3. Breaking the Habit

Gloria Carpeneto was born, as she puts it, to a ritually-correct and card-carrying Roman Catholic lower middle-class European immigrant family. Baptized four days later, Sept. 14, 1947, at St. Anthony of Padua in northeast Baltimore, she attended the parish grade school with four brothers and sisters and graduated from the all-girls Seton High School on Charles Street at a time when students were "still wearing nurse uniforms," she recalls with a laugh.

When she accepted a vocation with the Sisters of the Good Shepherd in Peekskill, New York, it surprised her family. Not because she was becoming a nun, but because she was leaving Baltimore and moving to New York.

"As you much as you can, at 17 years old, hear a call from God, I did," Carpeneto says. "The Sisters of the Good Shepherd worked primarily with women, victims of domestic abuse, and 'delinquent' girls. They were out in the world, and that was very attractive to me. Even as a teenager, I really liked social service work."

But after two years, Carpeneto, then Sister Gloria Ray, questioned whether the ordered life was a good fit. "It was the way convents were organized at the time, the structure. I wasn't happy with the system. It really pushed me back home." By no means did she ever question her faith.

Her first job upon returning was in the Chancery office of the Archdiocese of Baltimore and Lawrence Cardinal Shehan. In the evenings, she finished the undergraduate work she'd begun at New York's Fordham University at another Jesuit institution, Loyola College.

"I didn't question Church doctrine then, not the role of women in the church or anything," she says. "Not like today when we talk about the 'stained glass ceiling.'"

Indeed, she could not have imagined, 40 years after departing the convent, she'd hear a new religious calling, leading to ordination as a priest—as well as ex-communication by the Vatican.

Last summer, the petite, gray-haired, 61-year-old grandmother took part in a ceremony in Boston with two other women and claimed holy Orders as a Catholic priest. Several hundred supporters attended the July ordination, which the Archdiocese of Boston immediately denounced.

Despite facing ex-communication, Roman Catholic Womenpriests have ordained 35 female priests, seven deacons, and one bishop in the U.S. since 2002. In Canada and Europe, where the movement began, they have ordained another 20 bishops, priests, and deacons, all in accordance with historic apostolic tradition, they maintain.

Together with Annapolis resident Andrea Johnson, who claimed Catholic priesthood in 2007 in a similar ceremony, Carpeneto leads Mass—outside the auspices of the Archdiocese of Baltimore—on the third Sunday of every month at a Protestant church in Catonsville. Typically, 30 to 40 people, including men, women, and families, attend services, and Carpeneto estimated 100 supporters receive their email updates.

Some people have asked her why she and the other women didn't just leave the official Roman Catholic Church and, for example, join the Episcopalian Church or another mainline Protestant denomination that ordains women to fulfill her calling.

"The simple answer of why I didn't choose to leave the Catholic Church is that I've been a Roman Catholic since I was four days old. It's not just my religion, it's my culture, like Judaism is for Jewish people," Carpeneto says. "All of us [in the women's ordination movement]

15

love the Roman Catholic Church and our choice is to reform from within rather than walk away.

"We've all said this is our family."

4. To Haiti

In a battered, industrial corner of the Baltimore harbor, at the end of a gravel road filled with pallets, cast iron pipes, steel cables, electrical cords, and cargo boxes, four-dozen people huddle in the cold, dark, early-morning hours to wish the U.S. Naval hospital ship *Comfort* well as it prepares to set steam for Haiti.

Meanwhile, Steve White sits at dock's edge with a walkie-talkie, directing his tugboat crew as they lower two 35-ton diesel generators on deck. By the time the sun has come up, the *Comfort* is almost ready. Fifteen welders and electricians are the last off ship. They've worked 36 hours without sleep.

The 894-foot ship with red crosses on its sides will carry 560 medical personnel, four X-ray machines, a CAT scan, and as much as 5,000 units of blood to the earthquake-ravaged country, where they will treat hundreds of the most severely injured.

Trying to stay warm in a gray, hooded U.S. Navy sweatshirt, Lauren Wishart of Severna Park looks out as another tug pushes the *Comfort* to open water. Her son, Lt. Aaron Wishart, is aboard.

"He's stationed in Norfolk, and I saw him yesterday," she says. "He told me he'd be down there a minimum of two months. I'm doing what a mother has to do, seeing him off."

A crane lifts away the gang blank. Lineholders pull thick, 120-foot ropes off the bow and stern bollards. "If you've got a pair of gloves, feel free to lend a hand," Jim Tighe, from Dundalk, jokes with an onlooker.

Rosalie Smith, 65, and Audrey Smith, 68, best friends from North Baltimore, attended an NAACP meeting last night where a hat was passed to collect donations for victims of the earthquake.

"You feel so helpless," says Audrey Smith. "But we wanted to come down. It tugs at your heartstrings. I wish we could go with them and cook and serve meals to the troops."

5. Friend of the Court

Jerry Lawler met Ricky, then 13, shortly after he'd been removed from his latest foster home and placed in another residential institution. "His foster care mother basically said, 'I can't deal with him anymore,'" Lawler says.

A volunteer with the Baltimore nonprofit CASA, an acronym for Court Appointed Special Advocates, Lawler was assigned to Ricky by the Baltimore City Family and Juvenile Court. He was supposed to get to know Ricky, floundering seven years after being taken from his mother because of neglect, and serve as another set of eyes and ears in his life. He would represent Ricky's interests in court hearings, the educational system, and the medical and social service communities.

A clinical psychologist by profession and father of two grown children, Lawler was nonetheless nervous before their first meeting.

"I think all the volunteers wonder, 'What if I can't relate to my kid? What if they don't want to see me? What if they yell at me or get pissed off at me?'"

Ricky didn't yell or get angry. He barely spoke.

"He was guarded. Withdrawn. No swagger. Just 'I'm not going to tell you anything,'" Lawler recalls. "I'd ask how he was doing, and he'd say, 'Okay.' I'd ask if he wanted to go to McDonald's: 'Okay.' Want to go to the Inner Harbor? 'Fine.'

"It was six months before we'd be driving somewhere that he'd tell me what he'd done the previous night. Another six months before he'd tell me anything he was feeling," Lawler continues. "This was a kid who'd learned not to trust people because they'd let him down so much."

Foster kids often move from placement to placement with few belongings, even photos of their siblings and families of origin. However, one possession Ricky allowed Lawler to view offered insight behind his silence.

"He kept a compiled 'book' of himself, awards from completing different programs, and he had family pictures in there," says Lawler, adding Ricky has had 16 various placements since entering the foster system, including stays with five sets of foster parents. He had pictures of each foster family, two dogs he loved at one home. A professional picture of himself as a baby, pictures of his half-siblings, his grandmother. And a photograph of his mother, a heroin and crack addict and North Avenue prostitute.

"It's heartbreaking," Lawler says. "He's proud of her, believe it or not. He wants her to get clean—to be a mom—and be with her more than anything."

The honorable David B. Mitchell, then Administrative Judge of the Juvenile Division of the Baltimore City Circuit Court, established CASA of Baltimore in 1988. The program, operated by the University of Maryland School of Social Work before becoming an independent agency, pairs volunteer advocates with foster children in crisis. Today, CASA volunteers impact the lives of more than 200 children each year. Children's names in this story have been changed to protect their privacy.

Opening a thick, three-ring binder on his South Baltimore kitchen table, Lawler points to meetings with ever-changing Department of Social Services caseworkers, group home supervisors, school counselors, therapists and family involved in Ricky's life. CASA volunteers learn the child's history in order to build a relationship. Lawler files status updates and makes recommendations at court hearings as necessary. He shows up for important events.

"Last year, I attended his junior high graduation," Lawler says. "That was a big deal." This year, he helped him through his freshman year of public high school. Over two years, he's become the constant in Ricky's life.

"He passed everything but algebra, which he's taking this summer," Lawler says. "He's reading at grade-level. There's no way I can back out now."

6. Golden Hours

Several minutes before the helicopter's estimated arrival, two nurses take a dedicated elevator to the roof. At night, they can spot the helicopter a dozen or more miles away and watch as a small light comes into view. If the accident occurred in Southern Maryland, for example, it will appear off in the distance past M&T Bank stadium. On a bright, glaring day like this, the medevacs pop into view more suddenly, dropping down upon R Adams Cowley Shock Trauma Center with surprising swiftness.

Not unexpectedly, on this Labor Day Weekend, accident victims, assault victims, and transfers from other hospitals begin arriving Friday afternoon.

At 2:51 p.m., it's a 48-year-old man, crushed by a tree. At 3:40, it's a patient who fell from a tree while intoxicated. At 5:14 p.m., it's a motorcyclist, found in the woods with a severed leg, who is flown in. His leg arrived next to him in a cooler but could not be saved. Four minutes later, a 36-year-old female arrives. An unrestrained back-seat passenger involved in a car accident, she'd been ejected from the automobile.

Later, an 81-year-old woman arrives. She'd fallen while riding a bike. One minute after her, a 22-year-old woman who'd been pushed from a car comes in on a stretcher. At 8:30 p.m., a pedestrian is flown in after being struck by a tractor-trailer. At 10:35, a gunshot victim, with bullet wounds to the neck, is brought in after being found unresponsive in alley. He dies two hours later.

By 10:45 p.m. Friday, 15 people had been admitted. By 5 p.m. Saturday, another 24, including a 15-year-old who been shot in the face below his left eye.

As the boy is wheeled into a bay, accompanied by police, conscious and wide-eyed scared, blood dripping from his face, neck swollen with fluid, a dozen and a half doctors, fellows, residents, nurses, and trauma technicians surround his stretcher.

In a well-rehearsed choreography, the teenager's clothes are cut off by one nurse as another asks for his mother or father's phone number. An I.V. is started. His blood pressure is checked. Blood is drawn. Doctors examine him for exit wounds. Blood is suctioned from his mouth. An anesthesiologist begins to sedate him, so he can be intubated. Stable at the moment, he's readied for X-rays.

"I see where it is," Dr. Deb Stein says, minutes later, examining three-dimensional images on her computer screen and staring at a bullet lodged in the teenager's lower neck/upper chest area. "But how did it get there?"

Fortunately, the bullet ricocheted down after entering his face and not into his skull.

Fifty years ago, Dr. R. Adams Cowley, a pioneer in open-heart surgery, developed the first clinical shock trauma unit in the country, putting together a small staff and equipment—including two, and later four, beds—at the University of Maryland Medical Center. It was known as the death lab, at first, until patients given up for dead began to survive. Cowley is credited with coining the idea of "the golden hour," or as Dr. Thomas Scalea, Shock Trauma's physician-in-chief and the driving force for the past 13 years, explains, "the concept that trauma is a time-related disease."

By the end of the three-day weekend, the total was 107 patients. Many were discharged within a day or so, but the 104-bed hospital remained filled. As usual.

Most U.S. trauma centers typically treat about 3,000 to 3,5000 patients a year. Shock Trauma treats more than 8,000 annually, the largest facility of its kind in the U.S.

Ultimately, Labor Day Weekend proved not so dramatically different than other summer weekends. The 13 trauma resuscitation bays and critical care beds often get filled, with patients doubling up.

"We all have very definitive roles, and I think as a result, we provide a very high level of care," says Stein, who has worked at Shock Trauma since 2002. She also stresses the hectic pace, while not for everyone, fits her personality.

"Some people like knowing what to expect. I like not knowing what is going to happen every day," she says. "But the other thing I love, too, is seeing people get better."

7. Miles of Charm

Nervously hitting nearby port-o-potties, re-lacing running shoes, double-checking race belts and carb packets, 5,000 marathoners squeeze onto Russell Street, behind Camden Yards' leftfield wall.

On a crisp morning, thousands more line the sidewalks, shouting encouragement and wishing friends and loved ones well. Moments later, the national anthem blares, the Bromo Seltzer Tower clock strikes 8 a.m., and then suddenly a "BANG" releases the penned herd. Confetti pours down, and Gov. Martin and Katie O'Malley enthusiastically wave to the now flowing mass of humanity.

It's the 10th anniversary of the Baltimore marathon, a 26.2-mile jaunt up and down the city's rocky pavement from the ballparks to Druid Hill, from Federal Hill to Patterson Park, Lake Montebello, and Mount Vernon.

"I've been training for this for the last three years," says Baltimore City firefighter Robert Duckett Jr., 34, prior to the start up South Paca Street. "I missed the deadline two years ago. Last year my training got interrupted and I did the half-marathon."

Filling out a mesh jersey, the 5-foot-10, 230-pound former Edmondson High football player looks like a mini version of Ravens' fullback Le'Ron McClain. "Five years ago, I was right about 300 pounds," he adds. "My goal is to finish."

Behind Duckett, an Elvis impersonator jogs in a white jumpsuit, offering, "Thank you—thank you very much," to on-duty police officers. Ahead, there's someone running in a tuxedo and a couple of women running in tutus and tiaras. One very tall marathoner juggles three balls the whole way without ever breaking stride.

Along the route, runners pass students cheering outside their schools, wise guys hold up signs at mile 18 and 19, asking runners, "Who Needs Toenails?" and reminding them, "No One Made You Do This."

In East Side neighborhoods, families cheer from porch steps. In Charles Village, two fans in full-body tiger suits dance to "Eye of the Tiger" from *Rocky* and high-five runners, while another nearby couple hands out 400 pounds of gummy bears. Through Lexington Market, crowds high-five and fist-bump ragged runners. At the finish line: congratulatory kisses.

"You look at the city today, see all that history, too, and I mean, it's beautiful, and it can be emotional," Duckett says after finishing in just over six hours. "The best thing is that you see all these different people, all the diversity. And everybody is cheering for everybody," he says. "We are not like that every day. We are not good to each other every day like this. But, you know, we could be. We could be."

8. The Wheel

Surrounded by floor-to-ceiling bookshelves and scattered six-inch thick tomes, four reference librarians sit at desks organized in a square configuration, facing each other. Plugged into computers and phones, the librarians answer questions from Baltimore, the state of Maryland, and, literally, the world—as they come in via telephone, email, and text message.

In the center of the desks, within arm's reach of each librarian, spins what is affectionately referred to as "The Wheel." Completed in 1969, The Wheel is a welded, seven-foot-tall, circular bookshelf, stacked with 800 reference titles, including *The Dictionary of Classical Mythology, Facts About the States, The Baseball Timeline,* and *Larousse Gastronomique,* a leading culinary resource first published in 1938.

Queries come from students and academics, and most are part of some rigorous research endeavor, but people also regularly call for crossword puzzle help, last night's winning lottery numbers, or yesterday's Orioles score. Other queries are more eclectic.

"Someone once asked, 'Where do people go when they're dead?' Another asked, 'Am I my cat's mother?'" recalls library professional assistant Maggie Murphy, explaining all questions are taken seriously and provided the most credible answer found. "With the person who asked if they were their cat's mother, we quoted a biology textbook that stated a cat is the product of two cats, and therefore she couldn't possibly be the cat's mother." Psychologically or philosophically, Murphy noted, there may be a different answer.

At the moment, a fresh query arrives asking if Gustav Holst's orchestral suite, *The Planets*, included a movement for Pluto—de-planeted several years ago by the International Astronomical Union. Murphy shared with her client that Holst penned the suite between 1914 and 1916, before Pluto received planetary status.

Medical and legal queries are common, but Sonia Alcántara-Antoine, information services manager, cautions that those queries also point to the limited nature of the reference librarian's role. "As librarians, we can't give medical or legal advice," she says. "We can cite medical or legal text, but we can't interpret. We can't go there."

9. Old School

Baltimore City College graduated its first coed class the same year Cindy Harcum, the school's new principal, started junior high. In love with literature and the humanities, she wanted to go to the school known as The Castle on the Hill. Not that it would be easy.

There were admission standards and, even worse, the commute from West Baltimore to Waverly.

"It took three buses and an hour and a half," Harcum recalls. "If the No. 22 went by twice and it was full, I took the subway downtown and went up from there.

"I wasn't going to let distance stop me, but that wasn't new," she adds. "After Gwynns Falls Elementary, I'd gone to Roland Park Junior High. I'd been doing it since I was 11."

Founded in 1839, City College counts three current Maryland Congressmen as alumni: Rep. Elijah Cummings, Rep. Dutch Ruppersberger, and Sen. Ben Cardin. Mayors William Donald Schaefer and Kurt Schmoke, philanthropists Joseph Meyerhoff, Morris Mechanic, and Zanvyl Krieger, and two-time Pulitzer Prize winner Russell Baker are also City alumni, along with dozens of judges, state legislators, scientists, educators, and journalists.

Harcum's grandparents immigrated to Baltimore from the West Indies. Her father finished high school in the city six years before desegregation and moved from job to job until, at 40, he earned a degree from Morgan State, landing a position with the federal Department of Transportation.

"He always stressed education," says Harcum, noting her sister and older brothers also earned college degrees. "It was understood that you would do well in school."

With her English literature degree from the University of Maryland, Harcum returned to City College to teach in 1997. Eventually, she ran writing seminars at several city high schools, developed curricula, trained teachers, and oversaw SAT readiness preparation at City. In 2004, she began coordinating the International Baccalaureate and Advanced Placement programs. A year later, she was named an assistant principal.

Last August, amid declining test scores and national rankings and the arrest of a City College staffer on sexual abuse charges, Baltimore City schools CEO Andrés Alonso reassigned principal Tim Dawson and asked Harcum if she'd take the job on an interim basis.

As an alumna, she brings a natural connection with the students to her new position. Open and direct, she also brings the credibility of having walked in their shoes.

"If they tell me they're late because of a bus, I tell them to get up earlier," Harcum says. "Nothing will be given to you here."

10. Bienvenidos

Nicolás Ramos came to the United States when he was 16, picking broccoli and cauliflower on a Texas farm and loading boxes of cucumber, squash, cantaloupe, and watermelon into refrigerated trucks. With his brother Carlos and a friend, he eventually socked away $700, enough money to buy a wood-paneled Ford station wagon from a nearby junkyard. Leaving the farm in search of better prospects, the Coahuila, Mexico, native discovered a different group of Latinos in San Antonio—established middle-class families.

"In San Antonio, I met people who looked like me, but I didn't understand why they didn't speak Spanish," laughs Ramos, now 51 and the owner of South Broadway's popular Arcos Restaurant. "It was disarming. I said, 'We've got to go North where there are more white people and better economic chances.'

"I picked Memphis, Elvis Presley's town," he continues, shaking his head at the randomness of it all. Unlucky in Tennessee, he and his brother headed for Arkansas, then east, with five other Mexican buddies crammed into the station wagon, to Georgia and South Carolina. "We were day laborers, standing outside the 7-Eleven." Finally landing in Laurel, hired for Route 1 construction gigs, genuine opportunity arrived. "A lady showed up one day and said, 'Hey guys, we want to get you worker's permits,'" Ramos says. "We came in from the shadows."

He and Carlos, now deceased, purchased a functional pickup truck and took English classes. In 1986, President Reagan signed the Immigration Reform and Control Act, providing amnesty and a path to citizenship. Four years later, Dry Wall and Painting by Ramos opened in Upper Fells Point at a time when the Latino community barely registered a blip on Baltimore's radar.

"When I came to Baltimore, there were two Latino businesses on Broadway—La Botanica, a tiny, pharmacy/convenience store, and La Internationale, a grocery/discount store," Ramos says. "Since 1990, we did a lot of construction work."

Married at St. Michael's Church (a longtime home for Baltimore Latinos before it was closed due to age), he bought his first home at 17 St. Ann St. with a personal loan for the down payment from a church deacon. Eventually, Ramos bought 10 buildings, including the one at 129 S. Broadway that houses Arcos. Recycling heavy beams and hardwood from Fells Point and Canton homes, pews and frosted glass from a Washington, D.C., church that he rehabbed, Ramos spent four years crafting the bar, tables, chairs, doors, and patio inside his restaurant. He added authentic Talavera tiles and Mexican artifacts and photographs, finished the original brick interior, and launched Arcos for Cinco de Mayo in 2005.

Today, Ramos has four children, including a daughter at Dickinson College. He's served on the Governor's Hispanic Affairs Commission, as president of Baltimore City's Hispanic Business Association, and as part of Mayor Stephanie Rawlings-Blake's transition team. He's hosted events for Gov. Martin O'Malley, former New Mexico Gov. Bill Richardson, Rawlings-Blake, and Odette Ramos, who ran for city council this year.

"Do you know what Arcos means?" Ramos asks. "Arches. Arches connect two points. I wanted to bring a little bit of culture, food, and ambience of Mexico to Baltimore. I saw the potential and fell in love with Baltimore. Looking down from Johns Hopkins to Fells Point, I could see the possibilities. But on Broadway, there was prostitution, crime, and drugs [in the '90s]. You couldn't walk the street at night. Now, we call it Latino Town or Spanish Town, and everybody sees what I saw."

11. Slumlord Justice

Carol Ott had enough. "Maybe I woke up on the wrong side of bed that morning," she says. "I don't know exactly what pushed me over the edge."

For years, the feisty, 5-foot-1, mother of two dutifully attended Pigtown neighborhood meetings. Each time, the same topic—the shuttered shopping center at the intersection of Washington and Martin Luther King Jr. Boulevards—came up. It was bad enough that the community's grocery store had departed. Now, across the street from the Welcome to Pigtown mural at the Southwest Baltimore neighborhood's gateway, the abandoned shopping center had degenerated into an open-air drug market, and the portico alongside the long-gone Save-a-Lot had, for all intents and purposes, become a homeless camp.

"When I moved there in 2000, the grocery store was still open, but it closed several years later and became an eyesore, garbage strewn everywhere," Ott recalls in the living room of her rowhouse. "Nobody was maintaining it. A doctor and his business partners, including at least one other physician, owned it, and were doing nothing to improve it. Apparently, they wanted an extraordinary amount of money for the property, and, meanwhile, the drug activity kept up."

Frustrated at another community meeting one night—"we had, like, five different neighborhood groups then, and I went to most of them"—Ott stood up and walked out, swearing she was done with meetings.

"There's got to be a better way of dealing with this," she remembers thinking. "It was typical of neighborhood meetings anywhere, city or suburbs, doesn't matter. Same people, same complaints, nobody steps up. I figured I'd force the shopping center owners' hand and make it public on the internet."

Not long after reaching her boiling point in late 2008, Ott launched her slightly infamous WordPress blog, Baltimore Slumlord Watch. The blog, which includes pictures Ott takes of abandoned properties as well as "reader-submitted" photos of abandoned homes, provides information on the legal history and housing violations of blighted properties, their impact on the surrounding neighborhood, contact information for local elected officials, and the names and addresses of negligent owners. It's direct, data-base researched, and at times, just a bit snarky, like Ott, who typically goes vacant-house hunting in jeans and bright red Converse high tops, generally toting a cellphone camera—and box cutter, for protection. It's not a coincidence, she notes, that vacant homes attract crime. (Until this story, Ott maintained her anonymity as the person behind Baltimore Slumlord Watch, partly for fear of retribution toward her family.)

Her initial post outed the Timonium doctor listed as the resident agent for the company that owned the then-vacant Pigtown shopping center and listed the hospital where he had surgical privileges. From there, the plan to goad one irresponsible landlord into accountability grew into a citywide housing resource. Ott regularly posts updates on Baltimore issues like lead paint and fire-department station closings, as well as vacant housing efforts in other cities.

Today, Baltimore Slumlord Watch, with 12,000 to 15,000 hits a month, possesses genuine social media clout. Friends and followers on Facebook and Twitter include City Council President Bernard C. "Jack" Young, Baltimore City Del. Keiffer J. Mitchell Jr., and Maryland Attorney General Douglas F. Gansler, among other politicos, not to mention numerous housing advocates and journalists. Not all are necessarily fans, however; one local columnist and talk-show host, Ott says, blocked her Twitter account after describing the blog as a negative portrayal of Baltimore.

Emails from property owners, unsurprisingly, are nasty, but generally threaten legal action, not physical harm. "I get, 'Dear Mr. Slanderer,' a lot," Ott says with a laugh. "I'm like, if you're going to threaten me, at least get the legal term right if you want me to take you seriously. It would be libel. Then again, I'm very careful."

Postscript: In 2018, Carol Ott transitioned to a job with the Fair Housing Action Center of Maryland, where she serves as the director of tenant advocacy.

12. A Dream Un-deferred

Gustavo Andrade lifts up a megaphone and asks several hundred Latino students and young adults outside of East Baltimore's CASA de Maryland an important question. *"He vivido en Estados Unidos de América salir por mas de seis meses des del el 15 de junio de 2007* (Have you lived in the U.S. since 2007 without leaving for more than six months)?"

Andrade, a senior CASA organizer, then asks those in line if they have a high school diploma, GED, or are enrolled in school or a career-training program. Finally, *"Estuve presente en EE.UU. el 15 de junio de 2012?"* (Were you present in the United States on June 15, 2012?)

That last day, June 15, is significant because it's the day President Obama signed the Deferred Action for Childhood Arrival executive order. The directive—albeit with many stipulations—allows young immigrants brought here by their parents and facing possible deportation to apply for a temporary work permit.

Nineteen-year-old Diana Garcia, who came to Maryland from Mexico a decade ago with her mother, is one of those seeking to apply (cost: $465) for the two-year "deferred action" deportation reprieve. Bright, attractive, and bilingual, she graduated from Annapolis's Broadneck High School in 2011.

"They say it could take a few days to several weeks after the applications are sent in to find out if it's been approved," she says. "We'll see. This is a great opportunity. We all know that."

Garcia says she would like to study medicine and become a holistic health practitioner. Currently, she's employed at a gas station whose name she's afraid to reveal.

"If I can drive, work legally, I can get a better job," she says. "Then maybe I can afford in-state tuition."

Later, inside one of CASA's small conference rooms, stacks of paperwork in hand, Garcia spends an hour and a half with trained volunteers documenting the schools she's attended, her medical vaccinations—even offering proof of her Catholic Sacrament of Reconciliation—to show she's been in the U.S. continually for at least the past five years. Afterward, she waits as everything is photocopied and scanned.

"I didn't understand when I was little that I was illegal. It wasn't until high school, when my friends started to drive and get jobs, which I couldn't, that I began to realize I probably couldn't go to college either," she says. "You're really happy watching all these good things happen for your friends, you truly are, but at the same time, it's really hard."

13. Blast Off

Moshe Hochman is getting precious few touches during a Saturday scrimmage on the indoor turf at DuBurns Arena. The Baltimore Blast, five-time Major Arena Soccer League champions, are holding their first open tryouts in two decades this morning, and 53 would-be pros—ranging from age 18 to 45—take their best shot at their boyhood dream. Most are local, but an assistant coach at Evergreen State College has traveled here from Washington State; another hopeful is scheduled to fly in from Brazil.

Normally a forward, but recognizing he's stuck on an inferior squad, the 29-year-old Hochman, an Israel-native and locksmith by trade, switches to defense in an attempt to flash some skills and catch head coach Danny Kelly's attention. Aggressive and quick, he manages to distribute a couple of sharp, no-look passes upfield to teammates, who nonetheless fail to convert the plays into scoring chances.

Meanwhile, opposing goalkeeper Jeff Estep, who plays in the Sunday night men's league here with the Dundalk Soccer Club, keeps up a steady chatter on the field, directing his teammates, some of whom has limited indoor experience.

After their match, Hochman and Estep, 33, sit near one another in the metal bleachers, catching their breath and eyeing the competition in the second scrimmage. Estep, whose had a good day in the net, recognizes Hochman from their Sunday night league and informs him that a couple of former Blast players he knows encouraged him to try out. Then he reminds Hochman that their respective rec clubs play against each other on this same field tomorrow night.

"You better be ready," Estep says, smiling. "We haven't lost to anybody this season."

Hochman, coming to grips with the fact that a professional soccer career isn't likely in his future, grasps a sore foot. He suggests that the match against Estep's team should be postponed.

"I'm going to be too tired after two days of tryouts."

(Postscript: Neither Hochman or Estep were signed by the Blast, but Estep later caught on with the Harrisburg Heat, where he played professionally for five years.)

14. Pin-Up Girls

As the Motorettes close a rocking set of Motown standards, 14 mostly young, mostly tattooed women step in front of the stage outside the Dundalk Moose Lodge. Dressed in back-seam stockings, bullet bras, peep-toe pumps, tight skirts, and vintage blouses—and primped with winged eyeliner, bright-red lipstick and retro-inspired "half updo" hairstyles— they're competing for the prestigious title of Miss Mobtown Greaseball.

The pin-up contest winner is promised, among other gifts, a professional photo session with Atomic Cheesecake and a portrait in *Retro Lovely* magazine. She'll also appear at several events over the next year, such as Baltimore's annual Night of 100 Elvises at Lithuanian Hall.

The concurrent car show attracts some 600 classic automobiles and hot rods on a picture-perfect early fall Saturday afternoon. But the day was as much about putting an updated twist on post-World War II style as it was about rebuilding late model Fairlanes and GTOs.

Naturally, a big crowd turns out for a gander at the pin-up girls. "A lot of these girls certainly would not have been comfortable living in the 1950s, barefoot and pregnant in the kitchen, not having the choice to work," says Stacy Barich, owner of Atomic Cheesecake in Parkville. "But they can appreciate the aesthetic. Besides, it's also just fun to dress up and be a girl and embrace your femininity. In those days, they wouldn't have liked being 'ogled'— today, they're like, 'That's right! I got it.' They've turned the tables."

The sideshow announcer calls out Stacy "Firecracker" Bucklaw, and the brunette hairstylist from Hanover, Pennsylvania, saunters to the microphone to big applause. Wearing a hand-painted skirt and yellow halter top, sporting a Betty Crocker tattoo one on shoulder and a U.S. Navy tat on the other, she's an easy pick by judges for the finals.

"It may only be the Mobtown Greaseball," she says later, smiling, glamorous behind orange, cat-eyed sunglasses. "But I feel like Miss America."

15. Illuminati

Under a hazy, pre-Superstorm Sandy moon, thousands of costumed kids and families fill Patterson Park for a Saturday night parade like none other in the city. As the Raya Brass Band, of Brooklyn, New York, warms up their accordions, tubas, saxophones, and bass drums, a black hearse with a dead-eyed, tuxedoed driver, various ghosts and goblins, and later, a half-dozen giant white mice on stilts arrive in line behind the band.

Following an afternoon of hayrides, live music, art installations, chili, barbecue, funnel cake, and lantern-making workshops, the 12th annual Halloween Lantern Parade begins its park march to big cheers. Several dogs with neon, glowing collars jump into the mix along the way, pulling their owners in with them.

"I love it," says Matthew Fass, Raya Brass Band accordionist and, coincidentally, music director for the annual New York Village Halloween Parade. "The New York parade started just like this, 39 years ago, as a small neighborhood parade in the West Village, and just kept growing. This has the same community-building spirit."

As the procession stretches forward in the dark, lanterns constructed from decorated plastic bottles and the occasional streetlamp illuminate the parade's underworld characters, as well as the wild dancing and drumming of the Baltimore Rockers and Baltimore All-Stars Marching Bands.

"I moved to the city two years ago," says one of the young women, dressed, with 15 college friends, in red, white, and blue Harlem

Globetrotters jerseys, shorts, and headbands. "To me, Patterson Park is like the epicenter of all the good things that are going in Baltimore."

After the parade, in front of the Pulaski Monument park entrance, acrobatic, flaming-baton twirlers entertain the departing crowds. Most people on hand don't look too anxious to leave.

When someone in their audience asks the name of the troupe that the flaming baton-twirlers belong to, one of the male twirlers shakes his head: "Oh, were not in an organized group or anything," he explains. "Just a bunch of friends who got together for fun."

16. Weddings Rings

"If we pass gambling and not this, I'm moving to D.C.," a woman jokes, *or maybe half-jokes*, inside the Marylanders for Marriage Equality election night party at Baltimore Soundstage.

At 10:25 p.m., news on the large-projection TV reports that with almost 70 percent of the precincts still out, the margin supporting gay marriage has slipped to 51-49 percent. Nearby, Dawn Trotter claps to boost her own spirits as much as anything else. Others search Facebook and Twitter for updates. At 10:40 p.m., 50-50 on Question 6 scrolls across the screen. Trotter, elbows on the table, hands covering her mouth, leans into her friend Colleen Pleasant Kline: "50-50," she whispers.

Wearing her lucky Ravens T-shirt—partly in homage to linebacker Brendan Ayanbadejo, who publicly supports gay marriage rights— Trotter sips a Coors Light. Her partner, Diana Bennett, two seats away, takes the news more stoically. In between, Kline, the couple's Hunting Ridge neighbor, seems most nervous of all. "They said if it passes, I can officiate," she says, smiling to break the mounting tension.

At 11:17 p.m., the crowd leaps to its feet as Barack Obama, who came out in favor of same-sex marriage this summer, is reelected as the 44th President of the United States. "Whatever happens," says Bennett quietly, referring to Question 6 and hugging Trotter, "it's validation."

And then, a few minutes later, it's 51 percent in favor again, now with nearly three-fourths of the state majority reporting in favor. But still, no official word.

Finally, at 12:16 a.m., although WBAL still hasn't "called" Question 6, Del. Maggie McIntosh, Del. Mary Washington, Del. Luke Clippinger, state Sen. Rich Mandelino, and Del. Heather Mizeur—five openly gay legislators—as well as Mayor Stephanie Rawlings-Blake and Gov. Martin O'Malley take the stage to announce the passage of Question 6 beneath yellow and black balloons that have been waiting all night to be released. Along with Maine, Washington, and Minnesota, Marylanders are among the first ever to support gay marriage at the polls.

Dawn embraces Diana, and at the same time, tries to video record the celebration onstage, with little success. The iPhone in her hand is shaking. Tears are running down her cheeks.

17. President Street

Another body cannot possibly squeeze into the packed house at James Joyce's Irish Pub & Restaurant, an early anchor in Harbor East when it served its first Guinness pint and plate of corned beef and cabbage a decade ago. Leading the pub's 10th anniversary party onstage this November night, in his familiar-to-Baltimoreans, tight black T-shirt, Gov. Martin O'Malley strums his guitar and leans into the microphone, taking his band, O'Malley's March, through an energetic set of Celtic ballads and Irish-tinged rock songs, including a cover of The Pogues' "Dirty Little Town."

> *Dreamed a dream by the old canal*
> *I kissed my girl by the factory wall*
> *Dirty old town*
> *Dirty old town*

The song, cast in a struggling industrial city, couldn't be more appropriate for O'Malley, who performed here at the pub's opening as then-Mayor of Baltimore, when Harbor East was still mostly empty warehouses and desolate docks. At the time, the city's crime and homicide rates were becoming the stuff of legend in the HBO series *The Wire*—an image O'Malley fought like crazy and a show that gets his ire up to this day. Now, however, the holiday lights decorating the hotel, restaurant, and gleaming office buildings behind him in the pub's front glass window seem almost symbolic, an affirmation of the burgeoning upscale district, the city's potential for wider rebirth, and even O'Malley's political career, which is experiencing something of a revival tonight.

He'd suffered through a disappointing General Assembly earlier last year when legislators ignored or punted much of his agenda, barely managing to pass a "doomsday" budget just before midnight on the session's final day. But a week earlier, on election night, O'Malley rebounded remarkably. The governor had thrown his full weight behind several risky, hot-button referendum issues—Maryland's same-sex marriage law; the Dream Act (to assist undocumented immigrants with in-state tuition); an expansion of gambling; and a new, partisan congressional map—and won on all four measures.

On top of those victories, as then-head of the Democratic Governors Association, O'Malley had advocated tirelessly for President Barack Obama in his reelection bid, frequently appearing on Sunday talk shows to square off with the Republican opposition. In the aftermath of Obama's victory, O'Malley's effective stumping added to the perception of his growing political momentum. Almost immediately after the votes were counted, political pundits, on the basis of O'Malley's referendum victories and increased national stature, put him on the short list of 2016 Democratic contenders with former Secretary of State Hillary Clinton, Vice President Joe Biden, and New York Governor Andrew Cuomo.

"I saw him play at McGinn's on Charles Street, which became Mick O'Shea's, when he was playing there regularly," says Ellen Muth. "He's debonair, handsome the way JFK was in the 1960s."

Her daughter, Lane, standing next to her between sets, also saw O'Malley play many times when he was mayor. "I told my mom then, 'He's going to be president in 10 years.'" Not necessarily because of any legislative achievements, Lane admits, but because of one of O'Malley's most commented-upon attributes as a politician, "because he was charming and appealing."

Standing at the corner of Harford Road and the Alameda, announcing that he was running for mayor in June of 1999, O'Malley's political future was hardly guaranteed—as is often posited, given his sturdy good looks and marriage to former Maryland Attorney General Joe Curran's daughter—let alone destined for a White House bid. He entered the race late, not jumping in until after former NAACP head Kweisi Mfume announced he was staying out.

Perhaps it's worth noting, for those who believe in such signs, that the James Joyce's Pub is located on President Street.

Postscript: O'Malley suspended his 2016 presidential campaign following a poor showing in the first presidential primary in Iowa.

18. More Menorah

"That's my rebbe," smiles Yitz and Sora Fleischman's youngest daughter, gesturing toward a 4-foot, gray-bearded, plastic rabbi in a Russian fur hat on display at her porch.

About an hour after Sabbath ends, families begin gathering at the Fleischmans' home, which is literally bringing the light of Chanukah to its Pikesville neighborhood. Yellow, blue, red, and green bulbs outline the fence, while bright white lights spell out "THE CHANUKAH HOUSE" in block letters atop the first-floor awning, and an 11-foot menora fills a corner of the front yard. There's a train garden, Jewish snowmen, and blown-up toy dreidel amid a wide mix of kitschy decorations, including a near life-size fiddler on the roof; a flying, yarmulke-wearing "Hershel" Potter; and an Adam Sandler-figure belting out, "It's so much funnukah to celebrate Chanukah . . ."

There's also a glass-enclosed, 3-foot Barbie on the lawn, lighting a menora. Why? As the display notes, Barbie was the creation of Ruth Handler, a Jewish businesswoman, who named the doll after her pre-teen daughter Barbara. Nearby, Sora Fleischman's mother passes out homemade sugar cookies shaped as the Star of David, dreidels, and menoras.

Soon, members of the Ohr Chadash Academy arrive for the First Night ceremony. Principal Akevy Greenblatt helps two of his third- and fourth-grade students oil-light two large menoras, and then, he and Yitz lead everyone in the reciting of the Hanerot Halalu.

Afterwards, the kids head over to pester the aforementioned, diminutive "Chanukah Rabbi," known for his sense of humor, with questions—per custom.

"Do you have an iPhone?" asks a boy.

"Yes, and I have the Angry Birds app," replies the ancient rabbi (Yitz's uncle via hidden microphone). "I play all the time."

"What's your high score?" another child shoots back. As the near life-size, plastic rabbi, who somehow possesses a twinkle in his eye, hedges, a dozen or so kids burst into laughter.

"How old are you?" asks one young girl.

"I'm very old," comes the answer in a Yiddish accent. "You should live to be as old as me."

19. Baltimore vs. Brooklyn

"I have been here once or twice, and for some reason, I like Baltimore," deadpans Matthew Zingg, a Brooklyn poet, as he steps to the stage at the Windup Space in Station North. "It sort of has a small, non-descript place in my heart."

Outside the performance space at the corner of North Charles and West North streets, a group of artfully disheveled 20- and 30-somethings, mostly in knit caps, plaid shirts, jeans, and eyeglasses, stand near filled bicycle racks, smoking cigarettes. Inside, the tables and bar are packed for literary "competition" between poets from New York's most populous borough and Charm City. Despite the serious, highbrow reputation of poetry, that doesn't mean there aren't funny asides and wry observances about urban life in both locales.

"We're city people," says Allyson Paty, Brooklyn's second reader. "We pull an invisible bubble out of our own heads and create a protective space around us."

A copy of the *New York Post*, always good for a laugh, sits nearby.

Before intermission, Alicia Puglionesi of Baltimore, taking requests from the audience, reads from her "non-verbal" dictionary, a project she's been working on for a year. She highlights the contradiction in defining actions, which are inherently non-verbal, with words. Someone requests a word from her dictionary beginning with the letter "I," and she chooses to describe "information," comparing the term and its movement to a person: "It comes," Puglionesi says shyly behind her large frame, '80s-style glasses, "and never says where it went."

Later, Eric Nelson, self-deprecatingly admits he's actually not from Brooklyn but Queens, which he refers to as "the land of pleasant living," which of course generates a chorus of boos from the Natty Boh-loving hometown crowd. Bearded and slight, with an open striped sweater vest over a mismatched button-down shirt, Nelson recalls his last visit to Baltimore several years ago with a couple of friends for another poetry reading.

"It was at the Hexagon Space, and we'd stayed overnight," Nelson recalls. "The next day, the morning after the reading, we're walking down the street toward our car and a big jeep pulls up alongside us," Nelson recalls, "and this guy leans out and says, 'Die hipster scum.'

"We still laugh about that."

20. Everything Must Go

On a cold, muddy morning outside the former United Steelworkers Local 9477, men sip complimentary coffee in paper cups before stepping onto chartered buses for a tour of the property that once housed the world's largest steel mill. Hilco Trading, which bought Sparrows Point in a bankruptcy sale, is offering previews of the mill's vast stock of heavy equipment, machinery, trucks, and tools for an online auction of "an industry," as one visitor—a former Bethlehem Steel worker here—puts it.

At the first stop, everyone exits the bus and two Colorado reps from EVRAZ North America, which operates several smaller mills, inspect 200-ton transport trucks known as "slab haulers." A rep from O&K American Corp, headquartered in Japan, is also aboard—along with several retired or laid-off Sparrows Point workers, coming for a last glimpse of the corrugated warehouses, tin mills, machine shops, rail cars, and loading docks.

"I came here in 1962, right out of Kenwood High School, into an apprentice program," says Lawrence Knachel, glancing out a bus window. "We had 27 softball teams. Shipping side used to play the steel side after work."

Inside a drafty repair shop, a former steelworker, in the hot tin mill for 39 years, mans a security post, earning a few last nonunion wages before the place becomes completely barren. A Midwestern manufacturing rep asks what caused the plant's closure. The ex-steelworker gives the question some thought and shakes his head inside a yellow hard hat. "Everyone has a different reason," he says finally.

"I'll tell you, though, the other day I got home, and my wife was crying. 'My grandfather worked there all those years,' she says. 'My dad worked there all those years,' she says. 'You worked there all those years, and now you're [there] shutting it all down.'"

Postscript: In 2018, Amazon opened an 855,000-square-foot "Fulfillment Center" at Sparrows Point.

21. Pinball Wizard

After 16 games on six pinball machines, including a wooden-rail, Art-Deco beauty from 1958, the National Pinball Museum's "old" pinball machine tournament comes down to the final ball of the last game. Gregg Giblin, a 56-year-old Baltimore plumber, jostling the machine for good caroms, and Mike McGann, 37, a Zen-like software engineer, both lead 48-year-old computer analyst Jack Hendricks by a wide margin.

Crouching, with his left foot forward, Hendricks catches the silver ball with his right flipper, holds it a second, and then sends it ripping through a spinner up the right side—racking 100 points for each rotation. He tries again and misses once, but then spins it twice in a row with deft shots from his left flipper. Next, in almost perfect succession, he cuts down three "drop targets" on the machine's top left side with pops from his right flipper.

Eventually, the machine gives in, discharging a single loud "knock," indicating bonus points and a free game—and victory for Hendricks.

"Good ball," says McGann.

"That's it," says Giblin. "You got it."

Like many of the 40 registered players, Hendricks also competes in a Free State Pinball Association league, which reports tournament results to an international governing body. "I'm ranked 1,844 in the world," he laughs, putting his career pinball earnings at $78.

"I grew up playing at the Greyhound bus terminal in Sunbury, Pennsylvania, riding my bike from my grandparents' house, while my mother worked. "I've got some of the same model machines I played there in my own basement now—set up in the same order that they were at the bus terminal."

22. Adults Only

Inside the Maryland Zoo's chandeliered Mansion House, schmoozing among 90 couples in suits and cocktail dresses, Jane Scheffsky shares several chuckles with a laughing kookaburra, sitting on a volunteer's arm. With a spot-on imitation of the bird's crazy, Woody Woodpecker laugh, Scheffsky keeps prompting the bird into faster, louder chortling. "I lived in Australia [the kookaburra's native country] for seven years," smiles Scheffsky, the zoo's assistant director of group sales, explaining the natural rapport with her new friend.

Nearby, a different woman misunderstands, momentarily, that a girlfriend was not referring to her husband when she was overheard commenting on another male guest's pungent odor. "Oh, I wasn't talking about Todd," the friend apologizes. "I was talking about the porcupine."

The couples are here, however, not just to meet a few animals over hors d'oeuvres and Chardonnay but for the sold-out Valentine's Day lecture, Sounds of Sex.

Lindsay Jacks, a zoo animal keeper, delivers her presentation, the Sound of Love, with accompanying videos of mallards, macaques, and whooping cranes—who mate for life—and other species, in the caterwauling throes of copulation. She highlights a male mouse, standing on his hind legs, singing "like Barry White" to woo a female partner.

She notes kinkier behavior as well, such as a penguin stopping to gawk at two other penguins having sex in public, so to speak. She shows a clip of "panda porn," which is actually used by zoo professionals to encourage the seemingly cuddly bears, who have a small window of fertility, to procreate.

Later, she notes female primates will, at times, consciously increase their volume of noise to "help" male partners ejaculate sooner rather than later.

"I think we have all been there ladies," deadpans Jacks, originally from Alabama, in a sweet Southern drawl. "For me, it's usually so I can watch *The Walking Dead*, and it's coming on in 10 minutes."

23. Sweet Trees

On a blustery, biting Sunday afternoon, Sheryl Pedrick is leading a Maple sugaring tour—mostly parents and their young kids—at Ladew Topiary Gardens, and she explains that other trees produce sap as well, just with lower sugar concentrations. According to legend, a Native American squaw first discovered the sugar maple's precious sap after her husband left a tomahawk planted in a tree, Pedrick says.

Fifty years ago, the gardens' founder, Harvey S. Ladew, placed several sugar maples up the hill purely for aesthetic reasons. But blowing seeds from those trees produced other maples in the woods away from the gardens—now, decades later, old enough to be tapped.

Jocelyn Weinbaum and sister Courtney Nurre, who grew up in Vermont, have brought their husbands and children. Each fills a gallon jug of Maple sap to turn into syrup at home. "My mom made syrup in our kitchen," Nurre says. "We used to pour it into the snow and eat it like candy."

Traipsing through the mud, Pedrick shows the kids how to use a hand drill to make a hole in a tree and insert a tap, known as a spile. Another volunteer demonstrates how the watery sap is traditionally boiled over an open fire, down to a thick, sweet-smelling consistency.

But it's the parents, reconnecting to their childhood memories, who remain more engaged than the kids. A towheaded girl repeats for a third time, "My toes are freezing," and finally, Pedrick asks everyone if they're ready to go inside to eat pancakes with 100-percent Ladew maple syrup. The group enthusiastically nods their heads. Except for Nurre's son.

"I'm still my chewing my gum," he says.

24. Basketball Diaries

Towson trails Hofstra, but former Tiger forward Chuck Lightening isn't worried. "These guys can play," he assures another alum. "This is their last game, and they're feeling that."

Lightening's referring to the Towson mens' final game this season, but it is also the last ever at the 37-year-old Tiger Center Arena. Next year, the team moves into a $75-million, multi-purpose facility. With two dozen other former players, including several from the first team to play here, the 1976-77 squad that went 27-3, and former coach Terry Truax, who led Towson to three straight conference titles and back-to-back NCAA tournaments, Lightening is among those introduced at halftime.

There are other memories, too, of this gym. Ray Charles, Styx, and Bill Cosby all played the Towson Center. Sugar Ray Leonard and Marvin Hagler's 1987 fight was shown here on closed circuit TV, and President Barack Obama came last season to watch Towson play Oregon State, which is coached by his brother-in-law.

Ultimately, the Tigers rally, completing the greatest turnaround in NCAA history, going from a 1-31 mark last season to finish 18-13 and in process, give the Towson Center a proper send-off. As he watches the comeback, Truax reminds former guard Quintin Moody—who, of course, doesn't need reminding—that his three-pointer on this floor sealed Towson's epic 1995 upset of Louisville.

"The fans stormed the court," smiles Moody.

Meanwhile, Lightening recalls when Truax, at his family's kitchen table, told his mother that he was offering her son a college scholarship. "I wasn't sure what to do after high school. Then I transferred and sat out a year," says Lightening, an explosive, if occasionally inconsistent, performer, who once scored 29 points in a near-upset of Syracuse and hung 26 on Ohio State in the NCAA tournament. "Good players were arriving, and he could've given away my scholarship, but he kept his promise.

"He yelled at me every day in practice," continues Lightening, a Towson Hall-of-Famer and Ellicott City IT staffing agency owner today. "Some things he said probably would bring [criminal] charges today," he adds with a laugh, "but I'm grateful he did it."

Did Truax, who built a reputation as a mentor who cared as much about his players' grade-point average as their scoring average, actually yell at his star forward at every practice for three years?

The retired coach doesn't turn his head from the game. "He needed it."

Postscript: Terry Truax passed away in 2015 after suffering a stroke.

25. Nether World

Stepping from his "wheat paste mobile" (a battered, pale blue compact), the street artist known as Nether unfurls his latest work. It's a 7-by-5-foot black-and-white drawing of a fictional character he's created—the dark, unseen city employee who secretly nails the (real) ubiquitous red "X" marks on Baltimore's vacant rowhomes and buildings deemed unsafe for firefighters.

Nearly every house on both sides of this West Baltimore block has a red "X" on its boarded windows.

Sometimes the 23-year-old travels by bicycle, with a basket attachment holding his bucket of homemade paste in place, while he straddles his 16-foot pole and brush, riding, he jokes, "like Harry Potter." Today, he drove because he needs his collapsible ladder.

Meanwhile, a girl, maybe 10, in a pink sweater, large black-rimmed glasses, and a big Afro, peers from a door in one of the few inhabited homes behind him. A couple of dolls, a ball, and several plastic cars sit on her front stoop, and her younger brother, still in his school khakis and blue shirt, leans out to watch, too. Nether takes just 15 minutes to set his ladder and paste his poster, alternately dipping his brush into the gooey bucket and pushing it across his two-piece poster, placed side-by-side on the boarded window across the street from the kids.

Suddenly, the image of a bandana-masked man, hammer in one hand, red "X" in the other, stares down from the vacant brick rowhouse, as if the character had been caught in the act on the near-desolate street. As Nether steps from the ladder, making sure he hasn't missed flattening any spots, the little girl opens her door. "I like your art," she says. Her brother agrees. "I like it, too."

"Thank you," Nether responds, turning around. "Do you like to draw?" he asks the children, who nod, affirmatively.

"Well, you know, I'm sure you'd get in trouble if you drew on the walls inside your house," Nether tells his young audience. "But I bet if you drew outside on the sidewalk or on the walls, no one would mind."

Postscript: Justin Nethercut and Elise Victoria founded Arts + Parks in 2017, an organization that seeks to blend street art and purposeful landscaping to create holistic spaces for Baltimore neighborhoods.

26. Sneaker Show

"How much for these?" asks a 20-something man, gently holding a pair of red Nike Air Jordans IIs, originally released in 1986.

"Gimme a price," responds Ahmad Bennett. "I'll work with you."

"How much do you want for these Grant Hill's?" chimes in another, looking over a pair of Fila hightops from the former Duke star's Orlando Magic days.

Bennett, a vendor with two tables full of vintage 1980s and early 1990s NBA shoes—plus a rack of Bulls and Celtics warm-up jackets—is selling his gear at the packed, third annual Baltimore Sneaker Show. "This is what I do," Bennett says, explaining that he tracks down sales of vintage and limited-edition sneakers online and through his network of connections. "Basically, it's hustling."

More than 1,200 people have shown up at the Shake & Bake Family Fun Center, paying $30 to peruse the best sneaker collections in the city and beyond, mingle, eat, and dance. With disco lights overhead and local hip-hop artist Greenspan pushing a beat, it feels more like a night at a club than an afternoon inside an old gym.

Cameron Wecker, a 22-year-old Elkridge Furnace Inn manager, ultimately wins the $500 prize for the best collection. Wecker first began collecting sneakers when he stopped growing for several years as a child, his feet remaining the same size for a long period. Then, following successful treatment for his rare genetic condition, the 5-foot-5 winner began collecting again after he and his feet (size 8) stopped growing naturally.

His prize shoe? An autographed left foot, size-23 game sneaker, worn and sent to him by Shaquille O'Neal when the future Hall-of-Famer played for the Miami Heat.

"You can't really understand how big it is until you see it," Wecker says. "It's nearly two feet long. It's wider than my chest."

27. Poor People's March

"We're coming together today to stand up for a working-class agenda," says Rev. Cortly "C.D." Witherspoon, leaning into a microphone in a light drizzle on a trash-strewn vacant lot. About 150 people, some from out of state and all in comfortable shoes—including union members, Occupy protestors, immigrants, and civil rights activists—gather around the Baltimore chapter president of the Southern Christian Leadership Conference. Some are here to highlight specific claims of police brutality—46-year-old Anthony Anderson died from injuries suffered during an arrest in his lot last fall—and others protest attacks on voting rights. Everyone wants more jobs, more investment in public education, and better pay for low-wage workers.

They're preparing to walk to Washington, D.C., in commemoration of the original Poor People's March 45 years ago this weekend. Their route will take them past City Hall, across Martin Luther King Boulevard, and down Route 1. They'll sleep in College Park before arriving in D.C. on Sunday.

Civil rights attorney Faya Touré, founder of the National Voting Rights Museum in Selma, Alabama, follows Witherspoon to the mic. "My brothers and sisters . . . we cannot be single focused. Some of us just want to fight for welfare rights, employment rights, jobs, environmental rights, but there is . . . one struggle."

Witherspoon leads the marchers, holding "JOBS NOT JAIL" and "WORKER + IMMIGRANT RIGHTS NOW" signs through East Baltimore. He alternates between call and response chants ("What do we want? Justice! When do we want it? Now!") and speaking directly to curious residents, either passing by or looking out their windows toward the commotion.

"Hard-working people of East Baltimore," Witherspoon says, glancing up past Tench Tilghman Elementary/Middle School and a block of rowhouses, both of which have seen better days. "We give tax breaks to developers and corporations to build their headquarters, but where is the investment in our neighborhoods? In our community? In our schools?"

"Amen," says a woman leaning out of her rowhouse front door.

28. Alcohol Free

Channeling Jerry Garcia with his gray beard and sunglasses, Scott W. strums "A Friend of the Devil." Next, Romana S., a young woman with long, ginger hair, steps to the stage and delivers a passionate (if ironic) rendition of the traditional Irish drinking song, "Johnny Jump Up."

Oh never, oh never, oh never again.
If I live to a hundred or a hundred and ten,
For I fell to the ground and I couldn't get up
After drinking a quart of the Johnny Jump Up.

More than 400 people fill Tall Cedars Hall in the Putty Hill Shopping Center for the 54th Annual Sobriety Show, organized by the Baltimore Intergroup Council of Alcoholics Anonymous. It's a low budget affair—$1 admission, with pizza, hot dogs, meatball subs, soda, and homemade cakes. Kids dance and run around the edges of the hall while the crowd, clearly enjoying a good time, banters at intermission and generously applauds favorite performers. The amateur acts, following months of rehearsals, vary from earnest to cool, including a killer cover of The Chantays' surf guitar classic "Pipeline." In a towering blue Marge Simpson wig, Shelley C. croons Patsy Cline's iconic "Crazy."

"Look at everyone laughing and smiling," says Joe P., an old-timer, sober 33 years since following a former drinking buddy into AA. "Now imagine if there was an open bar here, with these people drinking. They'd need the National Guard to break up the place."

29. Tour Dem Parks, Hon!

"You just rode under the oldest railroad bridge in North America," says Ed Orser—who literally wrote the book on the Gwynns Falls—to two-dozen bicyclists touring Charm City's parks, mill valleys, and streams. Pedaling past the granite B&O bridge, listening to the "falling" stream, Orser stops at Winan Meadows, named after Thomas Winans, who made a fortune building Russia's first railroad and put his estate here.

"Where you're standing right now would've been a four- or six-lane highway if people hadn't fought to preserve this area," Orser says. "Route 70 ends not far from here. It's 2,000 miles the other way to Utah, and plans called for it to go downtown and meet I-95."

Approaching a small, picturesque dam in historic Dickeyville, several riders get off their bikes for photos, shocked they're still within city limits. "I'm flabbergasted," a young woman tells two friends.

The 25-mile tour, organized by Eli Pousson, Baltimore Heritage's director of preservation and outreach, is a sub-event of the annual Tour Dem Parks, Hon! ride, which has attracted a record 1,300 participants this morning. The ride loops through 745-acre Druid Hill Park and the Jones Falls Trail, later heading toward Federal Hill.

Of course, it isn't all parks and streams in Charm City. Stopped at a traffic light on East Baltimore's once notorious and now simply downtrodden red-light district, Pousson notes that nearby St. Vincent de Paul's once held a regular 2:30 a.m. Mass for the printers and strippers who both pulled late shifts in the neighborhood.

"I've wanted to organize a vaudeville and burlesque bike tour for a year and a half," Pousson says, glancing dejectedly around "The Block." "But sometimes those things look better on paper than they do in reality."

30. Water Cure

Two-dozen curious environmentalists, taking a bike tour of something described as the Harris Creek Watershed, stop pedaling and pull up in front of the Patterson Park branch of the Enoch Pratt Free Library. Their tires come to a rest over several large, metal stormwater grates.

They've already visited the Real Food Farm on the grounds of Lake Clifton High School, where they were told the watershed's headwaters begin. They've stopped and perused Duncan Street's Miracle Farm, built on a vacant block in East Baltimore. They've ridden south past the Baltimore Recycling Center, Collington Square Park, the Reggie Lewis Memorial Basketball Courts, and bustling but trash-strewn Frank C. Bocek Park.

However, there's been no sign—visible or otherwise—of Harris Creek.

Not until a whiff of putrid air emanating from the aforementioned storm grates smacks Joy Goodie, atop her bike, square in the nostrils. "Oh, it smells bad," blurts Goodie, turning her head just before the stench hits everyone else, including her husband and two kids. "It's repugnant."

"That's Harris Creek," deadpans Leanna Wetmore, program coordinator with Banner Neighborhoods and a tour volunteer with organizer Ben Peterson. Wetmore notes the creek now runs entirely beneath the city, long ago co-opted into the massive underground storm-water system. "The water's visible if you look down there," Wetmore adds, as a few brave souls take a peek. "When there's a really big storm, the drains back up and flood this whole area. It can move cars parked here."

Hard to imagine today, but Maryland Historical Society paintings from the late 1800s actually show boats sailing on the creek through Patterson Park to Canton and the harbor.

Peterson explains to the group—still slightly stunned by the odorous discovery of Harris Creek—that the city's century-old sewage pipes (some made of wood) run parallel to equally antiquated stormwater pipes. When the outdated sewage lines inevitably bust, raw waste flows into the stormwater lines, entering the harbor untreated. And when thundershowers just as inevitably overwhelm the stormwater system, trash and chemical pollutants from streets, rooftops, and pavement get whisked downstream.

Of course, it's not just buried Harris Creek that is regularly debased, but the Jones Falls, Gwynns Falls, Middle Branch, and Patapsco River, among other harbor tributaries. At the tour's end, where Harris Creek empties into the harbor, not far from Canton's Waterfront Park— where residents in days long gone swam and crabbed and local clergy dunked their flock in full-immersion baptisms—frustrated activist Raymond Bahr calls healing the harbor, "mission impossible."

By coincidence, the morning following the Harris Creek bike tour, the Waterfront Partnership releases the most comprehensive report ever on the harbor's water quality. The grade: C-. Those who compiled the report, however, admit the harbor was scored on a large curve. The C- indicated that the harbor's overall water quality was acceptable only 40 percent of the time; a score of 50 would've been considered a mid-range C, indicating that water quality met acceptable standards on half of the days.

"As it was, in our system, the grade was just percentage points above a D+," says Baltimore Harbor Waterkeeper Tina Meyers, who assisted in compiling the report card. "If you used high-school grades, it would be Fs all the way from zero to 60 percent."

31. Pump It Up

Crowds cram Charles Street's sidewalk in Mount Vernon, straining for a better vantage. The 2013 Baltimore Pride Parade just ended, and now Segway-driving city police are clearing the street for the annual High Heel Race. At stake: a two-foot trophy, $1,100 in prizes, gift certificates, and Champagne.

"Payless," says Greg Mazzeo, explaining where he found size-11 black heels. "I'm wearing ugly black socks so they're snug and I can run." Chuck Stanley jokes that his pumps came from "Sal-vay"—i.e., the Salvation Army. "Painted them red to match my shorts."

The race is short, Read Street to Eager Street, but tough—a dead uphill sprint, including some jostling elbows before the pack separates. Jay Cruz, who has won previously, accidentally gets smacked in the face early. However, his good friend, Steven Powell, in brown pumps beneath coordinated camouflage pants, breaks free and wins going away. Shirtless, Powell cartwheels across the finish line.

"He's been training for three months, in heels, on a treadmill," Cruz says, begrudgingly, as Powell, a choreographer who ran high school track, gathers his awards.

The winner nods affirmatively, appearing slightly embarrassed.

"With ankle weights," Cruz adds.

Nearby, Stanley, who takes a very respectable fourth, remains out of breath. "I'm going to be 43 years old," he says. "I'm ready for a drink for Crissakes."

32. Pilgrimage

Folklorist Elaine Eff struggles momentarily with the karaoke machine that's serving as her microphone and speaker. The bus tour she's leading, the Painted Screen Pilgrimage, is sold out. She passes out maps.

"We're in the heart of Highlandtown," she says, "going to the Lourdes of Painted Screens."

Heading down Eastern Avenue, Eff points to examples in several rowhouse windows and screen doors, including a glorious image of Patterson Park's pagoda, drawing "oohs and aahs" from inside the bus. She provides brief neighborhood histories as well, ultimately reaching the birthplace of the painted screen: East Baltimore's St. Wenceslaus community.

Here, across from the Italianate church, in a neighborhood once known as Little Bohemia, Czech immigrant and butcher William Oktavec painted the first screen window 100 years ago, advertising his produce and meats. A few doors down, mother and homemaker Emma Schott saw Oktavec's handiwork and a light bulb went off.

"You mean, my husband can sit inside in his underwear, drink a beer, read the newspaper, and no one walking by can see him?" Eff says, mock-imitating Schott. Eff is highlighting, of course, the sidewalk proximity of rowhouse living rooms and the practicality of screen art before air conditioning.

Oktavec painted Schott a red mill alongside a stream, and soon enough, everyone on the block wanted a painted screen.

The tour also weaves past the former McElderry Park rowhome of Johnny Eck, a legendary "half-man" circus and sideshow performer who became an Oktavec screen painting protégé; then Canton, where a number of original screen paintings remain.

"There's one my great uncle did," Troy Richardson says during the tour, pointing to a lighthouse image in a window. Richardson's grandfather Ted and great uncle Ben both became screen painters in the folk art's 1940s and 1950s Formstone heyday.

Earlier, the Creative Alliance showed Eff's 30-minute documentary, *The Screen Painters*. In the film, William Oktavek Jr., whose brother, Richard, and nephew, John, carried on the family tradition and whose works are part of a revival in Highlandtown, talks about his butcher-turned-artist dad and the rowhouse folk art medium he launched.

"What I like about it is what I like about Baltimore," Oktavec says. "It's like Babe Ruth and baseball—that things like this can exist here and endure."

33. Setting Precedent

In the garage beneath the downtown law offices of Shapiro Sher Guinot & Sandler, Larry Gibson lifts a piece of luggage loaded with hardcover copies of his award-winning book, *Young Thurgood*, from his trunk. He intends to wheel the heavy bag up Charles Street to the city courthouse for a book signing with local bar association members. But first, the 71-year-old Gibson chats with a parking attendant, who wants the attorney to present his book to his church.

"I'm saving the last day in June for you," says Gibson, nodding. "Let's get it confirmed. The calendar's filling up."

By his count, Gibson has done 44 signings since the book's release last December. Walking north past the Hotel Monaco, he stops and notes that this is the old headquarters of the Baltimore & Ohio Railroad—the company name still engraved over the archway—for which the future Supreme Court Justice Thurgood Marshall and his father once worked as dining-car waiters.

Weaving through traffic, Gibson, without a hint of resentment, recalls his own experiences growing up in segregated Baltimore, such as getting kicked out of a recreation center with his older brother and cousin. "We were leading both the ping-pong and pool tournaments," he says, laughing. "That's what made me mad." He talks about setting pins at Stoneleigh's duckpin lanes—"where I wasn't allowed to roll a ball"—and working on a bakery truck as a teenager. "We made deliveries to places—like Highlandtown—that I didn't know existed, and I thought I knew every neighborhood in Baltimore," Gibson says, with another laugh. "We also delivered different kinds of bread, like pumpernickel, that I'd never seen.

"Before I went to work in the Carter Administration, for a background check, they asked for all my addresses, and I realized we moved every 18 months," he continues. "Of course, I'd only known all the Black neighborhoods."

In 1956, however—two years after Marshall, a Baltimore native, won the landmark Brown v. Board of Education desegregation decision—Gibson entered City College high school. Voted the storied institution's first African-American class officer, he moved on to Howard University, becoming a student civil-rights leader, motivated, he says, by a basic desire to "fully participate" in life. After Columbia Law School, he was the first "negro," as the Baltimore News-American reported, appointed to clerk for a federal judge in Maryland in 1967. And then Gibson clerked for Venable, Baetjer & Howard, one of the state's two biggest law firms. His goal at the time was to buy his parents, a janitor and a cook, a house. He recalls that period now, before his presentation in the courthouse's Barr Library, where he spent long hours researching cases as a Venable clerk—and where he was diligently working when he learned Rev. Martin Luther King Jr. had been shot.

With Baltimore convulsed in riots following King's assassination, Gibson instead decided to join the city's top Black law firm, Brown, Allen, Watts, Murphy & Russell, and immediately set out to elect the first Black leaders—including two of those partners listed above—to citywide offices. Quickly developing a reputation as a high-energy, no-holds-barred, grassroots organizer, Gibson served as campaign manager for Joseph Howard, who became the first Black judge on the Baltimore City Supreme Bench and the first African American to win a citywide seat in the fall of 1968—just seven months after King's death. In the next election cycle, Gibson directed the campaigns of Milton Allen, the first African American elected Baltimore State's Attorney—and the first to hold a chief prosecutor's position in a major

U.S. city—and William Murphy, who won a Municipal Court judge-ship. Paul Chester, whose campaign Gibson also directed, became the first African-American circuit-court clerk the same year, 1970.

Finally, the young organizer and his law firm supported Parren Mitchell, who became the first African American from Maryland elected to Congress in 1970. In two years, the color of Baltimore's political landscape had begun a transformation.

"I had every intention of working for Venable; there was an expec-tation that I would. But then Martin Luther King was shot, and I'm thinking, 'Why am I going to work for the establishment?'" Gibson says. "And I changed my mind."

34. Guns for Gigabytes

Inside a velvet rope, on the sidewalk outside West Baltimore's Cultural Arts Center, an ominous line forms on a hot and eerily quiet Saturday afternoon. A man standing in front reveals that he's carrying, hidden in a purple Ravens blanket, an Armi Jager AP-15 assault weapon. Behind him, a man holds a .22 caliber rifle wrapped in newspaper. Nearby, a woman reaches into her purse and pulls a pistol from a sock. Someone else lifts a firearm from a beer cooler. Further back in line, Frank Lipira takes a revolver—"concealed" inside a manila envelope—out of the waistband of his jean shorts.

Like the others, Lipira's exchanging his gun for a Dell laptop, courtesy of the nonprofit Digit All Systems. Organized with the Mayor's Office of Criminal Justice and SWAT team members from the police department, the guns for computers event is believed to be the first of its kind in the U.S.

Lipira, who witnessed shootings growing up in Park Heights, is concerned his children might find his handgun—or that it could be stolen. But he's not sure who in the family will get the laptop. "My daughter is 9 and wants it," he says. "So does my wife."

There's live music, fried chicken, and potato salad inside as the crowd waits to receive their computers. Digit All Systems employee Toni Klatt, handing out laptop vouchers as weapons are turned it, takes the stage for a moment.

"I want to thank everyone who is here," she says. "My fiancé, my son's father, was shot to death earlier this year," she continues, tears coming to her eyes. "I don't want another 18-month-old child asking where their father is."

35. School Girls

For the 29th year on this date, Max Obuszewski stands at evening rush hour on North Charles Street and holds up a grainy, blown-up, black-and-white photo of Hiroshima that was taken shortly after the Enola Gay dropped the first atomic bomb.

"Those who cannot remember the past are condemned to repeat it," reads the quote from philosopher George Santayana, captioning the photo on Obuszewski's poster. Two-dozen others, including a mom toting two kids, join the quiet—other than supportive honking horns—annual commemoration. The location near The Johns Hopkins University is meant to simultaneously protest the school's drone-weapon research, and the small event is also an opportunity to highlight the dangers not just of nuclear weapons but nuclear power— for example, the ongoing Fukushima radiation leaks.

Still, as Obuszewski glances around at the sparsely attended demonstration, he can't help but wonder what happened to the anti-war, anti-nuke movement. "I took a bus to New York in June1982, and there were a million people in Central Park for an anti-nuclear demonstration," he says, with a good-natured laugh. "Where'd everybody go?"

Afterward, demonstrators head to the nearby Friends Meeting House where 81-year-old Setsuko Thurlow shares the horror she witnessed as a 13-year-old Hiroshima schoolgirl: "People walking like ghost-like figures, flesh hanging from their bones, holding their eyeballs in their hands . . . others on the ground, begging for water, stomachs bursting open."

When she's finished, Thurlow sits to watch a 15-minute Hiroshima documentary made last year by another schoolgirl, Meher Hans, when she was a Ridgely Middle School eighth-grader. For the project, Hans interviewed Thurlow by phone, but the two are now meeting for the first time as the Hiroshima survivor watches the short film, also for the first time.

In the dark Friends Meeting House basement, Thurlow's voice suddenly calls out as scenes of the rubbled, desolate city—including a lone stone archway and half-steeple—pan across the screen. "That's my church!"

36. Hacking It

Behind the junkyard and strip club, in a cramped industrial garage off Pulaski Highway filled with saws, gears, drill presses, and duct tape, but also a high-end laser cutter, 3D printer, 5-foot functional robot, and laptops, Jason Morris ducks his head in the door to "oohs and aahs." Morris, sporting new Google glasses, happily lets the guys (it's all guys tonight, except for one woman) try on his computerized eyewear at the Baltimore Hackerspace's weekly open meeting.

"A hacker space," founding member Myles Pekala explains, refers to a place where you take one thing or several things and repurpose those things into something else." It doesn't mean breaking into CIA computers.

Hunkered at crowded tables, amid beer bottles and chips, collective members (pitching in $30 a month for access to tools and fellow hackers' various expertise) mostly work on personal projects. Mark Haygood, a retired city police officer, joined two years ago, seeking software help with his walking robot with George Foreman grill feet.

Meanwhile, Pekala, a research scientist, builds wheel housing for a 2.5-horsepower go-kart for an upcoming racing series in New York. "It'll go about 30 miles per hour. Helmets are required on the course," he says. "Most of us here weigh around 200 pounds though, and we need to find someone lighter to drive. Somebody's wife or girlfriend."

Nearby, Terry Kilby tweaks his mini-drone helicopter, which he employs with a high-definition camera to shoot unique aerial images, including the mysterious face on Mount Vernon's Washington

Monument, long-rumored to be modeled after someone other than Washington, but impossible to see from the park below. "It doesn't look like Washington," says Kilby, bringing up the photo on his iPhone. "More like Andrew Johnson on the $20 bill."

37. The Dome

The youngest boys, 8 or 9 years old, in the shadows of a corner church, some row homes, and a few vacant buildings, practice their dribbling on the broken sidewalks between games. During the action, they lean in against the fence around East Baltimore's iconic basketball court, known as "The Dome," straining to catch a glimpse of one of the "big kids" driving to the hoop.

Beneath the pavilion-style tin roof that gave the outdoor court its nickname four decades ago, some 400 fans fill the bleachers. The Dome looks different than it did when future NBA stars Muggsy Bogues, Sam Cassell, Carmelo Anthony, and, further back, Skip Wise starred here. Under Armour and the NBA renovated it last year with a new floor, fiberglass backboards, and fresh paint. But the soul of the place remains unchanged.

"This is where your rep is earned," says Dane Goodwin, an organizer of the annual Bmore Hoops All-Star event, including tonight's John Crowder National Game, featuring top high-school athletes on their way to college programs. A promising 6-foot-8 power forward, Crowder would've played in this game but was fatally shot three years ago before his senior year at Our Lady of Mount Carmel.

With a minute to play, his team clinging to a 59-58 lead, City College's Kamau Stokes grabs an outlet pass and bursts down the left side. With opponents in full chase, the 6-foot guard suddenly leaps from one of the lower free-throw blocks and dunks a ferocious right-hand slam—just the kind of play the kids outside the fence and fans inside came to see.

"When I was little, I looked up to John [Crowder]," Stokes says, holding the game's MVP trophy. "I knew him well. He got shot and wasn't able to live his dreams. I'm working on it."

Postscript: Kamau Stokes helped lead Kansas State to the NCAA Tournament in 2018.

38. Lady Day Way

In a cramped Upper Fells Point alley, Joe Rizza—T-shirt, jeans, and gray O's cap—sips from a can of beer in a foam koozie, studying a pile of broken blue tiles laid out in front of a cinderblock wall. Within reach sits a metal cart with mortar, putty knives, grouting tools, and a hammer for breaking tiles and mirrored glass.

"I started this with white dinner plates, some I stole from my kitchen," says Rizza with a smile. "I'm sure people walking by wondered what the hell I was doing."

Rizza's mosaic of Billie Holiday in full voice—white plates representing the iconic gardenias she wore in her hair—stands steps from her childhood row house. The work, which portrays waves of sound morphing into bluebirds as the piece moves down the street, is part of a larger effort to memorialize Holiday in the neighborhood where she grew up. At Durham and Pratt streets, there's a recently completed four-story mural of the singer, and there are plans to rename the block Lady Day Way—not that life in Baltimore, or elsewhere, was a fairy tale for Holiday, born to a 13-year-old mother, raised largely by relatives, and raped as a child here on Christmas Eve.

"None of the pieces have been cut, they're all broken, and I've stared at them sometimes thinking there's no way to make them fit," says Rizza, who lives around the corner. "I've done drawing, painting, photography, and just started working in mosaic when this project came up. But it felt right. She was using that brokenness to make music, to escape, to fly. That's what she's doing right there."

39. Well Read

Retracing the footsteps of old Baltimore's men and women of letters, a dozen curious folks, donning corduroys, sweaters, and light jackets on the first cool day of fall, gather at the brownstone birthplace of muckraking journalist Upton Sinclair. In front of what's now the American Heart Association Building on North Charles Street, Michele Alexander, leading the Maryland Humanities Council-sponsored Literary Mount Vernon Walking Tour, notes that Lewis's chronicle of the meatpacking industry, for example, "is why we have meat inspectors working today."

"Well, not *today*," a tour member chimes in—a nod to both the recent government shutdown and salmonella outbreak—drawing nervous chuckles.

The group stops by Edgar Allan Poe's former West Mulberry home and visits the former homes of Gertrude Stein and H.L. Mencken, as well as the Stafford Hotel, where F. Scott Fitzgerald stayed while Zelda sought psychiatric treatment at Sheppard Pratt. Also on the itinerary: the performance space of 1923 Pulitzer Prize poet Edna St. Vincent Millay, who said, "It's not true that life is one damn thing after another; it's one damn thing over and over."

Later, inside the dark wood and marbled columns of the five-tiered George Peabody Library, curator Paul Espinosa opens a massive tome—two-and-a-half feet in length—of Latin Mass hymnals handwritten in 1430 in Spain. He points to the words "*Gloria patri, et filio*," meaning "Glory to the Father, the Son," and then the abstract symbol, not to be spelled out, according to ancient tradition, for the Holy Spirit.

The pages remain well preserved, albeit white on one side, yellow on other. But not from age. "Each page was made of calfskin—the yellow side is the hair side; the white side, the skin side," Espinosa explains, turning a page. "A book this size would've been very expensive to make," he adds. "It would've taken a whole herd."

40. The Duchess

Looking through Attman's Delicatessen's glass counter window, the first stop on Baltimore Heritage's Bakeries and Immigration tour, catering concierge Elaine Gershberg calls attention to the "coddies" stacked near the predictable lox, bagels, all-beef hot dogs, and salami. Observant Jews don't eat shellfish, and the codfish, Old Bay, and potato treat, Gershberg explains, "became known as the Jewish crab cake."

"This used to be Corned Beef Row," she tells the group gathered in Attman's Kibbitz Room, adding that Lombard Street out front used to travel one-way in the opposite direction. But, as the story goes, it got turned around by a politically connected former delicatessen owner intent on moving his store from last to first on the once well-trod thoroughfare.

"There were seven delis on this street," she says, gesturing toward the Lloyd Street Synagogue, the country's third-oldest standing synagogue and now home to the Jewish Museum of Maryland. "Horseradish Lane, where my family, the Tulkoffs, made horseradish, was across the street."

The tour continues to DiPasquale's on Gough Street, established 100 years ago and also still family-owned. The group orders espresso and homemade pine-nut cookies, called *pignoli*, and fresh focaccia, gnocchi, and lasagna to carry home.

"The original Esskay's (the Baltimore meatpacking company founded in 1858) was down the street and used to run their hogs through this alley," says Joe DiPasquale, whose grandfather arrived from the small Italian town of Corropoli to work on the railroad but ended up opening an Italian market in heavily German Highlandtown. "No one knows why he settled here," DiPasquale laughs.

At Hoehn's Bakery on Conkling, 61-year-old Sharon Hoehn Hooper, in an apron, welcomes everyone into the bakery founded by her grandfather in 1927. That year marks the date the bakery's massive brick-oven hearth, nicknamed "the Duchess" and still in daily use, was embedded into the rear kitchen wall. Hopper began finishing and filling donuts here when she was 12.

"After high school, I'd gotten a clerical job at an insurance agency, which I liked and it paid well. Then somebody quit and my father asked me to come back. He said, 'I'll match what they're paying you, plus free room and board, and you don't have to wash dishes at home.'

"That was it," she says with a shrug and smile. "That was as close as I got to getting out."

41. Sci-Fi Channel

For the 50th anniversary episode of Doctor Who, the iconic BBC television series about an adventurous alien in human form—a time and space traveling good "doctor"—120 members and friends of the Baltimore Science Fiction Society squeeze into the old Aldine Theatre. Closed since 1954 because of the advent of TV, and home to the society since 1991, the Formstone, former fourth-run movie house makes a cozy venue for the global, 94-country simulcast of *Day of the Doctor*.

Some 11,000 volumes of science fiction and fantasy literature, stacked high in bookshelves, plus DVDs and board games, ring the viewing area, currently filled with folding chairs and a rowdy audience.

In hosting the *Doctor Who* event (devotees are referred to as "Whovians"), the sci-fi nonprofit, founded in 1963, naturally hopes to attract a few new members. Prior to the screening, social media coordinator Alexander Harris highlights, for example, the group's regional Balticon convention, the Ray Gun book club, game days, and writing groups. And, in three weeks, Harris adds, there will be the annual holiday decorating of "the Dalek"—a 6-foot-6 papier-mâché and plastic replica of an extraterrestrial cyborg race from, coincidentally, *Doctor Who*.

"A compromise between our Christian and Jewish members about a dozen years ago," Baltimore Science Fiction Society board chairman Dale Arnold explains with a chuckle. "It's not the holidays until the Dalek is decorated."

42. True Meaning

"*Habari* (How are you)?" Maulana Karenga booms in Swahili, greeting the crowd overflowing the Reginald F. Lewis Museum's theater and balconies.

"*Nzuri* (Good)!" comes the response. Close to 1,000 people have turned out for the all-day Kwanzaa event, and those who cannot find a place to sit or stand watch Karenga via video in the Africa-themed "marketplace" outside the auditorium.

Born Ronald Everett, not far from the Eastern Shore birthplaces of Frederick Douglass and Harriet Tubman, Karenga founded the weeklong "celebration of the good in the world" and African culture 47 years ago. Active in the Black Power movement and a scholar today with two Ph.D.s, Karenga explains Kwanzaa is a means for African-Americans to "reaffirm our rootedness" in African culture and "reintroduce African communitarian values."

"That's Kwanzaa," he says.

Karenga's African-wisdom teaching is followed by Baltimore's Sankofa Dance troupe, local beatboxer Shodekeh, and Griot storytelling. Throughout the day, "Mama" Sallah directs craft workshops, including weaving traditional red, black, and green Kwanzaa mats.

"I've celebrated Kwanzaa since 1976," Sallah says. "In West Baltimore, in those days, you went house to house celebrating Kwanzaa every night. If you did it right, it took three days of cooking to prepare—chicken, fish, collard greens, sweet potatoes, corn bread, bread pudding, rice pudding, banana pudding, apple pie—150 people might come by.

"At every house, there was one room to put the kids, and it would be a party all night," she continues with a laugh. "Now it's too commercial."

43. Last House Standing

A decade and a half ago, photographer Ben Marcin hiked, not hitchhiked, from Baltimore to Philadelphia, traversing as many remote farms and wooded areas as possible along the way. He estimates he's completed more than 5,600 hikes, two each weekend, one mid-week, give or take, for the past 40 years, mostly in the counties surrounding Baltimore. But his meanderings also include far-flung places like Guatemala's Mayan highlands, rural Mexico, India, and Montenegro.

His first pilgrimage, at 4 years old, began at the kitchen door of his family's house in Augsburg, Germany, where he was born. "I crossed over the railroad tracks, cut through a cornfield, went through some woods, and walked into town where I asked a traffic cop at an intersection to get my dad," he recalls in his second-floor, Bolton Hill brownstone studio. "I was out of gas and wasn't sure how to get home."

Since earning an economics degree from the University of Maryland, Baltimore County, he's held down a job at the Social Security Administration for the past three decades, but he's always had this other side, the solo expeditioner part, that is also linked to an artistic impulse.

He tried watercolor painting initially—"Looks easy, but it's not"—and didn't buy his first camera until he was 27. Like many people, the first photos he took tended to be travel pictures from exotic destinations. Later, self-taught, he began playing with color and infrared images and eventually had three shows at Hampden's Gomez Gallery, which closed in 2003.

He's now 55, and although his hair has grayed, he remains as fit, restless, and curious as ever. Over the years, however, his photography has turned closer to home, more inward, "to stories," as he puts it. Begun in 2010, his series *Last House Standing*—large-scale portraits of literally the last rowhouse standing on different city blocks, often no more than two miles from his own home—is currently on display at C. Grimaldis Gallery. The acclaimed series is also garnering the first international attention of his career, with reviews from the United Kingdom, Italy, Germany, and China, not to mention cultural observers like *The Paris Review*, *Slate*, and *Wired*. The stark, unsentimental photos manage to reveal both the decay and ghostly beauty of some of Baltimore's iconic rowhouses and their fading environs.

"Monuments," Marcin calls the withered, three-story, last turn-of-the-century rowhouses, "to dead neighborhoods."

In many ways, Marcin's *Last House Standing* photographs are more remarkable for what they leave out than for what they show. There are no cars in front of the homes in the barren streets, and, except for the occasional air-conditioning unit or bed sheet in an upstairs window, few signs of life, if any, can be seen in the pictures. Some of the homes are boarded up and appear to be vacant; others are clearly inhabited.

There are no leaves on the trees nearby, no clouds or sunshine in the backdrop, just overcast, dull skies in nearly every photograph. There is rarely even a street sign or lamppost in the frame, and there are no people. But the most obvious things missing are the neighboring homes—leaving the jarring juxtaposition of a house that is 15 feet wide and 40 feet tall standing by itself in an empty lot. "No engineer or architect would design a structure like that," says Marcin, who moved to the U.S. when he was 10. "They were meant to be attached to something else.

"The irony isn't lost on me," he adds. "All the traveling I've done, and, in the end, what I find most compelling has been right here all along."

44. Poe Love

As barren trees cast shadows over Westminster Hall on a late Sunday afternoon, those arriving to salute Edgar Allan Poe's 205th birthday gently place roses and pennies, per tradition, around the macabre poet's burial memorial. (In 1865, Baltimore school children began collecting pennies to move Poe's body from an unmarked grave to its current resting spot.)

A festive Irish folk song kicks off the occasion, followed by remarks from Poe House curator emeritus Jeff Jerome. Beneath a spotlight, actors in period costumes, including Emily Cory in black evening gown and cape, perform readings of the despairing poet's best-known works, for the 60 or so visitors crowding the small burial area, including "Annabel Lee," "The Raven," and "Alone."

From childhood's hour I have not been
As others were; I have not seen
As others saw; I could not bring
My passions from a common spring.

After the presentation, those gathered—some have come for decades to the annual event—stay for a raffle of original concrete pieces from Poe's old Amity Street home and a couple of Poe-themed birthday cakes before beginning a tour of catacombs under the historic hall.

"I've been coming since the 1970s," says Jo Ann Irick Jones, holding one of the sought-after black frosted cakes, decorated with red roses and the iconic image of the sunken cheeked, sad-eyed poet. "This was where my husband—he's now passed—and I came on our first date. We both loved Poe. We spent the rest of the day driving around Baltimore, talking and getting to know another. To me, this is a romantic place."

45. Pet Friendly

"DO NOT handle the dragons without permission," warns a sign.

"Will the hedgehog show its face?" asks Melanie Osborne, taking smartphone photos of the scaled, shelled, hairy, and quilled creatures at Repticon—the two-day reptile and exotic animal show, returning for the fourth time to the Maryland State Fairgrounds. "How much is the iguana?" Her daughter, she says, may be in the market soon for a pet.

"My sons want a lizard, a snake, and a chameleon. We've had two lizards—and lots of turtles and frogs—in the past," the Severna Park native explains. "Basically, we're allergic to cats and dogs."

Nearby, a teenager touches a big, ugly frog, poking it harder a second time. "Does it bite?" he asks.

"Yes, it eats mice," says the exhibitor.

Others check out the neon geckos and pet the boas and pythons curled around vendor's necks. Bearded dragons, a vendor assures, actually make quite nice pets. "They'll stay on your shoulder or sit on the windowsill in the sun." A Halethorpe-based AR Reptile House vendor explains he and his partners actually keep 25 snakes in their rowhouse basement. And breed rats (for feeding). "The neighbors are pretty cool about it," he says.

Meanwhile, Paige Zinderman, a Carver Center for the Arts & Technology senior, happily allows a four-inch, eight-legged tarantula to creep back and forth across her hands. "Aren't they poisonous?"

inquires a middle-age man, nervously looking on. 'No, venomous,"
the spider's owner clarifies. "Blowfish are poisonous, in that if you eat
one, you get poisoned. Things that are venomous bite you. They have
fangs."

"Oh."

"I like cats, too, but have you ever been to a cat show?" asks
Zinderman. "Cats are [all] pretty much the same. I like the way the
snakes move. I like that are a hundred different reptiles here.

"And look around, I fit in," she adds. "The people are weird."

46. Ring Tone

"There's nine matches and only three have been approved for weapons," Dan McDeVitt reminds the motley crew of tough guys, heels, cheap-shot artists, Samoans, and "Black Wall Street" thugs—some doing push-ups for a last-minute pump, others pulling on Lycra singlets and elbow pads. The Joppatowne Plaza Shopping Center venue normally serves as home to an Amish flea market, but tonight it is hosting the Maryland Championship Wrestling's 16th Anniversary Show.

McDeVitt, an ex-villain wrestler known as "Corporal Punishment" and MCW's co-founder—and realtor by day—also approves one wrestler's request to take three folding chairs in the ring. Then he cautions everyone about the venue's slippery tile floor: "If you throw someone through the barricades, they'll end up in the first row."

Meanwhile, 64-year-old WWE Hall of Famer Jerry "The King" Lawler, who famously put comedian Andy Kaufman in a neck brace in the 1980s, poses for photos with a line of fans stretching to the door. Later, just before intermission, Lawler, still built like a keg of beer, enters the ring to battle "The Pinnacle" Shawn Patrick. Despite his age and a 2012 heart attack, which occurred while *announcing* a show, Lawler trades body slam after body slam with Patrick, an Ocean City hotel manager by day, before finishing him off with his signature pile driver.

Kelly Bell, a 290-pound, longtime MCW wrestler, retiring because of vertebrae issues, notes being a good wrestling heel isn't easy.

"I always started with a bad joke, but you walk a line," says Bell, who fronts the popular Kelly Bell Band in another life. "Years ago, I grabbed the mic and asked a good ole' boy crowd what Pink Floyd and Dale Earnhardt had in common. The punch line? 'The last hit for both of them was 'The Wall.'

"Too soon [after Earnhardt's death]. My tag-team partner and I needed a state police escort out of the building."

47. Land of Pleasant Living

A light snow falls on Fells Point's railroad tracks as mostly thirty-something couples pile into a heated chartered bus for a Saturday tour of Federal Hill and Locust Point. Not a history tour, per se, but a Re/Max-sponsored home-buyer's expedition of exposed-brick living rooms, granite-counter kitchens, ceramic-tile baths, and panoramic views from two-tiered rooftop decks.

"Not sure you're all going fit into that house," smiles an elderly man, stepping onto his marble stoop as the couples traipse into the rehabbed rowhome next door. Upstairs, M&T Bank Stadium's purple seats are visible from a brand-new deck. Below, across the alley, a stout older woman in sturdy shoes shakes out a carpet.

The bus itself feels out of place here, struggling to navigate the narrow streets in "the neighborhood once known as South Baltimore," as one real estate broker on board puts it. There's also a lot of unappreciated local history passing outside the black-tinted windows—an original painted screen on East Gittings Street, the former Southway duckpin lanes—now condos—on the corner of Hamburg and Charles, where Babe Ruth once rolled, the Cross Street Market, the 1890s brick and brownstone public school repurposed as the contemporary School 33 Arts Center.

In truth, the tour never quite reaches Locust Point, which as everyone who grew up on the peninsula will tell you, begins at Rallo's Restaurant on Lawrence Street—even though Rallo's is gone, too, and it's Big Matty's Diner now. It's unfortunate because if there is one place you'd like to take a busload of soon-to-be Baltimoreans to help them understand everything that underlies this town's singular character and eccentricity, it's Locust Point, the first official point of entry for the state of Maryland. Baltimore was born here.

Indeed, you can make the case that nearly everything we think of as quintessentially Baltimore— Bawlmerese, blue crabs, Old Bay, Edgar Allan Poe, H.L. Mencken, Corned Beef Row, Billie Holiday, Pennsylvania Avenue, the Block, Preakness hats, Camden Yards, Natty Boh—came out of the roiling mash-up of Old South heritage, blue collar jobs, and the new influx of immigrants from what were once the busiest immigration piers below the Mason-Dixon line.

"Absolutely, you can trace it all back to the blending of Southern culture and migration, Northern industry, and the influx of European immigrants—first mixing at the port and its neighborhoods," Mary Rizzo, an American Studies Ph.D. and editor of the Public History Commons website, says later. "Baltimore's character, its uniqueness, the dialect—all of it—is a kind of amalgamation of these very different things coming together, with a little Appalachia thrown in," adds Rizzo, who has studied, in particular, the city's love affair with the working class "Hon" women of old Baltimore. "It's all threaded through these neighborhoods."

But even Formstone—the ersatz siding that John Waters infamously dubbed the "polyester of brick"—goes unappreciated as a peculiar Charm City legacy among the out-of-towners looking to take advantage of Baltimore's relatively inexpensive housing market. "I guess some of the homes were done in large stone because it was cheaper than brick?" inquires a young Capitol Hill lobbyist, sitting next to his wife.

"Actually," explains another real estate agent, pausing perhaps to hide any disappointment with his would-be client's lack of familiarity with local culture, "that's a facade."

48. Home Front

Inside the marbled War Memorial Building, about 200 people, including current Maryland National Guard soldiers and a dozen and a half surviving members of Maryland's historic, all-Black, 231st Transportation Truck Battalion, are celebrating the unit's 135th anniversary. Later, there will be a wreath laying at the Negro Heroes of the Unites States statue at City Hall.

Also on hand, a descendant of "Buffalo Soldier" 1st Sgt. Augustus Wiley, who served in the 9th Calvary Regiment after being born into slavery in Reisterstown.

Dubbed the "Monumental City Guards" when the unit received recognition as an all-Black independent militia company in 1879, the truck battalion was called to active duty during the Spanish-American War, both World Wars, and the Korean War. "The 231st Battalion was the first U.S. National Guard unit to land in Pusan—Dec. 31, 1950," retired Sgt. 1st Class Louis S. Diggs, the keynote speaker, tells the audience.

A member of the 231st, Diggs recalls waking up in Korea after integration came to his unit's camp literally overnight—when troop losses and the arrival of new soldiers put Black and white soldiers in the same barracks for the first time—albeit two years after President Truman's order abolishing racial discrimination in the Armed Forces.

After Korea, Diggs spent several years in Japan and Germany, not realizing how little things had changed at home. "I'll never forget visiting my mother in Sandtown before leaving for Philadelphia, where I was stationed next," Diggs recalls. "She made me a big bag lunch for the drive—didn't have to look inside—whatever she'd cooked, I knew would be good. But after a ways, I open it and along with my food, I pull out an empty jug.

"I thought, 'What's this?' And then it hit me—she knew, even if I'd forgotten—there wouldn't be a bathroom on Pulaski Highway or Route 40 that I could use."

49. Animal Lovers

Eric Vocke, who runs the Baltimore Bully Crew, a volunteer pit bull rescue, expects more than 500 supporters tonight as he welcomes guests past the purple and black balloons, a statuette of 1998 Playmate of the Year Karen McDougal, and metal detectors. Ducking inside the packed Gentleman's Gold Club, Tom Petty's "Running Down a Dream" blares from the sound system as a young, blond, butterfly-tattooed woman twirls above the main bar.

"This is 'Tits for Pits,'" smiles Vocke, a chef by trade, referring to the 501(c)3's fourth annual fundraiser. "We'll raise 25 percent of our annual budget here."

Most of the $20 cover (there's more couples and women this evening that one might expect), plus a percentage of the beverage sales, goes to the organization's efforts at helping pit bulls, including some pulled from dog fighting rings. Meanwhile, former MMA fighter Gordon "Shotgun" Shell, who has offered to fight Michael Vick (the former NFL quarterback convicted for running a dog-fighting ring) for charity, is signing autographs and posing for pictures. There's also a "Lap dances for Second Chances" raffle.

Near the Baltimore Bully Crew T-shirts and merch table, April Doherty, a paralegal with the Baltimore County state's attorney's animal abuse unit, admits last year's event was her first venture to a strip club. "It was, um, interesting," she says. Her husband, Kevin, standing next to her, adds, "It's not really our scene. We're usually in bed by 9:30." Just then, an athletic young woman in nothing more than a

G-string and, incredibly, heels, lands a near-perfect backflip atop the bar, sliding down into a full split.

"I'd give that a 4.4," Kevin laughs over the music and appreciative applause.

"That," his wife leans in, "was badass."

50. G-d of Baseball

Squeezing in an appearance at the packed Bolton Street Synagogue between her 6 and 11 p.m. anchor duties, WBAL's Deborah Weiner shares a story about being a newbie journalist in the Deep South—and the regrettable advice she took at the time to use a non-Jewish last name professionally. Eventually, she was "outed" by a local politician, who told her, by the way, he loved *Fiddler on the Roof.*

The event, including a silent auction, food, and wine, is actually a themed Stoop Storytelling show—"It's Complicated: Stories about the Joys and Oys of Contemporary Jewish Life"—and benefits the synagogue's educational programs. Anecdotes include a blind date with Monica Lewinsky, being struck by lightning, a Jewish grandmother's acceptance of interfaith marriage, and one family's four-continent diaspora.

Also, one man's struggle to balance two religions: Judaism and baseball.

The Orioles' last game of the 2011 season, Ira Gewanter explains, began the night of Rosh Hashanah. Not that it should have mattered with the O's wrapping up their 14th straight losing season. Except the Birds, playing at Camden Yards, could knock Boston out of the playoffs with a win that night—a small victory perhaps to some, but not an O's diehard.

Staying at his parents' home that evening, "buried beneath the blankets with my wife trying to sleep in the bed next to me," Gewanter followed the game on his smartphone, tracking balls and strikes and base-running avatars. "Not streaming video," he says, "more like tele-graph." Such electronic devices, he notes, are prohibited on holy days by observant Jews like his father, who, of course, caught him.

"I was all sweaty [from hiding under the covers] and felt like a hor-rible person," Gewanter recounts. "Sitting on the edge of the bed, my father broke the silence first. 'What's the score?'" he asked me.

51. Bullets and Old Battles

Up to his knees in a carefully measured trench behind Patterson Park's pagoda, a field archaeologist gently shovels a spade's worth of dirt, dumping it into a wire screen for sifting. Scattered bricks already pulled from the trench, believed to be the former site of Jacob Laudenslanger's tavern/butcher's shop, are stacked on the nearby grass.

According to historical documents, the tavern/butcher shop—because of its vantage atop Hampstead Hill in what's now Patterson Park—served as headquarters for Gen. Samuel Smith, who oversaw the entire 1814 Battle of Baltimore. As the fireworks, made famous by Francis Scott Key, raged off Fort McHenry, crack British troops made their way up the North Point Peninsula, eventually heading east toward downtown Baltimore.

At Patterson Park, however, says Greg Katz, a field director with the Louis Berger Group, which is overseeing a six-week dig for non-profit Baltimore Heritage, some 15,000-20,000 volunteer and militia forces from all over Maryland, as well as Virginia, West Virginia, New Jersey, and Delaware, had built earthen mounds for the land defense of the city. (Nicknamed the "Best Backyard in Baltimore," the 137-acre park was formerly established 13 years after the would-be British invasion, following a donation of land by philanthropist William Patterson.)

Along with the bricks from Laudenslanger's building, artifacts found to date include old buttons and coins, and ceramics possibly used as chamber pots by the militia who camped here. Although a gun flint and musket ball, typically used by American militia at the time, have also been found, no shots were ever fired here during the Battle of Baltimore.

"The British troops got about one-third of the way across the park," says Katz, gesturing down the hill. "They'd already lost their commander in the Battle of North Point, saw what they were facing, and turned around."

Which, of course, doesn't mean shots were never fired in Patterson Park. Especially, in the park's turbulent history in the '70s, '80s, and '90s, before its revitalization in recent years.

"I've got a spent shell," offers a volunteer, pulling a small piece of metal from one of the wire sifting racks and handing it to another field archaeologist, who shakes his head.

"That's a .22."

52. Natural-Born Artists

In a crowded gallery not far from the Matisses and Miros of the Baltimore Museum of Art's contemporary collection, Lucy Dworak-Fisher stands next to her Japanese-style, black ink piece, "Fall Tree." It's a simple but elegant lined work with a few hand-cut, burnt orange leaves clinging to branches—more scattered around the trunk—set against an austere white-gray backdrop. Dworak-Fisher, in a cotton dress and sneakers, fingernails on one hand painted blue, is reticent, however, about discussing her piece.

"She does like to draw, but she's shy," her mother says. "She only agreed to four photographs."

A Federal Hill Preparatory kindergartener, Lucy's piece is part of the annual Baltimore City Public Schools Art Exhibition, which showcases 400 works from 90 public schools. Highlights include a found-object portrait of singer Lana Del Rey made of lipstick, broken pencils, bottle caps, crayons, and assorted bits of metal and plastic. There's also a detailed pencil study of an empty school hallway, an 11th grader's unsentimental street photography, and a middle school girl's conceptual sculpture depicting the complex world of social media.

Later, the Mount Washington School art teacher Rachel Brander, who explains the annual exhibition is as important to faculty as students—"All you go through in a year, how could you miss a day like this?"—comes across Lucy's "Fall Tree."

"What's that Picasso quote?" Brander asks rhetorically. "'All children are artists. The problem is how to remain an artist.' All kids are artists until third grade, and then they start noticing that their work doesn't look like someone else's and they become self-conscious," Brander says. "School beats [their natural creativity] out them, too. That's the art teacher's job—to put it back in."

53. For Whom It Stands

In the Reginald F. Lewis Museum theater, 10 local people share personal stories, many bittersweet, inspired by the American flag in a program called O Say Can You Feel, related to the current *For Whom It Stands* exhibition. When she considers the flag, Joyce Dennison, a veteran, retired Baltimore City teacher, and former Maryland HIV/AIDS hotline director, recalls protesting segregation at the Northwood Shopping Center as a Morgan State student and the Pine Street jail where she was locked up. She also recalls former U.S. Congressman Barbara Jordan's words: "What the people want is very simple. They want an America as good as its promise."

Walter Jones recites Langston Hughes's poem, "I, Too, Sing America" and Roderick Howard II recounts the life of Charles Ball, a Calvert County slave who escaped, enlisted, and fought in the War of 1812, only to be captured and sold back into slavery.

Ella Pope reads a letter from her younger brother Calvin, written Aug. 24, 1968, 100 days before his tour in Vietnam was scheduled to end, and just before he was killed. "I could read between the lines that he was anxious to come home," she says, fighting back tears as the handwritten note is projected overhead.

Finally, John Wesley Milton, spokesman for the Baltimore City of Civil Rights but a native Mississippian, describes growing up across the street from Roy Bryant and J.W. Milam, the men who murdered 14-year-old Emmett Till. "Everyone knew them," Milton says. "They were the overseers in the field where we all picked cotton." He also recalls later holding an American flag at a march when he was about Till's age—until police officers ripped it from his hands. "Meanwhile, the people cursing us were waving rebel flags."

"I flashed back at that moment to second grade, when we stood and recited the Pledge of Allegiance every morning. And I thought, 'What's wrong with this picture?'"

54. Metal Age

By 10 a.m., while health conscious, organic-food loving crowds sip freshly ground coffee and cheerfully sort through locally grown produce at the Baltimore Farmers' Market & Bazaar, a darker horde (literally—dressed almost entirely in black T-shirts) gathers outside a vacant lot across the street.

This is the final day of Maryland Deathfest XII—billed as "America's biggest metal party of the year"—and soon 4,000 tattooed and pierced fans of doom, death, speed, black, stoner, thrash, and grindcore (no music genre has more subgenres than metal) will be headbanging below the Orleans Street overpass.

Today's big-name acts include Sweden's Candlemass and the U.K.'s Uncle Acid and the Deadbeats, but Charm City's own Misery Index gets the sunburned mosh pit roiling early with a deafening, scorched-earth set. "This is my sixth Deathfest, and I came to see about 10 bands, but Misery Index was one of them," says Pedro Velazco, a sportswriter who has driven from Kokomo, Indiana, for the four-day festival. "I'm 43, and I still call myself a death metal kid."

There are loads of merch tables here, along with beer, margarita, and vodka lemonade stands and labels, like Relapse Records, offering their wares. By mid-afternoon, the food vendors, such as Zombie Barbeque, Headbanging Hotdogs (100-percent vegan), and Pork Lord Tacos—with upscale Bluegrass Tavern executive chef Tim Dyson manning the grill—are getting busy.

"Oh yeah, different crowd than we get in Federal Hill," Dyson laughs. "This is for fun—'Pork Lord' is my nickname at the restaurant. I was in a band in high school, too, and we played this shit. I love it."

55. Going to Pot

Inside a Westin BWI hotel conference room, would-be entrepreneurs, older than you might think, take copious notes as Brent Tageson discusses the finer points of his profession. Dressed in slacks and a golf shirt, Tageson could pass for a corporate CEO, but he is, in fact, a Northern California marijuana grower. Eight years ago, he was busted in a raid, but today he's working for the Cannabis Career Institute, introducing others to a rapidly changing industry.

"If you take all the moisture out," he cautions, explaining proper curing techniques while gesturing to photos of large marijuana plants on the screen behind him, "all you have left is plant material. And what you want is the cannabis oil."

The $300, all-day workshop comes on the heels of Maryland's recent decriminalization of small amounts of marijuana and revision of the state's medical marijuana initiative. After Tageson discusses cultivation, his partner, Aaron Silverman, addresses the retail side of the business as it is currently playing out in California and Colorado. Some here are clearly already growers—"Sure, I'm interested in potentially opening a dispensary, but I do like to garden as a hobby," says one gray-haired man—while others are attending for personal, medical, or purely entrepreneurial reasons.

"I was recently diagnosed with bladder cancer," says another middle-aged man. "I'm an insurance agent."

Kal Shah, a Hindu businessman, smiles when asked why he's interested in pot. "Well, I've never smoked marijuana," he admits. "But

I'd consider opening a dispensary." The good-natured Shah chuckles. "Why not? I don't drink and I own several liquor stores, and I don't eat meat and I own two Subway franchises."

Postscript: The medical marijuana industry in Maryland ended its first year of operation in 2018 with $96.3 million in sales.

56. Wind and a Prayer

Filing out of morning Mass at St. Leo the Great Roman Catholic Church, led by Bishop Denis Madden, some 400 Little Italy parishioners gather for the traditional Feast of St. Anthony street procession, keeping a 110-year-old promise to the medieval Franciscan friar. As flames moved east during the Great Baltimore Fire of 1904, which destroyed more than 1,500 buildings in its wake, Italian immigrants were told to evacuate.

"Sparks were coming into the neighborhood," says Jerry Elliott, president of the St. Anthony's Society of St. Leo's. A number of worried faithful, however, went to the church and removed St. Anthony's statue—the same one that remains in the church today—carrying it to the nearby waterfront and praying that their homes and church be spared.

"When the winds changed overnight, they decided to hold a festival every year in honor of St. Anthony," explains Elliott, adding that although he's Irish, he is "married to an Italian girl" with Baltimore roots.

After the procession, the statue is placed beneath a tent for prayers to the saint and donations to the poor.

"I haven't missed [the festival] since I arrived from Sicily in 1967," says Anthony Staiti, 74, after pinning $5 on the statue and receiving a small St. Anthony medallion.

"When I was sick as a child, my Sicilian mother prayed to St. Anthony every day and lit candles until I was better. As a boy, she used to dress me up in a brown robe with the white rope belt like him, and I'd march in the procession there.

"She told me when I grew up, it was up to me if I wanted to keep praying to St. Anthony," Staiti continues. "I do it for her. But it's worked, right? I'm still here."

57. Boyz to Men

Lt. Colonel Melvin Russell is addressing several hundred men at the edge of Leakin Park on a warm Friday night, the setting sun catching the gold trim of his police hat. "This city belongs to all of us," Russell implores the crowd, preparing for a 9.5-mile anti-violence march from one end of the notorious North Avenue to the other—and back. "It's your presence, your being out here that's going to turn this city around. You can't be afraid of the kids that you used to give freeze pops and bags of chips to."

Earlier, Mayor Stephanie Rawlings-Blake noted her 20-year-old cousin was killed in a robbery last year.

As sirens and several "12 o'clock boys" fly past, organizer Munir Bahar, who launched the initial 300 Men March after a string of shootings last June, adds that change requires time and commitment. "Like a slow-cooked meal, it takes a lot of attention."

Then, the men, nearly all African American, most wearing black "300 Men" T-shirts with "Baltimore's Anti-Violence Movement" emblazoned in block white lettering across the back, begin their journey. Onlookers shout encouragement, cars honk in appreciation, and the march's female supporters hand out water bottles every few miles.

"It gets real when you come back up under I-83 and see that hill, and you know there's two miles to go," laughs Ian Smith, his shaved head already glistening with perspiration. Smith is also keeping tabs on Divine Harris, a Fort Worthington Elementary fifth grader. "Even when his older brother backed out, he told me he still wanted to do it," says Anita Harris, Divine's mother, waiting for him at the Baltimore Cemetery, the halfway point. "We've lost a lot of friends and family to violence."

"He took my walking stick and he was off," Smith tells his mother. "I had to catch up to him."

Postscript: Less than a year later, following Freddie Gray's death while in police custody, Baltimore's per-capita, large-city homicide rate rose to the highest in the country.

Riverside Park
East Randall Street
August 11, 2014

58. Up Hill Climb

Raised with six siblings in a narrow rowhouse in South Baltimore's historically Black Sharp-Leadenhall neighborhood, Elijah Cummings can recall any number of indelible childhood experiences. Beyond attending a poor, still-segregated elementary school, he was among the first children to integrate the Riverside Park swimming pool in the summer of 1962.

"People were throwing bottles, rocks, and screaming," he says, shaking his head, "calling us everything but a child of God."

He remembers running home on Sundays from the church where his father was a preacher to listen to Martin Luther King Jr.'s speeches on WWIN-AM radio. He also remembers being a teenager and getting stopped by police while returning home one night—from his job at the Baltimore Country Club—past the citywide curfew following the 1968 riots.

But there are other memories, seemingly less profound at the time, which also left their imprint.

"My father, a former South Carolina sharecropper who moved north so his children could be better off, worked long hours at Davidson Chemical doing manual labor," recalls the 63-year-old congressman, sitting in his midtown Baltimore office. "And he was happy to work, and to work overtime to make money to support us. But when he came home, he used to sit in his car, sometimes for an hour. Everyday. It didn't matter if it was 80 degrees, 90 degrees, or 5 degrees.

"We all knew not to disturb him, and it's funny, too, there were not a lot of cars in the street in those days," laughs Cummings, himself a tireless worker by all accounts. Years later, Cummings continues, he asked his father—although he suspected the reason—why he sat in the car. "He told me that he was often treated badly at work, dealing with discrimination, and he didn't want to bring those things, any bitterness, into our home," Cummings says, pausing and getting emotional. "He did not want to make us victims as well. He always came into the house with a gentle smile."

He is recalling this story as he's asked about his dust-up a couple of years ago with Rep. Darrell Issa, the House Oversight Committee chairman, which went viral and thrust Cummings into the national spotlight. (Cummings was the committee's ranking Democratic member at the time.) A half-billionaire California businessman, Issa cut off Cummings's microphone during a key IRS hearing, literally making a slashing motion with his hand across his throat to signal sound technicians during Cummings's opening statement. It was an egregious act, arrogant and disdainful, and a clear violation of House procedure. Anyone in Cummings's seat would've been understandably angry, ready to throttle Issa. But Cummings maintained his composure (his father, who passed away a decade and a half ago, certainly would've been proud), trying only to make his case, passionately—for the Baltimore congressman is nothing if not a man who wears his heart on his sleeve.

"It's not just my voice that was being shut down," Cummings says. "Remember what I said: 'I represent, we represent, over 700,000 people.' What about *our* voice? 'Shut it down [Issa said].' That's not the Democratic way."

The controversy could've played out very differently in today's hyper-politicized social-media environment if Cummings had overreacted. Instead, Issa issued a public apology the next day and the episode proved a galvanizing moment for Cummings, with people stopping him in airports across the country to tell him that they appreciated the way he handled the episode.

"Of the many things I learned from my father—and neither he nor my mother completed elementary school because they went to work in the fields—was to treat everyone with equal respect and not to speak or act out of anger," Cummings says. "Because when you do, the person only hears your tone; they don't get the message.

"And," Cummings adds, tapping a finger to the table for emphasis, "you'll lose sight of the bigger picture. You'll get so caught up in *who* you are fighting, you'll forget *what* you are fighting for—and it's the what that is important."

59. Bunny Tales

"One of the comedians, Jackie Gayle, called me 'the Yiddisha Bunny'—I'm from Northwest Baltimore's Jewish ghetto," says 68-year-old Sharon Bernstein Peyton, recalling the summer 50 years ago when she went to work as a cocktail waitress at the *Mad Men*-era Playboy Club when it opened on Light Street. "And when I had my hair down, and because I didn't wear a lot of makeup, he called me 'the Beatnik Bunny.'"

Peyton had thought she wanted to go to art school, which she did, attending the Maryland Institute College of Art for a year after graduating from Forest Park High School in 1963. But once at MICA, she saw how talented everyone was and suddenly a career in art didn't look like a good bet. Certainly tuition didn't look like a great way to spend her parents' money, given her doubts. "All I knew was I didn't want to be a teacher, nurse, or secretary, and those were the jobs available to women."

Then her boyfriend saw an ad for the soon-to-be Baltimore franchise of the Playboy Club—the latest addition to Hugh Hefner's burgeoning string of nightclubs—and suggested she apply. "I finally got up the courage to go down there," Peyton says. "The money was two or three times better than I could've made elsewhere."

There's no denying the club's incredible male chauvinism—it's Playboy's foundational value, after all. However, there's also no denying it was an exciting place for an unsophisticated 18-year-old girl, rubbing shoulders with pro ballplayers, movie stars, entertainers, politicos, and the three-martini-lunch business crowd. "The feeling of being there at the very beginning was that it was 'cool,'" Peyton says. "You never thought of blue-collar Baltimore as a cool place in those days. This was the coolest thing I knew."

Cool enough that Hefner and his entourage flew in on his private jet for the opening party. ("Very shy," Peyton says. "Conversation was like pulling teeth.")

It's fitting that almost exactly a half-century since the Baltimore Playboy Club opened, the 2014 International Playboy Bunny Reunion, which several former local bunnies plan to attend, will be held in Baltimore this month.

In hindsight, the Baltimore Playboy Club's run from 1964 to 1977 is remarkable for any number of reasons—including hosting break-through comedians Flip Wilson and Richard Pryor and singers such as Jerry Vale and Al Martino. Well-known, well, playboys, such as Robert Mitchum and Joe Namath were sure to stop in on their way through town. And the bunnies themselves became mini-celebrities, participating in parades, charity golf outings, and visits to Walter Reed National Military Medical Center accompanied by Cab Calloway and Bert Parks. But most remarkably perhaps, the club somehow managed to span three distinct and rapidly changing eras in American culture. Its 13-year existence stretched from the end of Camelot and the innocence of "I Wanna Hold Your Hand" to the Vietnam War and Summer of Love, and finally, to the Equal Rights Amendment movement and *Ms.* magazine.

"You know what's funny?" Peyton continues. "I think Playboy figured they'd get 'girl-next-door' types who were kind of passive, and what they really got were a lot of 'girl-next-door' types who were go-getters. It was a daring thing to do in those days to become a Playboy bunny."

60. Cinema Al Fresco

As the sunlight fades behind Ciao Bella, a gathering crowd, many toting picnic baskets and wine, or pizza from nearby Isabella's, settles into the canvas chairs in the empty parking lot next door. Fifteen years ago, Little Italy's restaurant owners were at their wits' end over the huge, bare billboard outside Ciao Bella's—a planned mural had turned into a zoning dispute—until Da Mimmo's Mary Ann Cricchio had an epiphany after catching a movie, *al fresco*, in the old country. By a small miracle, she says, the third-floor bedroom window of Ray Lancelotta's rowhome (then owned by his uncle, John Pente) turned out to be the perfect height and distance to throw a 35mm film onto the billboard's blank canvas, giving birth to the annual Little Italy Open Air Film Fest.

Per tradition, the final evening's film is *Cinema Paradiso*, the story of a Sicilian filmmaker and his beloved boyhood theater's projectionist. After Cricchio introduces the film (not last year's shortened version, which drew protests, but the original, three-hour cut), Rick Huether, upstairs in Lancelotta's bedroom, discreetly loads a Blu-ray disc into a digital projector. The state-of-the-art equipment replaced the cast-iron, 35mm projector several years ago, Huether, who works for Astro Events, admits out of earshot of moviegoers.

"We could put the projector anywhere now, but people like to point out the white bulb in the window to friends who've never been to the festival," he says, gesturing to just such a couple.

Meanwhile, Lancelotta, who's been watching Cricchio's introduction from a sidewalk bench, ducks inside his living room. "I've seen all the movies," he says with a guilty smile. "I'm watching the Orioles tonight. They're having a great year."

61. For Love of Country

The musket and cannon fire is so loud on the banks of the North Point Peninsula that some of those watching the action, including former steelworker David Crews, wear earplugs. Behind each shot, a putrid cloud of white smoke blows forth—not out to the nearby Chesapeake Bay, naturally, but over the hillside crowd. "Oh man," says Crews, shaking his head, interrupted by the stench as he tries to photograph Dundalk's Defenders Day reenactment of the Battle of North Point. "That sulfur smell takes me right back to the 'L' furnace at Sparrows Point."

In 1814, some 4,000 hardened British redcoats landed here, planning to march to Baltimore and join the ships attacking the city. Instead, suffering key losses and slowed down by Maryland militiamen, they retreated after making it only as far as Patterson Park, where massive numbers of militia troops from the region were dug in. This afternoon, though, the British are giving as good as they get—standing firm in firing lines, lobbing volley after volley—before finally turning back.

Their sergeant's vocal commands, however, are shouted in a noticeably un-British accent, with "About face," for example, sounding more like "A-boot face!"

"We're Canadian, from Niagara Falls," Mike McAndrews explains. A bearded bear of a man, sweating profusely in his 23-ounce melton-wool redcoat, heavy gray slacks, and boots, McAndrews notes that in the U.S., it's difficult to find War of 1812 reenactors willing to portray the British. But in Canada, it's the other way around. "To us, the loyalists were on the right side of history," McAndrews says. "Look at whose picture is on our money. It's the Queen."

62. Hello in There

Dale Johnson leans his 20-year-old, pale-green Bianchi 10-speed against a Hampden porch, grabs three small trays—a hot lunch, a cold-cut dinner, plus fruit, juice, and milk—from the cooler atop his rack, and rings the doorbell. "How are you, Bruce?"

"I'm doing good," the middle-aged man answering the door responds, managing a smile while shakily grasping the food that Johnson has brought by. "Polish sausage and sauerkraut?" he adds. "I love Polish sausage." After briefly reminiscing about his college lacrosse days, Bruce mentions he's got a psychiatry appointment later and plans to take the bus. Johnson listens and nods before waving goodbye, off to his next Meals-on-Wheels delivery, part of a small, local, two-wheel program with other cyclists that he began two years ago.

"The best thing, really, is that it attracts younger volunteers," Johnson says. "The average age of Meals on Wheels drivers must be 77. I'm only 62."

Later, he hands a blind gentleman two meals and lets him know he may have found someone to help read him his mail on a regular basis.

At two homes, only a relative of the incapacitated recipient makes it to the door. With other deliveries, Johnson may be the only person some people see and interact with all day. "I've had a few clients who've died, which is sad, but you also meet interesting people," he says afterward, still in his bike jersey and spandex shorts.

His favorite client is Ms. LaRue. "She's 98, 5 feet tall, but she still has a spark about her," Johnson says. "She used to go ballroom dancing with her husband, and my wife has me doing that, so we compare notes occasionally. 'Tell your wife,' she said to me once, 'that Ms. LaRue thinks you have great legs.'"

63. Rain or Shine

Marvin "Doc" Cheatham stands with other volunteers in Matthew A. Henson Elementary School's lobby, next to a mural of Thurgood Marshall, Eubie Blake, Frederick Douglass, and other great Baltimoreans, including Henson, the first African-American Arctic explorer. This morning marks the fourth annual Michael Carter Men Reading in Baltimore City Public Schools Initiative, a series founded by Cheatham and named after a longtime city schools advocate. It's more about the male role models than it is about reading.

"This is the hook," says Cheatham, a former president of the Baltimore chapter of the NAACP. "The hope is the men will become more engaged with local schools."

Later, encouraging the children in Ms. Copeland's pre-K class to circle around him, Cheatham takes off his jacket and begins reading Dr. Seuss's *One Fish Two Fish Red Fish Blue Fish*. Then he stops himself. "Are you okay? Are you shy today?" he asks a boy in the back. "C'mon up here and sit next to me." Most of the children are enthralled, but Cheatham interrupts himself again, addressing another quiet boy. "C'mon, you come up here, too, and sit on my other side."

Finishing the tale, Cheatham, a retired government worker who grew up and still lives nearby in West Baltimore, echoes the words of principal David Guzman, reminding the kids they need to come to school every day, even when it's raining or snowing. "My name is Mr. Cheatham, which sounds a little funny, right?" he continues to rapt attention. "If your parents can't bring you to school, you tell them to call Mr. Cheatham, and I'll come get you."

64. Syndicated Fame

Anxious production assistants hustle in and around the wardrobe and prop trucks parked behind the Jarrettsville Volunteer Fire Company, serving today as the back lot of HBO's award-winning series *House of Cards*. Inside, 75 would-be extras chow on a catered breakfast before getting shuttled to the set—a nearby barn—where the real-life retirees, housewives, and cable guys will portray rural Midwestern voters.

Dressed in jeans, boots, and flannel shirts for a town-hall-style meeting, everyone is soon perspiring under the bright lights (water bottles are handed out), as stars Robin Wright and Kevin Spacey take turns delivering lines from the stage. "I know it's warm, so we are going to open this big door behind me," says Spacey, still channeling conniving South Carolina congressman-turned-President Frank Underwood during a break. "We'll let in that cool air outside," he tells the crowd of occasional thespians, soaking up the performance, in Underwood's thick, faux empathetic drawl, "to offset all the [political] hot air coming from this podium."

During the long stretches of downtime, many compare notes about recent extra work on HBO's *Veep*, also shot in Baltimore, and past gigs.

One local part-time actor recounts a no-line part as a waiter on the 1970s soap *Dallas*, serving J.R.—Larry Hagman ("I remember his cowboy hat to this day"); his TV wife, Linda Grey; and the woman who played Hagman's mother, Barbara, Bel Geddes. "Funny thing was, years later, I get a call from a friend I hadn't heard from in a long time. Guess the first thing he says. 'Were you ever on *Dallas*?' He'd seen a rerun somewhere.

"Of course, I asked him how I looked. He says in all seriousness, 'You totally nailed it, dude.' And we cracked up."

65. Heaven's Gate

Just inside the imposing stone and iron entrance, former city schools teacher Wayne Schaumburg is name-checking the "Who's Who" of Victorian Baltimore buried at Green Mount Cemetery, celebrating its 175th anniversary this year. On this picnic-perfect fall morning, Schaumburg notes those buried here include Johns Hopkins, Enoch Pratt, and Henry Walters, founders, of course, of the world-class university and medical center, groundbreaking library system, and thriving art museum that bear their names to this day.

Built on 68 rolling acres in East Baltimore's Oliver neighborhood, then considered "the countryside," Green Mount is home to stunning bronze works by major sculptors William H. Rinehart and Hans Schuler, as well as 65,000 people in repose. "But you won't find a lot of snappy epithets," Schaumburg says beneath the yellow and red leaves of the cemetery's massive trees. "The ones you do see usually refer to eternal 'sleep' or 'rest.' Life was hard then, and for Victorians, death was often viewed as a release."

Privately owned, Green Mount catered to Baltimore's upper-middle and upper classes—which doesn't mean that there haven't been controversial and colorful characters buried on the grounds. Elizabeth Patterson Bonaparte, once sister-in-law to Napoleon, is interred at Green Mount. Also among the buried: John Wilkes Booth, Lincoln's assassin; Johnny Eck, Baltimore's famous "half-man" sideshow performer; and Elijah Bond, patentee of the Ouija board.

Former Mayor William Donald Schaefer also purchased a plot, Schaumburg heard. But the City Hall icon of the 1970s and '80s later decided, apparently, not to be buried among the noted politicians, philanthropists, and industrialists. Instead, Schaumberg explains, Schaefer lies forever alongside his longtime companion, Hilda Mae Snoops, at Dulaney Valley Memorial Gardens Mausoleum.

"He's one that got away."

66. Time of the Season

On a damp Saturday, the morning after Halloween, two-dozen hearty folks and curious kids squeeze inside the warmth of Valley View Farms' garden center for the annual fall harvest Great Pumpkin Seed Count. For weeks, a couple thousand visitors have sized up Valley View's biggest pumpkin ever, a 1,725-pounder named "Gourdzilla," writing down guesses at the number of seeds in the behemoth. At stake: a first place $300 gift certificate to the garden center, which, with its exotic squashes—plus other vegetables, herbs, trees, shrubs, and perennials—has become something of a holiday destination.

Delivered by truck from "up the river" and the size of a small car, the pumpkin's walls are roughly a foot thick. (Valley View owners consider the exact birthplace of their giant pumpkins a trade secret.) In some northern states, and in Canada, where Windsor, Ontario, hosts an annual pumpkin regatta, similar gargantuan gourds are carved into canoes for fall harvest boat races.

Valley View's seed count goes back a quarter century now, beginning in 1989 with a relatively smallish 755-pounder. "Breeding," says retail greenhouse manager Carrie Engel, explaining the explosion in the size of the Sumo-like squash. "People ask, but we're obligated to return all the seeds back to the grower."

Counting duties actually don't take long: This year's total is 373, just below average. Although novice predictions go upward of seven figures, two years ago, only a single seed was found. The disappointment today, other than that the winner isn't on hand and will be notified by phone, is that Gourdzilla didn't make it here either. He over-ripened a few days ago.

"Where's the giant pumpkin?" one downcast child asks Engel during the count. "Oh, I am afraid we had to cut him open before he went bad. He's out back now," she says reassuringly, "resting in pieces."

67. Role Models

Hours before Michelle Obama's appearance at an Anthony Brown-Ken Ulman "Get Out the Vote" rally, Tamara Jones is mostly succeeding in keeping her 12-year-old daughter and friends content in line outside Baltimore's War Memorial Building. "Sandwiches, chips, juice, plus Halloween candy," Jones says. "And they all brought their iPads or devices to play."

The girls, however—Jones's daughter Riaine, Kayla Arrington, Nevaeh Donaldson, and Tara Lowery—don't know that the First Lady is actually going to be here today, which Jones has kept a surprise, offering Mayor Stephanie Rawlings-Blake as the star attraction. "My daughter loves the mayor," she says, noting that the sixth-grader at East Baltimore's Henderson-Hopkins school has volunteered alongside Rawlings-Blake at neighborhood events.

The mayor, in fact, is the first elected official to appear in the packed auditorium, followed by a roster of state Democratic politicos, including Lt. Gov. Brown, who eventually introduces the First Lady, sending the girls into a frenzy.

After a brief rallying speech, as Obama comes forward to greet the audience, the girls literally climb on the backs of nearby adults, thrusting their arms in the air for handshakes with the First Lady.

"I'm never going to wash this hand," exclaims one of the girls.

"I got squished," adds the smallest girl, Tara, 9, nonetheless smiling and holding up a smartphone video of Obama.

"Do you think she should run for office?" someone asks Jones, who scored a hug from the presidential spouse.

"Why not? She's smart, articulate, engaged in what's going on—even fashionable," Jones says.

Bursting into laughter, she catches herself. "Oh, you were asking about the First Lady, not my daughter," she smiles. "Yes, she should run, too."

68. Brass in Pocket

"Two weeks ago, program director Scott Mullins asked me into his office and closed the door," recalls general manager Steve Yasko, as anxious, former 1980s teenagers and twenty-somethings wait outside WTMD's studio for the station's weekly "Live Lunch" performance. "He leans back and folds his arms, like he always does when he has something—good or bad—to tell me. He says, 'We're 48 hours away from confirming Chrissie Hynde.' Hardest thing in the world for me not to tell anyone for two days."

Beloved for her tough but tender songs and persona, the legendary Pretenders frontwoman, true to form, comes out in black boots, torn jeans, and a black T-shirt. Promoting her album *Stockholm*, the 63-year-old sits down between two accompanying musicians, literally rolling up her sleeves for 45 minutes of classics like "Kid" and "Talk of the Town," as well as new material, her keening, seductive alto and attitude as distinct as ever. One moment, she is waving off an encroaching photographer, and the next, she's generously calling out Baltimore's All Mighty Senators—three of whom are in the audience and opened for The Pretenders on their 2003 tour.

Later, guitarist Warren Boes shares that the Senators—long established in the city's music scene but not a national act—had "no idea" how or why Hynde tapped them to fill the prestigious slot opening on the tour.

"We were intimidated but had to ask when we finally met her, 'Why us?'" he recalls. "She said she saw our CD and handed it to

[Pretenders guitarist] Adam Seymour for a listen. She said she told him, 'These guys must be good. They're not making it on their looks.'"

69. Christmas Cargo

Amid the Christmas decorations, tree, and holiday lights, sit hundreds of gift-wrapped shoeboxes, stacked along the walls of the cramped Stella Maris Seafarers' Center. Sent by local churches, schools, and charities, and filled with toothpaste, shaving cream, gloves, and scarves—as well as pens and stationery for writing home— some 1,500 presents will be delivered by volunteers to foreign seamen docked at the Port of Baltimore this season.

"The sailors come from all over the developing world: Sri Lanka, Indonesia, the Philippines, former Soviet Bloc countries, most working on eight- to 10-month contracts," says Monsignor John FitzGerald, who oversees the center, a mission of the Archdiocese of Baltimore. "It's a lonely life. They miss holidays, the births of children, and funerals of parents."

Part logistics hub, chapel (FitzGerald celebrates Mass in four languages), and internet cafe, the center provides services to 12,000 seafarers a year, many of whom email and Skype with family from its computers. Volunteer van drivers also offer seamen, often in dock for only 12 hours, the chance to refill prescriptions at pharmacies and, like the visiting Chinese seafarers today, to shop for themselves or loved ones at their favorite American stores like Walmart and Best Buy.

"Everything in the U.S., you can buy in China. Bose headphones, UGG boots, and iPhone 6, but it costs a lot more. [An] iPhone 6—$150 more," says Jianteng Li, 36, in heavily accented English as his shipmates pose for photos in front of the center's Christmas tree, still an exotic religious artifact in the ancient, officially atheist, East Asian country.

"My wife emailed me," Li shrugs and smiles. "She wants UGGs. Two pairs."

70. King for a Day

There is free ice skating here later for kids participating in Baltimore's 75th annual Doll Show, but right now, they're busy playing with their favorite dolls (the term is applied broadly) and looking forward to the contest. It's a beauty pageant of sorts for toys, and the rules are simple: entrants must be 14 or under and may only enter one doll in one category, such as foreign, antique, best stuffed, action figure, or most unusual.

"The judges ask the kids questions about their doll, which is great, because they get to talk about something they love and be taken seriously," says Trish Jefferson, who's been coming to the show since 1957 and is watching her granddaughter run around the rec room inside the Dominic "Mimi" DiPietro Family Skating Center.

One 5-year-old enters her obviously well-loved, stuffed panda, which she's had, she explains, since meeting the panda Tai Shan at the National Zoo.

"How old is your panda?"

"One-hundred and thirty," responds the girl, not missing a beat.

After the category winners receive their ribbons, two overall winners are named the show's official King and Queen. Along with trophies, they're handed authentic-looking crowns and seated in a throne for pictures. "Queen" Kimore Spencer, 12, won for her vintage, box-kept, African-American Barbie. Edward Clark, 11, won both "most unusual" and "King" honors for his dead baby shark, preserved in a jar. "A friend of my father's brought it from Florida," he says, proudly, noting it's a blacktip shark as he points out the telltale fin markings.

Afterwards, in line for skates, he adjusts the crown still atop his head.

"I've never ice-skated before," he admits, "but I'm not taking this off."

71. Baby New Year

"Somebody get me the time," pleads 58-year-old Bob Hosier, pacing in his rowhouse living room in a diaper, bonnet, and bib. Surrounded by friends and family—including an actual baby, whose diaper is being changed on the sofa—Hosier is nervously trying to sync the televised New Year's Eve ball drop in Times Square with the light-post ball drop he's rigged up in front of his house for the past two and a half decades.

"It takes 22 seconds for our ball to drop," explains Hosier, who, along with starting the audacious holiday-decorating phenomenon known as the "Miracle on 34th Street," appears each year as Baby New Year at midnight to expectant throngs. "If it took a full minute, I'd need a 60-foot pole, and the city wouldn't go for that."

Just before the climactic moment, Hosier, manager of a trucking company based at the Port of Baltimore, kisses his wife and daughter. Then, as fireworks fly, he opens his front door to wild applause, popping champagne as he waves to the crowd.

"There he is!"

"Hey, Baby New Year!"

"Oh, that's one sexy diaper!"

Fortified by 100-proof Old Grand-Dad, Hosier mingles with members of the fawning and, for the most part, only mildly intoxicated crowd, who offer toasts and kisses, rub his belly for luck, and pose for delirious selfies.

"You know," says an onlooker to his girlfriend, "waiting for him to come out of his house every year, it's like he's our version of Punxsutawney Phil."

"The difference," his date smiles, scanning the beefy, nearly naked Hosier, "is just a little less hair."

72. Historical Notes

"I won't be doing a lot of twirling," says Dunbar High School drum major Martuise Montgomery, a silver baton tucked into the nook of his elbow as he rubs his hands together before the start of the annual Dr. Martin Luther King, Jr. Parade. "I'm afraid I'll drop it. I'm freezing, but it's important to be here. We're marching to honor Dr. King's marches."

Despite the chill, deep crowds line the 10-block route and, moments later, Martuise kick-starts trombones and trumpets with pumps of his baton. Their first number, "Wade into the Water," is an old Negro spiritual, which Harriet Tubman used as a reminder to escaping slaves to get off the trail to prevent dogs from tracking their scents.

Nearly 70 groups follow Dunbar's lead, including the Buffalo Soldiers of the Baltimore Chapter 9th and 10th Calvary Association on horseback, the Baltimore chapter of Alpha Phi Alpha, which King pledged as a 23-year-old Boston University divinity student, and neighborhood marching bands like the Westsiders and Baltimore Go-Getters.

Among the songs blasting today is Stevie Wonder's "Happy Birthday."

"Many of our kids know that song but don't know that Stevie Wonder wrote it in 1980 because of the backlash against making Dr. King's birthday a holiday," says Charles Funn, Dunbar's band director. "That song swayed public opinion. I'm not just a music teacher," Funn adds, standing next to Martuise, who eventually worked up a sweat with his high stepping, as the band gathers near their bus afterward. "I was about their age when Dr. King was shot. I try to be a history teacher, too."

73. Dancing Days

Upstairs at Germano's cabaret lounge, author Rafael Alvarez is reading a short story he wrote years ago about a retired burlesque dancer named Jean Honus, a platinum blond who billed herself as the Jean Harlow of the Block and stripped until she was 56.

But the headliner tonight is Margo Christie, who recently penned *These Days*, a novel based on her own experiences dancing on the Block in the late 1970s and '80s. Amid clinking glasses and applause, accompanied by jazz guitarist Michael Joseph Harris, the red-headed Christie takes the floor in a vintage, sequined, lace gown and feather boa. The 52-year-old's only concession to the passage of time: reading glasses.

Among the passages she shares is a paragraph about the long summers on the Block—the slowest time of the year, she quickly learned. "August on the block dragged by hot and sleepy . . . Lenny [the bar manager] said men took their families on vacation during the summer but will be back with an appetite for some real fun in September."

A Denver transit bus driver for the past 16 years, she's enjoyed returning home to promote her book, which received an Amazon Breakthrough Novel award.

"I've been having great fun, but this isn't the first time I've been in a newspaper," she tells a reporter with a wry smile. "[Between dancing stints], I used to work at the Mustang Inn, and the *East Baltimore Guide* once named me the best-looking barmaid in Highlandtown. Of course, most of the barmaids in Highlandtown then were over 50 and I was 17."

74. Past as Prologue

The Johns Hopkins University sociologist Karl Alexander had come to Baltimore in the early 1970s with an interest in high-school graduates and their transition into the "real world." By 1982, however, he was squeezing his 6-foot-4 frame into pint-sized chairs at 20 public elementary schools across Baltimore City, on to something entirely new.

Doris Entwisle, an accomplished colleague whose career pursuits ran toward early education and childhood development, had gotten to know Alexander shortly after his arrival, asking him to help her edit an academic journal. The first female professor to eat in the exclusively male Hopkins Club, Entwisle was not afraid of breaking new ground and, soon enough, a marriage of sorts between their areas of expertise emerged. "It was a simple idea," says Alexander, speaking on what became known as the Beginning School Study, one of the most important longitudinal research efforts of the 21st century. "It was our intuition that if kids got off to a good start in school, things would continue to go well for them. But if they got off to bumpy start, it would likely have a chilling effect over the long haul."

Initially, the plan had been to track students' progress through the third grade. "Then, it dawned on us that we'd done the hard part," Alexander explains, with a chuckle. "We'd gotten permission from parents, teachers, and the school system, including access to school records. Why not keep going?"

Huddling with first-graders in empty classrooms and over cafeteria lunch tables—wherever schools could find space—the researchers asked some basic questions: "What do you want to be when you grow up?" "What kind of grades do you think you'll get?" "Do you like school?"

In hindsight, it seems astonishing that so little research had been done on the transition from "home child" to "school child," says Alexander, an outgoing and energetic, fatherly 68-year-old with clear blue eyes and a neatly trimmed white beard. "Sociology was focused on all the other major life transitions: high-school graduation, marriage, children, retirement, and aging. No one was looking at the first major transition in someone's life, which is going to school."

Alexander, Entwisle, and their tight-knit team of researchers would ultimately keep close tabs on 790 first-graders until they turned 28 years old, a feat unlike anything else ever attempted in the United States. *The Long Shadow*, their acclaimed book based on the study, was recently published, though Entwisle, who passed away in 2013 at 89 years old, did not live to see the culmination of their work in print.

At its core, the Beginning School Study, which largely included, but was not limited to, disadvantaged city kids, set out to determine who succeeds and why. Alexander, Entwisle, and Linda Olson, who started as a research assistant and ultimately served as co-author on *The Long Shadow*, examined each student's family and socioeconomic background. Twice each school year, they charted their progress, eventually chronicling their entry into the workforce and identifying patterns around who landed good-paying blue-collar jobs or completed college degrees and who struggled to find a toehold. But the broader context matters, too. As these kids entered first grade in 1982, U.S. cities, including this one, were collapsing.

As the kids matured into teenagers, the team's queries evolved to include questions about drug use, relationships, and sex, as well as job prospects and higher-education goals. They talked with the students' parents once a year, often making home visits, and later recorded extended interviews with students, who would occasionally cry as they looked back and reflected on their lives. Inevitably, the researchers trailed their subjects to juvenile detention centers and, later, to state prisons for interviews with the former first-graders. They also saw many of them start to raise their own children while still teenagers.

"We literally watched these kids grow up," Alexander says. "It became our life's work."

On a chilly winter night, Alexander, Olson, and longtime staff members Joanne Fennessey and Anna Stoll—a pair of sharp, sweet-natured, 4-foot-11 women in their 60s who became quasi-private detectives for all their chasing down of participants—gather for a post-publication, celebratory dinner at One-Eyed Mike's in Fells Point with a small group of the study's subjects. The "kids" are now 38 and 39 years old (it took a decade after the study to complete *The Long Shadow*), roughly the same age Alexander was, and a just a few years older than Fennessey and Stoll were, when the study launched. The faces have aged over time, but the mood is warm and friendly. The participants still recall the early questionnaires and the later, more in-depth interviews.

They also remember the annual birthday cards, although they only just learned the secret motivation behind those hand-written missives: to help the researchers maintain up-to-date addresses. "We knew if they bounced back, somebody had moved," says Stoll with a smile, as she looks around the table. "That's also why we always asked for the name and contact information for a family member or close friend, someone besides the parents, who would always know where the kids would be."

"Oh, I remember the birthday cards," says study participant John Houser III, a beer in his hand. "I thought it was neat every year. I thought, 'These people care about me.'"

Houser also recalls the gift cards to record stores like Sam Goody that researchers gave him after interviews when he was a teenager. "Ten bucks," he says, sitting next to fellow participant Jesse Fask, who nods his head of dreadlocked hair. "Enough to buy a CD or cassette tape in those days."

After growing up in Southwest Baltimore's working-class white enclave known as Lumberyard, Houser—a graphic designer who graduated from Frostburg State University ("I chose the farthest in-state school from Baltimore") with the assistance of Pell grants and student loans that he's still paying off—certainly counts among the study's success stories. Of the 30 or so kids he grew up with, several were into hard drugs by age 18 and 19, including one friend who died from an overdose. Just six or seven finished high school, and he's the only one who went to college. "Most of us started smoking pot around 14. There was a lot of that around," Houser says. "The hard drugs started coming in when we were around 16. You'd see junkies hanging around the neighborhood, stealing things, and crack was coming in. I saw children, basically, dealing drugs to kids' parents, and kids' mothers turning to skeletons and turning tricks."

Houser, who has read *The Long Shadow* and is anxious to talk about the results with the study's authors, says he only smoked pot, deciding at some point to distance himself from the lifestyle he saw swallowing up his friends by hiding out in his bedroom, listening to music, and reading comic books. He also recognizes that while his family was occasionally on welfare (his father was a union sprinkler fitter and on strike from time to time), he had two parents and other relatives nearby keeping him on track. "It made me realize, even before I had my own kid, I had parents who cared and parents who wanted to be parents."

75. Only Way

With a rebounding economy and falling gas prices, some 20,000 outdoors-oriented vacationers are expected at the 50th annual RV Show at the Maryland State Fairgrounds, the East Coast's largest retail show. The top luxury campers here run $400,000 and include granite-top kitchens, porcelain tiles, flat-screen TVs, premium audio systems, and heated-leather seats, but the industry's bread and butter remains in the $20,000 to $65,000 range, says Greg Merkel, owner of Leo's Vacation Center in Gambrills.

"My father Leo started the business 43 years ago after our first vacation in a camper," says Merkel, noting that families can still get into the market at $5,000 with a used, pop-up trailer. "After that, we went everywhere—Ocean City, Pennsylvania, Virginia, Delaware. The favorite was the 'Roller Coaster Capital of the World,' Cedar Point in Ohio."

Along with the massive vehicles filling the fairgrounds' exhibition halls, dozens of Mid-Atlantic campgrounds are represented—most of them familiar to Ruby Harbaugh, who bought her first recreational vehicle with her husband in 1968. Since then, she's bought nine more, all from Charlie's RV and Camping Center in Randallstown, where the energetic 81-year-old is also employed, answering the phone and working the floor.

"I've got a 36-foot, Itasca motorhome with an 8.1 Chevy Vortec engine, workhorse chassis, and five-speed Allison transmission," says the petite, blue-eyed grandma. "Drove 1,088 miles in two days over the Ozark Mountains last summer. Just me behind the wheel. I've been to Disney World 42 times, and I'll go this year. Don't know where else yet.

"My husband died in 2009 and had been in a home for six years when I bought this last RV," adds Harbaugh, whose license plate reads, ONLY WAY. "He told me, 'You keep on going, Ruby. You always were a better a driver than me anyhow.'"

76. No Small Deaths

Pigtown's Allied Binding Company, where they still bind real books, hosts tonight's "Diorama-rama" competition, a celebration of old-school storytelling in a box, hosted by the local arts group Wonder Commons.

The theme is Notable Last Moments, with judges including Jaime Kauffman, program director with nonprofit Art with a Heart, and Bruce Goldfarb, an expert on the Maryland Chief Examiner's Office's renowned Nutshell Studies of Unexplained Death dioramas.

"One goal with Wonder Commons," explains organizer Robert Marbury, author of *Taxidermy Art: A Rogue's Guide*, "is to get people who are non-artists to make things." That said, genuinely talented folks are here, such as Jim Doran, who specializes in making tiny dioramas in iPod cases and kitchen spoons.

Among the entries is an homage to recently departed Leonard Nimoy, featuring an anime figurine of *Star Trek's* Spock falling through strobe lights inside a parking cone to the "Final Frontier." Best in Show goes to game developer Shawn Cook for "We Were Dead Before the Ship Even Sank," featuring a water-color painted boat swaying between waves, enhanced by bottom-of-the-sea LED lighting, all inside a 6-inch box.

Meanwhile, the Cornell Prize, named for surrealist assemblage artist Joseph Cornell, goes to writer Zoë Nardo for "The Wire," which plays not off the acclaimed HBO series but The Flying Wallendas.

Her 2-foot tall cardboard frame depicts Baltimore's harbor, its row-house neighborhoods, and a high wire strung from the iconic Domino Sugar sign in Locust Point to the neon visage of Mr. Boh in Canton.

An accompanying poem tells the tragic tale of the diorama's thrill-seeking protagonist—only her tutu and legs visible after a head-first fall into the swirling water below in her notable last moment:

Halfway through she slipped and messed up the plan
She never made it to the one-eyed man.

77. Working Girls

"It was a serious time for everybody, and I took my job very seriously," Grace Henninger tells a packed auditorium at the Baltimore Museum of Industry, describing how she helped build B-26 bombers at the Glen L. Martin factory during World War II. "I learned right away that if you were working the rivet gun, the bracket had to be held very tight. Very little rework had to be done on my end," the blue-eyed 90-year-old says in a North Carolina drawl. "I loved my United States of America."

At its peak, 53,000 workers were employed by the Middle River aviation manufacturer, one-third of whom were young women like Henninger and fellow panelist Elsie Arnold, president of the Rosie the Riveter Association's Baltimore Chapter. Raised on a 500-acre farm, Henninger had followed an aunt here. Starting at 18, Arnold worked at Glen L. Martin for two and a half years and saved for nursing school. "The boys left for war and the women took over," smiles Arnold, who went on to a 40-year career at the Greater Baltimore Medical Center. "But we didn't think of ourselves as pioneers."

Later, Henninger recalls meeting her future husband, home on leave, at the nearby Essex A&P supermarket. They married six weeks later, March 18, 1945—almost 70 years ago to this day.

After his discharge, they ended up buying a four-room, one-floor house, initially intended as temporary housing for plant workers in a development called Victory Villa, where the streets were given names like Fuselage Road and Altimeter Court.

"There were extensive renovations over the years, but we raised our five children in that house," says Henninger, who worked on the assembly line at Westinghouse for 20 years after her children had grown. "My husband, Jim, died in 1999 from colon cancer from the asbestos at Bethlehem Steel. I still live in that house."

78. Bike Messengers

Riding lead, and wearing a bicycling jersey with "BALTIMORE" across its front, Mayor's Office staff photographer Mark Dennis is guiding, at about 20 miles per hour, a group of cyclists who left Newtown, Massachusetts, just two and a half days ago, down Pulaski Highway toward City Hall.

For the third year since the mass shooting at Sandy Hook Elementary School in Newtown, 26 cyclists, representing the 20 children and six educators killed by the single gunman, rally here on their way to Capitol Hill, where they'll remind legislators about the Dec. 14, 2012, tragedy and push for stricter gun safety laws.

Among the cyclists, four live in Newtown, including Monte Frank, the ride organizer, and Dr. Bill Begg, the emergency room doctor on duty the day of the horrific tragedy. Two riders have children who attended Sandy Hook, and two other riders lost a family member in the 2007 Virginia Tech shooting. Altogether, they're making 14 stops, from Harlem to one-stoplight towns, to build support for gun violence prevention.

Greeting the cyclists, Mayor Stephanie Rawlings-Blake notes that gun violence has long plagued Baltimore, adding that nearly every family, including hers, has been touched directly or indirectly by gun violence.

"What I learned that day as a doctor is that gunshot victims either die, become permanently disabled, or live with the psychological trauma of being shot for the rest of their lives," Dr. Begg tells the crowd.

"Most of the kids never had a chance," he says later, quietly, choking up and admitting that it has taken him a long time to process what he witnessed. "I had trained in Baltimore, at Johns Hopkins and the University of Maryland, two of the finest medical institutions in the world. And it was all useless that day."

79. Rare Bird

Outside the MASN television booth at Camden Yards, Jim Palmer is bouncing from side to side in the carpeted hallway, launching into baseball stories and bad jokes with practically everyone who walks by. One moment, he's recalling the time he watched, as a 20-year-old phenom, Moe Drabowsky strike out 11 in relief in Game 1 of the 1966 World Series, and the next, he's stopping former O's shortstop and broadcasting colleague Mike Bordick to comment on their nearly matching blue suits. "Hey, Mike—we look like we're in a union."

Fêted this afternoon because this season marks 50 years since he broke in with the Orioles, Palmer's tossing out the first pitch before the home opener in an hour, and he's either anxious or excited. Or he's got ADHD. The man can't sit or stand still.

He chats up front office VP Dan Duquette and official scorer Jim Henneman, whose history with the club, Palmer happily notes, pre-dates his own. When someone asks if he's been doing any throwing, he responds with a windmill circle of his right arm, a wisecrack about 50 Cent's infamous ceremonial toss last year that nearly plunked a photographer, and an anecdote about Joe Namath, a Florida buddy. "Joe's throwing out the first pitch at a spring training game in Jupiter the other day and he asks for advice. I tell him, 'Joe, whatever you do, don't go on to the dirt [meaning the pitcher's mound]. Does he listen? It didn't end well."

Later, he suggests to WJZ sports director Mark Viviano that he take the mound in his stead. "No one will notice," Palmer says. It's a funny nod, actually, to the fact that they occasionally get mistaken for each other, until Palmer feigns his iconic high-kicking motion—the one bronzed in statue behind centerfield—raising his left foot to improbable but graceful heights for someone who turns 70 this October.

And it's this constant motion and banter (no surprise to O's fans who is doing most of the talking), until Palmer takes the field. Making his way through the clubhouse, he trades jibes with longtime attendant Jim Tyler, fist bumps Adam Jones, and detours for a word with closer Zach Britton about anti-inflammatory medication. ("Purely preventive," Palmer assures a reporter, reading his sudden concern for the young star's health.) He ducks into Steve Pearce's BP session and scoops a loose ball, as former battery mate Rick Dempsey searches for a mitt.

Finally, with a tug on the hand railing (the first evidence that the tan, trim, and well-coiffed Palmer isn't completely dominating Father Time), he's up the concrete steps behind home plate, and announcer Jim Hunter introduces him to the sellout crowd.

He won 20 games eight times
He won three Cy Young awards
He won 268 games in an Oriole uniform
He's the greatest Oriole pitcher ever . . .

And ignoring his own advice to Namath, Palmer climbs atop the hill and fires a strike on the corner, because that's how Jim Palmer rolls. It may be fine for every other cranky-kneed ex-jock or ex-president to take the easy way out and toss from the grass, but not Palmer, who is also renowned as one of the game's all-time great (and most exasperating) perfectionists.

"I thought Dempsey did a good a job framing it," O's manager Buck Showalter chides him in the dugout afterward.

The most revealing exchange on Opening Day, however, comes during the fourth inning of the broadcast, as Palmer's anniversary cake is delivered to the booth. Play-by-by man Gary Thorne asks him to reflect on his years with the O's and the on-field ceremony, which included a $50,000 check from the team to Autism Speaks, a charity that Palmer's become involved with in recent years. It's a condition that his 18-year-old stepson, Spencer, with whom Palmer has become very close, suffers from.

"I want to take a moment," a clearly moved Palmer replies—which he got, as Manny Machado hit a high fly ball to center, collecting himself before going on to talk about his parents and the teammates that played behind him and thanking the Angelos family (which owns the club) for their generous contribution. What viewers didn't catch—not because of anything Palmer did but because the camera tracked Machado's ball to center—were his eyes welling up.

Thirty-one years ago at his press conference announcing that the Orioles had released him as a player, he had abruptly bolted from the room as his emotions rose, unable or unwilling to allow the public to see him in a vulnerable light at the time. If Palmer, who always appeared perhaps a little too well poised over the years—never a hair out of place—is finally allowing fans to see that life, like it is for most of us, is, at times, overwhelming and emotional, well, that's probably a good development.

"He's crying," MASN's director whispers in the back of the booth.

80. No Silent Spring

As leadoff man Alejandro De Aza steps to the plate, the unmistakable—and on this day, wholly surprising—sound of the Orioles' rallying cry echoes throughout Camden Yards. For the first time in major league history, there isn't a single fan at a game. Not officially, anyway.

This afternoon's contest is closed to the public following protests in the wake of 25-year-old Freddie Gray's death in police custody. However, two-dozen vociferous fans are stealing glimpses of the action outside the center-field gates, letting the Orioles know they're not quite alone.

"Give me an 'O,' Give me an 'R' . . ."

In fact, the strange thing is not what isn't heard but what is: everything on the field and from the dugouts. When a White Sox batsman hits a hard grounder to O's second baseman Rey Navarro, the ball can literally be heard smacking into gloves around the infield for an inning-ending, 4-5-3 double play. Players can be heard calling for fly balls and clapping and cheering each other on from the bench.

During the pregame press conference, O's manager Buck Showalter had joked about the umpires catching the normally unheard "sweet nothings" emanating from the dugout. Afterward, he jokes again about the starting pitcher hearing the bullpen phone ringing. But when asked what advice he has for Baltimore's young Black men, Showalter strikes a serious tone.

"I've never been Black, okay? So I don't know," he begins. "I can't put myself there. I've never faced the challenges that they face. . . . It's a pet peeve of mine when somebody says, 'Well, I know what they're feeling. Why don't they do this?' . . . You have never been Black, okay? So just slow down a little bit."

81. Rainbow Warriors

The nearly 40-year-old Gay, Lesbian, Bisexual, Transgender Community Center of Baltimore (GLCCB) moved into the Waxter Center last year, so it's appropriate that Baltimore Heritage's LGBTQ Walking Tour begins here. Beyond the neighborhood's gay bars and restaurants, Mount Vernon has long been home to gay-friendly institutions, activist Richard Oloizia notes, including the Waxter Center, which since 1991 has hosted the Chesapeake Squares—Baltimore's gay-friendly square-dance club—and the Emmanuel Episcopal Church, which first screened John Waters' notorious *Pink Flamingos*.

Across the street, Oloizia points out the old apartment of John Stuban, the founder of ACT UP Baltimore, who died of AIDS in 1994, and then Leon's, a gay bar since 1957, which for decades maintained a second, hidden entrance—to protect the privacy of patrons—through the straight restaurant located behind it.

At Mount Vernon Place, Oloizia recalls the city's first pride marches, and retired college professor Shirley Parry tells of the local lesbian women who founded the Bryn Mawr School for girls and secured the rights of women to attend The Johns Hopkins University School of Medicine.

The 90-minute tour ends near the Hippo, the popular disco that's set to become a CVS, and the rowhouse where Gertrude Stein lived when she attended Hopkins. Kate Drabinski, a University of Maryland Baltimore County gender and women's studies lecturer, notes that Stein faced misogyny at med school, which she wasn't great at—she was a writer, after all—but Baltimore is where she first fell in love with a woman and suffered her first heartbreak.

"She lived down the street there, but please don't go knock on the door because other people live there now, and that would be awkward," Drabinski cautions. "From experience."

82. Homeward Bound

"Feel how soft this bird is," says Dave Glorioso, handing a pigeon to a slightly nervous young girl outside at the annual Maryland Traditions Folklife Festival. "Go ahead. You can let him go, too. He'll find his way home."

Glorioso, 63, has been raising racing pigeons, aka homing pigeons, for four decades, keeping a couple hundred birds behind his house in Lansdowne. With his son, Fish, he's brought about 50 birds here.

Big races start as far away as Georgia, with the birds' speed calculated by how long their return flight takes. "Nobody really knows how they do it," Glorioso says. "I think it has something to do with the sun. On cloudy days, it takes them longer."

Pigeon racing used to be very popular in the city, Glorioso continues. The cradle of the sport was Europe, coming to the U.S. during the influx of early 20th-century immigration. The Baltimore Pigeon Fanciers Social Club, based in blue-collar Curtis Bay, has been around for more than half a century, but gentrification, among other factors, has taken a toll on the sport locally.

"Men would work in the factories, give the little money they made to their wives, and then go in the backyard and fool around with their birds," he says. "The women may not have been crazy about the hobby, but at least they knew their husband wasn't down the street at the bar."

When on form, avoiding hawks and hunters, the birds can make it back from, say, a race in North Carolina faster than Glorioso can in his pickup. Once, he pulled into his driveway after a six-hour trip—only to find them already there, waiting in the coop. "It's estimated they flap those little arms a million times during a 500-mile flight," he says. "I'm dead tired after driving that far. Of course, they're dead tired, too."

83. Signs of Life

"I run a lot, and the first time I turned down Bond Street and saw the Bond Street Wharf sign, I was blown away by the scale and color," says Samantha Redles at the Baltimore Museum of Industry, explaining the inspiration for her pop-up exhibition, *Not Yet Lost! The Art of Maryland Sign Painters*. "I knew there was a person who did that, who was behind that sign."

The three-story, BOND STREET WHARF lettering, integrated into the former warehouse's architecture and reappointed brick, was painted in 2008 by Brendon Brandon, whose efforts over the past half-century include other historic renovations, such as the former home of the E.J. Codd Company, which once manufactured boilers and parts for barges and boats also in Fells Point.

As part of the exhibit here, organized by Redles for her Maryland Institute College of Art Curatorial Practice thesis, there is also a screening tonight of the 2013 documentary *Sign Painters*, which recounts the craft's heyday and unsung mid-century practitioners before the mass adoption of vinyl lettering.

"It's definitely viewed as blue-collar, but it offered the chance to be creative and work with your hands," says Redles, whose show highlights six Maryland painters, including Clifford Olson. His best-known work included the whimsical Cloud Mattress mural on the company's former Guilford Avenue factory, which has since gone condo. Restored and visible from I-83, the painting depicts a woman lying alone in bed in a negligee and curlers, levitating above the city at night.

As a 14-year-old in 1934, armed with his paintbrushes, Olson had hopped a freight train out of his Nebraska hometown, ultimately landing in Baltimore. "Dad didn't quit until he was 76, after a stroke," his son Ole says later. "Worked all those years on swinging scaffolding without a safety line, shoveling snow off in the winter. I helped him sometimes in high school. He'd tell me, 'You'll be fine. Hold onto the brush.'"

84. Business as Usual

Like the ephemera sitting in the front windows—the papier-mâché bunny and evil clown dolls, the used hardcover on tiny surrealism and '80s vinyl from Afrika Bambaataa—Normal's Books & Records wasn't expected to survive the digital revolution, let alone celebrate its silver anniversary.

But crowded among the teetering stacks of books and bric-a-brac this afternoon, a real clown named Norma plays a kazoo as a young dad with dreadlocks tries to corral his son, and two men peruse albums and recall Left Bank Jazz Society shows at Baltimore's old Famous Ballroom. At the same time, in the store's backroom performance space called the Red Room—which is blue—the a cappella Sacred Harp choir is following a raucous noise band to the floor. (The Red Room, which has hosted hundreds of $5 shows since its inception in 1993, later birthed Baltimore's internationally acclaimed annual festival of experimental music known as High Zero.)

The shop's motto, co-owner Rupert Wondolowski notes, has always been "everything from the obscure to the indispensable." Its name comes from paid study work several of the early store founders did with the Baltimore Psychiatric Research Center, where control subjects in schizophrenia investigations were referred to as "normals."

"We started two doors down in a smaller space, but not a lot else has changed," Wondolowski says. "We did sell vintage bikes and clothes but ran out of room for that. The first year, it's true, John

Waters bought a bike here. This was before iPhones, so I don't have a picture, but in my mind, I can still see him wobbling off down the street in ragged glory."

85. Tiny Love Songs

The volunteer-run Natural History Society of Maryland—which is hard to miss, given the giant replica dinosaur out front—has its unusual collection of taxidermied wildlife, pressed butterflies, and sea turtle skulls on public display this afternoon. But today's main attraction is a presentation by entomologist Cathy Stragar called Summer's Singing Insects, about the katydids, crickets, and cicadas that make up the season's outdoor chorus.

Stragar, who works at the Bee Inventory and Monitoring Lab at the U.S. Geological Survey Patuxent Wildlife Research Center in Laurel, explains that many insects make music by a process known as stridulation, or rubbing body parts together at incredibly fast speeds. A male cricket, for example, uses one wing as a plane and the other as a scraper/bow, playing to attract female partners.

Cicadas, however, use a different method, popping an abdominal noisemaker called a tymbal, which can produce sounds over 100 decibels. "Males close their ears to literally prevent them from going deaf," Stragar notes. Some grasshoppers, she continues, emit supersonic sounds that humans can't hear.

As part of the lecture, the first in a bimonthly series at the Natural History Society, Stragar plays recordings of crickets and cicadas. She notes the local varieties of each as the small but rapt audience nods in recognition of certain familiar chirps and whistles.

"Recently, Jurassic-era cricket sounds were re-created," Stragar continues, adding that paleontologists have reconstructed the fossil wing structures of the modern cricket's ancestors. "These tell us a lot about what the world sounded like during that period," she says, hitting the play button on her laptop. "These are 165-million-year-old songs."

86. Hon Speak

Accompanied by a bald, mutton-chopped Elvis impersonator in a blue polyester jumpsuit, the 10 finalists at the annual Best Hon Contest take the stage one at a time for the talent portion of the show. Variously jitterbugging, hula hooping, and skateboarding across the platform, the surprisingly diverse group of women channel the working-class fashions and towering beehives of Charm City past, later blowing kisses and tossing Berger cookies to the adoring crowd on The Avenue in Hampden.

Most of the contestants perform ballads expressing their deep affection for their boyfriends, their football team, and their town. However, the eventual winning "hon"—Nikki Bass, an Aberdeen Proving Ground scientist by day—demonstrates how she helps her Department of Defense colleagues understand her "Bawlmerese" dialect.

It is worth noting that Bass, who grew up in Parkville, is also the first multiracial Best Hon of HonFest, the city's wild weekend street festival, covered over the years by the likes of *The New York Times*, *The L.A. Times*, and CNN. "Moms of the brown girls, the Latina, African-American, and Asian little girls entered in the [earlier] Miss Honette contest brought their daughters up to me and my mom," she says later.

Utilizing a classroom periodic table, Bass literally spells out "Bawlmer" for the crowd, letter by letter, employing element symbols. "*Ba*, for example, is for barium," she begins. "As in, 'It's best to *barium* flower seeds after Mother's Day, hon.'"

Donning safety goggles onstage to protect her eyes "from all the Aqua Net," she continues: "*W* is for tungsten, as in, 'You better make sure every pin is *tungsten* all the way, hon. Otherwise that hairdo won't hold together.'"

87. London Calling

"Are you ready, Mod? Are you ready, Rocker? Get set . . . slow down!" the starter yells, whipping down his arm.

With that, "mod" Janet Gripshover, in big, round sunglasses and knee-high stockings, oh-so-gently throttles her sleek Stella scooter as her "rocker" husband—in black T-shirt atop a 1970 Honda 350 motorcycle—does the same.

The annual Charm City Mods vs. Rockers is a celebration of the rival early-'60s British subcultures, which occasionally clashed on the front pages of London's tabloids. Festivities include vendor, club, and custom-builder displays and music from the bouffant-sporting Fabulettes. Bikes and scooters vie for awards in various categories, including best Retro, Modern, British, and Cafe Racer.

Cafe racers, lightweight motorcycles with dropped handlebars, got their name from disaffected youth racing from one cafe to another and back, organizer Tim Carter explains. "They'd put a song on the jukebox, and the idea was to get back before it was over."

The highlight "race," however, is literally a contest of who can ride the *slowest* until one competitor loses his or her balance. In their heat, Gripshover's burly, bearded husband puts his foot on the ground first—to the cheers of rowdy fans behind Dundalk's American Legion Post. "He'd moved up in line because he wanted to beat me, too," Gripshover says. "[But] I get a lot of practice maneuvering in and out of our alley in Mount Vernon."

88. Beastly Art

Surrounded by Egyptian mummies, a "unicorn" horn, Buddhist statuettes, a leopard skin (head attached), and a stuffed alligator, the Walters Art Museum's Joaneath Spicer explains to the packed Chamber of Wonders crowd that Renaissance noblemen often collected curiosities from around the globe.

"Partly, it was trophy collecting, like today, but they were also trying to understand God's plan. Astronomy has shown that the Earth isn't the center of the universe, as the New World and other cultures are being discovered by Europeans," Spicer says. "A squirrel might not be proof of God's handiwork, of a miracle, but a flying squirrel—that's a different story. That you'd have stuffed." (The spacious, renowned Chamber of Wonders installation is meant to evoke the type of collection that would have been the pride of a sophisticated, 17th-century European nobleman.)

The curator of Renaissance and Baroque Art, Spicer is hosting this evening's event, Memento Mori: A Night of Rogue Taxidermy, along with local taxidermy artist and author Robert Marbury and the Hampden shop Bazaar Baltimore.

Meanwhile, in the Sculpture Court, artists have created pop-up exhibits for an "alternative" taxidermy competition. Efforts include a pistol-toting rat standing on its hind legs, a mixed-media painting with actual pigeon wings, raccoon heads on dinner plates, and a loin-clothed "sacrificial" lamb nailed to a cross.

There's also a stuffed "jackalope," the fearsome, mythical creature of North America's Upper Great Plains, described as a jackrabbit with antlers, and a similar taxidermied "porculope" by artist Karen Nemes, who trekked from Indiana for the show.

"A friend found it [the deceased porcupine] alongside the road. I can't tell you how many times I got pricked sticking its needles back in," the unexpectedly bubbly Nemes explains. "I mean, I play with dead things. I'm just happy people here seem to like my work."

89. Blind Love

Of the three Christian virtues—faith, hope, and charity—"hope is the most elusive quality," says Rebecca Hoffberger, founder of the American Visionary Art Museum, as she addresses the preview audience for the museum's 20th anniversary installation, *The Big Hope Show.*

Many of the exhibition's 25-plus, self-taught artists are survivors of deep wounds and terrible personal ordeals, including childhood sexual abuse, alcoholism, mental illness, and blindness. Their works include everything from a small totem pole to scrapbooks to an antiwar painting about a Hiroshima survivor.

During a tour, artist Dan Patrell talks about losing his wife to ovarian cancer and the stained-glass mosaic he created while grieving. Their teenage daughter chose the "healing" stones used in the panel's windows, and Patrell embedded a Morse code message—"love is forever"—in the work's sunrays. He also mixed his wife's ashes into the mosaic's grout.

"I broke down when I finished," he says, choking up. "But they were happy tears."

Nearby, Romaine Samworth sits in a wheelchair beneath her colorful papier mâché sculptures, which include a young couple dancing, farm animals at play, and a regatta on Philadelphia's Schuylkill River. The 94-year-old Samworth lost her sight from a reaction to a smallpox vaccine at age 8, but the sculptures are remarkable in their detail, shape, and whimsy. The biggest tragedy of her life, she says, was when her oldest sister, Mildred, whom she adored, died.

"I loved my crayons and picture books as a child, and I cried when I lost my sight. I was devastated," says Samworth, who grew up on a Pennsylvania farm. "When I started to sculpt in the 1970s and 1980s, it was as if I were bringing those images to life. I could 'see' again in my mind."

Postscript: Romaine Samworth died in 2017.

90. Swimming Lesson

Near Shaarei Tfiloh synagogue, built 94 years ago by Jewish immigrants on Liberty Heights Avenue, Eli Pousson begins Baltimore Heritage's Black and Jewish Civil Rights bike tour of the city's once Jewish—now largely African-American—westside neighborhoods.

While American Jews overwhelmingly supported the Civil Rights movement, Pousson notes that in Baltimore, it was a complicated relationship at times.

Pousson highlights the migration of the city's Jewish population from its East Baltimore tenement roots to the Druid Hill Park area and finally, to Park Heights, Mount Washington, and Pikesville. Jews, Pousson points out, were also victims of Baltimore's notorious segregated housing laws, one reason they moved to the then-empty western city suburbs.

The ride passes the home of Abram Hutzler, who launched the family's iconic downtown department store, which was segregated like others in the Howard and Lexington streets shopping district. It also goes past the home of Walter Sondheim, who oversaw the desegregation of the public schools in 1954, and the former residence of Clarence and Juanita Jackson Mitchell, the unofficial first couple of Baltimore's Civil Rights movement.

There's also a stop at "public pool No. 2," once designated for Druid Hill Park's "colored" patrons—the only outdoor pool then available to the city's westside Black residents. Young white and Jewish progressives protested the park's segregated tennis policies in

193

1948, organizing an interracial tennis match, but the park's two pools remained separate until 1956. Later, in disrepair for decades, the pool—ladders and lifeguard chairs intact—was filled with dirt, topped with lawn grass, and transformed into a surreal memorial landscape by Baltimore artist Joyce Scott.

"Black kids are still three times as likely to be drowning victims—a direct result of discrimination. There was no place for their great-grandparents to swim, and that legacy has been passed down through generations," chimes in pediatrician Dr. Ralph Brown, who is along for this morning's ride. "I harp on that with everyone: 'Have you gotten them swimming lessons yet?'"

91. Bowling for Dollars

"These kids crowbar it, don't they?" says Dundalk-native Danny Wiseman, as a teenager from Great Barrington, Massachusetts, rips another big hook for a strike at Wiseman's Youth Scholarship Tournament.

A PBA Hall of Famer, Wiseman won the first of his 12 professional titles in 1990 at 22. (Incidentally, it was at Woodlawn's Fair Lanes Open, with ABC's Chris Schenkel making the call and Frank Robinson—yes, that Frank Robinson—in the house cheering.)

But today, he's hustling all over Middle River's AMF Country Club Lanes, trying to keep his tournament—which started at 8 a.m. and won't end for almost 12 hours—rolling. More than 150 budding bowlers are competing, including many top Mid-Atlantic youth, vying for nearly $25,000 in scholarship money.

The sport has changed since he was growing up, Wiseman acknowledges, but remains popular and competitive—especially among today's college-bound students. In fact, one of Wiseman's protégés here, Perry Hall's Bryanna Leyen, has already been offered scholarships from Vanderbilt and Fairleigh Dickinson universities.

Wiseman, who began bowling duckpins with his sister and father when he was 5, later walking to the old Dundalk Fair Lanes Bowling Center every day after school, never attended college. Before reaching the pro ranks, he hustled in what were called "pot" games in Northeast Washington, D.C.

"When I was 18, 19, making maybe $1,000 a night on Fridays and Saturdays, you'd bowl all night," he recalls. "I remember a few mornings driving home at 6 a.m. That's actually how one of my first [professional] sponsors learned about me."

92. Going to Graceland

The walls in the upstairs Jungle Room are draped in velvet leopard print, matching the snug dresses on a few of the bouffant-sporting women hitting the dance floor as Rob Kilgore belts out a cover of "Lawdy Miss Clawdy," one of the King of Rock 'n' Roll's early hits:

> *Well lawdy, lawdy, lawdy*
> *Miss Clawdy Girl,*
> *you sure look good to me . . .*

There are all kinds of bands inside the packed Lithuanian Hall, covering nearly the entirety of Elvis Presley's blues/country/rockabilly catalog on three floors this evening. There are also enough Elvis impersonators (this is the 22nd annual Night of 100 Elvises, after all) to match every incarnation—Young Elvis, Comeback Elvis, U.S. Army Private Elvis, Bloated Elvis—of the singer several times over. Although, truth be told, it is difficult at times to tell the unabashed fans dressed in homage to their idol apart from the professional Elvis tribute artists, also known as ETAs.

Also worth noting: this event typically sells out its 1,000-plus tickets.

"I have older sisters; I was weaned on Elvis," says Kilgore, who works for NASA by day. "In fact, in 1972, I visited a girlfriend in Memphis and went to Graceland with her. Elvis was asleep—it was 2:30 in the afternoon—so we couldn't go in the house. His uncle Vester gave us a tour of the grounds in Elvis's Ford Bronco instead."

Midway through the night, hula girls take to the main theater stage, a nod to the icon's *Blue Hawaii* period. Meanwhile, downstairs, near the Viva Las Vegas Lounge, the King's Kitchen Menu features Elvis-inspired favorites, including, of course, fried peanut-butter-and-banana sandwiches.

Carole Carroll, who founded the event, which benefits the Johns Hopkins Children Center, says she knew all along that the mash-up of an Elvis-themed holiday benefit couldn't miss.

"Elvis gave very generously to charities," she says. "And I never had any doubts about the ability of his legacy to draw a crowd. I remember years ago watching a television program where these people traveled up the Amazon, and the natives they encountered there only knew of Avon cosmetics, Jesus, and Elvis from the modern world."

Postscript: The 25th Night of 100 Elvises moved to the Lord Baltimore Hotel and now takes place over three days.

93. The Flock

"I grew up in Fells Point when this neighborhood was called Little Poland," says Anthony Monczewski, 70, the grandson of a Polish immigrant butcher, as he steps inside Holy Rosary Church. "They still celebrate Mass here in Polish."

Dedicated in 1928, the massive Romanesque shrine includes two-story, stained-glass windows, marble altars weighing a collective 49 tons, and a 3,000-pipe, mahogany-encased organ. On this Saturday, Monczewski's childhood church is one of seven historic, Southeast Baltimore immigrant churches open to the public while their holiday decorations remain in full swing.

Sacred Heart of Jesus, which celebrated its first Mass in Highlandtown in 1873, opened first this morning, enticing visitors with local pastries and coffee. Also included: Our Lady of Pompei in "little" Little Italy, St. Leo the Great in Little Italy, St. Casimir and St. Brigid in Canton, and St. Elizabeth of Hungary at Patterson Park.

Inside Our Lady of Pompei, a gorgeous 1923 church built for Italian immigrants and known for its neon-backlit statue of Mary (affectionately nicknamed "Las Vegas Mary" by some congregants), pastor Luigi Esposito smiles as he recalls an early sermon. "Father Lou," who recently celebrated 50 years of service to the parish, admits that as a young priest from Naples, Italy, he occasionally stumbled in his new language during Sunday's homilies.

"I was trying to express the idea of the shepherd helping a lost sheep back into the sheepfold—a very common Christian metaphor," he recounts. "Well, the Italian word for sheepfold is *ovile*, so I figured the English word was the one that sounded closest . . . and told the congregation that we must each help the lost sheep into the oven."

94. History Type

Sitting on a chair in front of a 7-foot-tall machine invented in 1884 called the linotype—literally "line of type"—Ray Loomis hits several keys, demonstrating how hot liquid metal forms molds for each letter. "It was mechanical, before electricity, when gas lines and a steam engine, usually in the backyard, powered its operation," says the 86-year-old Loomis, a printer with 72 years of experience. "It created the type that got taken over to the press, which is basically how things were printed for 80 years."

Thomas Edison called it "the eighth wonder of the world." One stunning effect: in the first decade of its use, American newspaper readership jumped nearly tenfold, going from 3.6 million to more than 33 million.

More than 150 linotype and letterpress enthusiasts, mostly including former printers and younger artists, are gathering inside the Baltimore Museum of Industry for an unveiling of the museum's renovated linotype exhibit and a discussion around the machine—and its inventor, Ottmar Mergenthaler—which launched the previous Information Age.

Michael Ponton, a Maryland Institute College of Art graphic design major, renovated the exhibit, making tonight's promotional flier from old linotype font. "I find inspiration in his story and accomplishments," Ponton says. "My Bolton Hill apartment is on the street where Mergenthaler lived. I walk by his house on the way to my internship."

A German watchmaker, Mergenthaler emigrated in 1872, arriving in Locust Point to join the U.S.'s burgeoning industrialization and, possibly, to avoid conscription into Otto von Bismarck's army.

"He was extraordinarily bright, making this complex machine out of mechanical parts when others struggled with similar efforts," says Frank Romano, author of *History of the Linotype Company*. "His biggest problem was that he never stopped inventing it. He kept changing his mind, believing he could do better. Drove people crazy."

95. Female Form

"A labor of love," says Jillian Storms, as she walks through the rich, detailed exhibit she has curated, *Early Women of Architecture in Maryland*, at the Enoch Pratt Free Library. Shedding light on a dozen pioneering women whose groundbreaking careers spanned from the 1920s through the 1960s, the exhibit includes portraits, biographies chronicling the steadfastness of their ambitions, and notable accomplishments, such as interior design at the National Academy of Sciences in Washington, D.C., as well as copies of their original drawings and renderings.

Among those profiled is German-born Poldi Hirsch, whose family fled the Holocaust before she went on to study architecture in Switzerland. She later emigrated with her husband, settling in Havre de Grace, where she designed numerous local buildings and private residences, including a still-standing mid-century office complex in which her husband began his medical practice.

Also included are Katherine Cutler Ficken and Rose Isabel Greely, the first licensed female architects in Maryland and Washington, and a reproduction of a Maryland Society of Registered Architects letter to Ficken. Dated May 2, 1938, the note advises that while she was "certainly eligible" to attend the organization's annual dinner and meeting, as the only woman in the society, she should check with her "good father" regarding the propriety of her attendance.

"We had a lot of trouble tracking her down," Storms says of Ficken, who designed the Solomon's Island Yacht Club in 1944, among other projects. "She'd adopted a 4-month-old son when she was 45, but she died in 1968 of cancer when he was 11. Our college research assistant was ready to give up when we finally found him. It turned out he'd kept a photo album of her work, including that letter, all these years."

96. Sister of Hoop

Institute of Notre Dame guard Amber Knapper-Jones darts to the wing just in time to tip an opponent's pass. Then, scooping up the loose ball, the diminutive senior dribbles the length of the floor, laying the ball off the backboard as she's knocked down, sending Towson University's packed SECU Arena into a frenzy.

On a night so frigid that walking through the parking lot feels like a brave endeavor, 3,400 fans are here for the 50th edition of "The Game," the annual match between IND and Mercy, a pair of Catholic girls high schools not especially known for their hardwood prowess.

The first contest took place at the Baltimore Civic Center (now the Royal Farms Arena) as a school basketball fundraiser before a Baltimore Bullets NBA game. IND won that first contest, 31-23, but now trails in the overall series.

This evening, led by Knapper-Jones—her key steal capping a 9-0 run—and sophomore Ja'Lyn Armstrong, who scored 14 points, IND wins again.

A lot has changed over the years, including girls basketball, which once played by half-court rules. Other things seem eternal, such as Sister Hildie Marie Sutherland behind the IND souvenir table. After her mother died giving birth to her ninth child, she was placed with the nuns at St. Mary's Female Orphan Asylum in her early teens. She received her own religious calling at 17 and has since spent the past 68 years doing whatever needs doing at IND, including running the school bookstore and making a locker-room speech before "The Game" a few seasons back after a request from the coach.

"I told the girls, win or lose, they will always be No. 1 in God's eyes," Sister Hildie says. "And I told them to keep their heads up, their hands out, and eyes on the ball and the player they should be guarding."

Postscript: Sister Hildie passed on March 14, 2019, 10 days shy of her 87th birthday, after more than 60 years of service to the Institute of Notre Dame.

97. Tale of Two Cities

"This mess really begins in 1910 with the City Council's first segregated housing law, Ordinance 610," local historian Lou Fields says as he drives through Freddie Gray's neighborhood, passing by several civil rights landmarks on the way. Fields notes that New Shiloh Baptist Church, whose congregation hosted Rev. Martin Luther King Jr. in 1953, hosted Gray's funeral last April. Getting out of his car, Fields walks through the bleak area near Gray's childhood home, where he and his sisters suffered lead paint poisoning, toward the Western District police station—built atop a playground, it turns out—where the first protests erupted while Gray remained in a coma following his questionable arrest and ultimately fatal police wagon ride.

"Thurgood Marshall, the Jacksons, the Mitchells all walked these streets. So did Billie Holiday," says Fields, pointing out several historic sites, including the former home of Baltimore's first Colored YWCA.

One of the last stops he makes this morning is at the Holiday sculpture, located between the fourth and fifth stops of Gray's unsecured ride in the back of the police van. Among those joining Fields here is artist James Reid, who created the striking bronze piece in 1985, capturing Holiday in full voice, which Reid describes as a "call to action." At that time, however, the City prevented Reid from installing the sculpture's original base panels because one panel is designed around the jazz singer's anti-lynching song, "Strange Fruit."

Black bodies swingin' in the Southern breeze;

Ultimately, the panels were added in 2009.

"A 24-year censorship fight," says the soft-spoken, 73-year-old Reid, who pumped gas as a teenager in this neighborhood. "The entire work is metaphorical, and the 'Strange Fruit' piece is more important than ever. To me, there's an evolution from the lynching of young Black men to mass incarceration of young Black men and police brutality.

"You know, I had a very strict mother," he continues. "And she taught me to be careful in how I move around a store and things like that. She told me to keep my hands close by my side and not to pick up anything until I was ready to buy it. Would you believe that I am still aware of that at my age now?"

98. Repository

About the same time Enoch Pratt Free Library CEO Carla Hayden welcomes visitors to the grand reopening of the Canton branch library, a young dad holding his daughter's hand sheepishly slides in with an armful of children's books. "We got them from another library, but you can return them to any branch, right?" he asks the woman behind the counter.

Opened in 1886 with Enoch Pratt himself in attendance, the Canton location is the last remaining branch of the original six libraries, but it had been closed for the past four years for renovations. (In 1882, in a letter addressed to the Mayor and City Council, Pratt offered a gift of a central library and six branch libraries—"for all, rich and poor, without distinction of race or color"—with an endowment of more than $1 million.)

Former *Baltimore Sun* columnist Russell Baker once described the cozy Canton branch as "a whimsical little cathedral, as it were, to the printed word." Former U.S. Senator Barbara Mikulski, who grew up in the neighborhood and whose family famously owned a Polish bakery nearby, later told an interviewer that she considered getting her library card at the Canton branch "a rite of passage into adulthood."

Among those on hand for the ribbon cutting is 95-year-old Mollie Katz Witow, who was born in Danzig to Jewish immigrants and came here often as a girl. She grew up above her father's grocery and butcher shop, regularly roller skating down Boston Street to the Can Company—when they still made tin cans there. After graduating from Goucher College, she entered into the Pratt's librarian training program.

"I remember I had to wait until I was 8 years old to get a library card," she says. "The librarian's name was Miss Gough, spelled the same as the street. She wore a voluminous black skirt, starched white blouse, and high-button shoes. The first book she gave me to read was called *The Keeper of the Flame*. It was about an American-Indian father who taught his son to leave little objects along a path so people would know to follow him."

Postscript: President Barack Obama named Carla Hayden the Librarian of Congress in 2016.

99. Root Shock

Oh, Baltimore
Ain't it hard just to live?
Just to live
—"Baltimore," by Randy Newman, 1977

The Difference, the musical duo of Curtis McGee and Malaika Aminata Clements, are singing a remix of Nina Simone's hit "Baltimore" before this afternoon's staged reading of *Last House Standing* at the packed Northwood Branch Library. It's a play about the ill-fated East-West Highway Expressway that became the known in the city as the Road to Nowhere.

Ultimately, the project relocated more than 1,000 families and businesses in West Baltimore, a period several audience members still recall.

Written and directed by playwright Sheila Gaskins, *Last House Standing* is set in 1968 on a rowhouse stoop. The central protagonist is a teenager named Evelyn who kisses her boyfriend for the first time only to realize he's moving away because of the coming highway— and she is, too. There are a million financial and emotional issues to wrestle with as neighbors count the families that are already gone and those that remain.

At one point, Evelyn's young cousin and pals run around as an Arabber plies his trade: "Strawberries, cantaloupes, watermelon, red to the rind"—all evidence of a close-knit community being torn apart.

"Oh man, that takes me back," says a man in the audience.

Though her divorced mother seems in denial that eviction is imminent, Evelyn gains strength after her grandmother appears in a dream to teach her about resilience. It's a message reinforced in her nighttime vision by the tree in front of her house, which morphs into a defiant, branch-waving, Black Power activist preaching a deeply funny soliloquy about the shared "root shock" experiences endured by trees and African-African communities.

The leafy London planetree, found all over Baltimore's rowhouse neighborhoods, raps about bending, but not breaking, in the face of oppression, ending with the chant "No Justice, No Leaves!"

"You know," says another older West Baltimore native, "I remember those trees, too."

100. Field of Dreams

Glenn Murphy is first in line. Decked in sweats and sneakers, the former high-school infielder pounds his mitt, lets out a whoop, and then bends down to field a half-dozen batted balls, all of which he scoops cleanly. The 56-year-old even handles a grounder up against the third base stands at Oriole Park, if a bit awkwardly.

On this chilly afternoon, he may be the oldest of the more than 75 would-be ball boys or girls vying for a position, but there's no typical candidate—schoolteachers, college students, and IT specialists are among those trying out. The only requirement is to be at least 18. At $8 an hour, a love for the O's is a given.

"I had Jim Palmer's rookie card," says Murphy, name-checking the Orioles Hall-of-Fame pitcher.

At the other end of the age spectrum is Annabelle Williams, whose all-time favorite Oriole is center fielder Adam Jones. "I'm only 17," acknowledges Williams, who also wields a fine glove. "But I turn 18 before the season starts."

The tryouts are brief. There's an introduction to the judges, who include Orioles staff and CBS Radio personalities Rob Long, Greg Carpenter, and Reagan Warfield, and then the field test.

"I used to have season tickets, so I'm super excited to be here," says Matt Fouse, 31, a Charles Village artist, who waits for his shot in the dugout as friends of various contestants take photos from the stands. "I gave up the tickets after we had our daughter. My wife's a night-shift nurse, but she said if I do get picked, we'll figure things out so I can do this."

101. Water Works

It's raining, but not hard enough to dissuade the volunteers, now putting on ponchos and hip waders. About 150 friends, neighbors, and students are gathering in John Long's yard for the annual spring cleanup of historic Bread & Cheese Creek, which this morning means trying to avoid getting wet from above as well as below.

"Amazing turnout, isn't it?" says the good-natured Long, loading metal signposts dug from the creek into a recycling cart. He launched the nonprofit Clean Bread & Cheese Creek in 2009 after purchasing his father-in-law's bungalow-style house, which sits alongside the stream.

According to local lore, Bread & Cheese takes its name from the War of 1812's Battle of North Point, when it served as a popular spot for soldiers to rest and eat their rations, although the true story behind the name isn't clear. Not in dispute, however, is that the creek, adjacent to Merritt Boulevard shopping centers, had been a mess for decades.

Over the past seven years, Long's army has pulled some 112 tons of trash from the 3.7-mile waterway, including 328 shopping carts, 429 tires, 92 bicycles, three bathtubs, a pool table, a seesaw, and an unopened bottle of Pepsi from 1986. Minnows, frogs, and even small snakes have since returned, notes volunteer George Fischer, whose school-age sons lend a hand during a final walk-through in the creek's shallow waters.

For many of the youngest volunteers, however, the environmental aspect of the cleanup takes second place to the chance to muck and scavenge around in the creek.

"I found a BB gun. That was pretty cool," says one local girl, drying her socks. "Last year, I found a car engine."

102. Sweet Memories

In the small waiting room inside the Wockenfuss Candies factory, visitors pull on hairnets as a video on a flatscreen TV explains how cocoa beans are extracted from football-shaped pods, which can grow close to a foot in length in Central America. "I can't believe how big it is," a middle-school boy says in admiration as he picks up one of the rough, leathery cocoa pods on hand.

Ultimately, the chocolate made from the beans inside those pods finds its way to Northeast Baltimore, arriving on 1,800-pound pallets in the form of 10-pound bars.

Today marks Wockenfuss's fourth annual factory tour, drawing close to 2,000 chocolate lovers for a behind-the-scenes look at how liquid caramel gets drizzled over cashews and then broken into bite-size patties, for example.

Launched 101 years ago by Herman Wockenfuss, a Prussian immigrant, the company has expanded to nine retail locations between Baltimore and Ocean City, while also growing its shipping service. But it's still a family-operated, locally owned enterprise, notes treasurer Janice Wockenfuss Motter, a fourth-generation staffer.

To her point, most people on the tour appear to either know one of the employees working this morning or recall when the factory was still located in nearby rowhouses. (Wockenfuss confectioneries include caramel apples, fudge, and lollipops, as well as fruit-shaped marzipan, crystallized ginger, and mint nonpareils.)

"I ate Wockenfuss candy as a child, too," says Gail DeNicolis as two women hand-dip marshmallows into a creamy vat of chocolate behind her. DeNicolis has worked here for nine years after a career in special education.

"When I was 4 or 5, my aunt walked me to the original storefront on Belair Road at Easter. During the holidays, we get requests from all over the country from people who grew up in the area and want to send Wockenfuss chocolate and candy to their family. I know why: the taste reminds them of their childhood. Same as me."

103. Not Sitting Still

At Triangle Park, the narrow, grassy oasis between Pennsylvania and North Freemont avenues, the ninth annual No Boundaries Coalition block party is in full swing.

Among other performers, two raucous local marching bands, New Twilighters and Baltimore Christian Warriors, are attracting appreciative crowds to the stage area. There's also mosaic-making and face-painting for kids, as well as produce from a new community stand, Fresh at the Avenue, for sale.

Originally founded as the Boundary Block Party, named to highlight the geographical, racial, and economic divide between largely white, upscale Bolton Hill and Central West Baltimore, those early efforts eventually gave birth to the No Boundaries Coalition, which is also shuttling residents to the polls today for early primary voting.

To that end, just a little farther down Pennsylvania Avenue, pastor C.W. Harris is climbing onto the fire escape ladder alongside the Jubilee Arts building. The 66-year-old lifelong Sandtown resident isn't climbing down, however, but up to the top, where he promises to remain until 500 of his neighbors cast a ballot.

The roof of the three-story Jubilee Arts center, which Harris founded, has been equipped with a tent and portable toilet but little in terms of creature comforts.

"After what happened last year [referencing the death of Freddie Gray and subsequent uprising], a bunch of us met right there," Harris says, pointing across the way to St. Peter Claver Catholic Church.

"Everybody said politicians don't listen to the community because no one votes, but no one knew how to inspire more people to vote. Finally, I said, 'Look, I'll go up on the roof until people vote.' I was willing to do anything. So, here I am."

Postscript: After Harris's five days on the roof, Sandtown turnout more than tripled from the previous election.

104. Old New Age

A passerby would likely miss the plain white door hidden a half-dozen steps above the renowned C. Grimaldis Gallery. The gold-stenciled lettering on the glass simply reads "The Theosophical Society" along with, curiously, a seven-digit phone number. The small, nondoctrinaire, wisdom-seeking society, which promotes the study of philosophy, comparative religion, and metaphysics, has been here so long, it predates area codes.

This afternoon, in fact, the organization, at its current location since 1929, celebrates the 100th anniversary of its chartering.

Highlights today include a talk by Tim Boyd, the current president of the international Theosophical Society, and a presentation by archivist Janet Kerschner, who displays a 1939 photo of this very meeting room, sending members seated on folding chairs into convulsive laughter.

"Even the ferns are in the same place!"

The original Theosophical Society was formed in 1875 in New York City by Helena Blavatsky, a blue-eyed Russian spiritualist; Col. Henry Steel Olcott, an early American convert to Buddhism; and an Irish-born lawyer named William Quan Judge. The Society's original objectives remain: to form a nucleus of the universal brotherhood of humanity, to encourage the study of comparative religion, philosophy, and science, and investigate the unexplained laws of nature and powers latent in man.

In his address, Boyd credits the Society for being among the first to introduce Eastern terms, such as yoga, karma, and reincarnation, into the Western lexicon.

Kerschner then traces theosophy's Baltimore "boom" from the 1920s through the 1950s, which topped out at 73 members for the organization and included Sunday radio programs on WITH. Today, there are a little more than two-dozen people, albeit an eclectic group of artists, retirees, hippies, community organizers, and graduate students, on the chapter's Listserv.

"I first came in 1971," says Carl Hurwitz, a clinical psychologist with a gray ponytail. "We've been dying a slow death ever since that's just taking a very long time."

105. Amphibious Art

A giant orange squid pedals downhill and splashes into the water at the Canton boat launch, drawing big cheers from the overflowing crowds gathered on the grassy banks. The squid is soon followed by an Alexander Calder-themed "Mobile Mobile" and another human-powered amphibious vehicle named "Wheel of (Mis)fortune."

But then a giant unicorn—built and driven by Oakland Mills high school students atop mountain bikes—capsizes. "It's cold, it's cold!" a boy bellows, pulling himself onto the dock.

Meanwhile, a girl on the team smiles and breaks into a short backstroke.

"This is our second year," says Oakland Mills teacher Skip Yarn, referring to the 18th annual Kinetic Sculpture Race, the have-to-see-it-to-believe-it event presented by the American Visionary Art Museum. "But it's the first time we attempted the water entry. On a positive note, our steering on land has improved quite a bit."

More than mere whimsical art farce, the "race" is also equal parts endurance contest and engineering challenge. The 15-mile trek from Federal Hill to Southeast Baltimore and back doesn't just offer a spin in the Inner Harbor but requires traversing sand and mud pits at Patterson Park on totally human-powered works of art. The machines can be simply bicycles with pontoons, manned by a single brave soul, or they can be well-engineered, sophisticated vehicles stretching 50 feet long. Pilots, known as "Kinetinauts," compete for awards, such as Grand Mediocre East Coast Champion, the top honor, and highly prized Next to the Last Award.

"This weighs about 4,000 pounds when the nine-person crew is aboard," says David Hess, captain of a sea- and street-worthy vessel coined "The Golden Eyedra." "It's made from an '87 Suzuki Samurai, so it's also got four-wheel drive. The frightening part is going downhill at 35 miles per hour."

The Arbutus Middle School entry this year is a four-wheeled sculpture named "Monsters of the Middle School Brain." The enormous papier mâché "brain," sitting above the team of bicyclists, depicts the daily horrors of cafeteria lunches and school bathrooms, as well as subjects like bullying.

"Up through fifth grade, everything is easy," says sixth-grader Tressa Salava, explaining the sculpture's origin and theme. "Then all of a sudden, there's all this homework and kids towering over you. Middle school is pretty terrifying."

106. Blast from the Past

Fifty years ago today, Frank Robinson launched a home run off Luis Tiant that not only cleared the left field wall but 50 rows of seats, landing in Memorial Stadium's parking lot. The only HR ever knocked completely out of the park in the Orioles' history on 33rd Street, the titanic shot was considered such a momentous feat that Robinson received a minute-long standing ovation, and a week later, a flag reading "HERE" was placed atop the bleachers to mark the spot where the ball sailed from the park.

"The [one-minute] ovation the fans gave me after I trotted back on the field following the homer was the thing I remember most about my years in Baltimore," Robinson said later. "I knew then that I had been accepted."

Memorial Stadium, of course, was torn down after the team moved to Camden Yards. However, a popular amateur ballfield has since replaced it, with home plate and left field closely aligned to the old diamond's configurations. So, on this windy afternoon, local resident Mark Melonas is hosting a second flag raising to commemorate the golden anniversary of Robinson's epic blast.

The replica "HERE" flag that Melonas commissioned is even made by the same company that produced the original.

"I wasn't born yet in 1966, which was also Frank's first year with the Orioles. But my dad, who was 17 then, told me how much he meant to Baltimore," says Melonas, 41, a furniture maker.

Robinson, later Major League Baseball's first Black manager, initially had difficulty buying a house in segregated in Baltimore. Once he did, however, he led the O's to their first World Series title that same year, delivering a 410-foot homer in the series-clinching 1-0 win at Memorial Stadium.

"I was sitting in left field that day," recalls Mark's dad, Jim Melonas, now 67. "It flew two rows over my head."

(Postscript: After Frank Robinson died in 2019, former Orioles' teammate Brooks Robinson released a statement: "As a player, I put Frank in a class with Willie Mays, Hank Aaron, and Mickey Mantle. He was the best player I ever played with. When he came here in 1966, he put us over the top. He was a great man and he will be deeply missed.")

107. For Love of Country

Once a way station known as the Immigration House for turn-of-the-century newcomers to America, the wooden trunk on the floor of this three-story, red-brick boarding house reveals much of the building's history.

Gold lettering on the trunk, one of the artifacts on exhibit at the new Baltimore Immigration Museum, which is hosting an open house this afternoon, reads "Bremen-Baltimore Sept. 25 Dampfer [steamship] Rhein." It's a telling inscription pointing to the historic Atlantic route that carried 1.2 million mostly German and Eastern European immigrants to Locust Point between the Civil War and World War I.

Above the trunk, a black-and-white photograph shows a young man with a bushy mustache, a cap, and an overcoat sitting amid duffle bags and cheap suitcases shortly after arrival.

The culmination of years of work by Nicholas Fessenden, a former Friends School history teacher, and his wife, Brigitte, a German-born preservation expert, the budding museum documents Baltimore's immigration saga, which has been largely overshadowed by New York's Ellis Island. The immigration pier itself was constructed by the B&O Railroad, which, in part, hoped to attract Central and Eastern Europeans to the burgeoning Midwest where it was building an expanding network of tracks.

On this day, Locust Point residents stop by in a steady stream, as do other visitors interested in learning more about their city and, in some cases, their own family's backstory.

"I'm German on my mother's side," says Frank Tewey, whose ancestors lived nearby. "My great-grandmother's family told her, 'Never marry a sailor; they all leave.'" But she did—another German immigrant named Gerhardt—and, indeed, he left, heading home to Deutschland to claim a small inheritance. He returned, however.

"My great-grandfather joined the German navy in order to come back and then jumped ship to be with my great-grandmother," Tewey continues. "Good thing he did. One of their future children, my grandmother, had 63 grandkids when she died."

108. Senator Barb

Look at the first half-dozen times Sen. Barbara Mikulski's name appears in *The Sun,* and you can learn almost everything you need to know about her. It's all before she ever ran for an elected office.

In 1962, a Mount St. Agnes College alumnae reunion announcement mentions that a "Miss Barbara Mikulski" will be assisting in organizing the event. It's exactly the type of unglamorous assignment that a go-getting, 25-year-old woman signs on for: a ton of phone calls, errands, and lots of networking possibilities. Two and a half years later, "Miss Barbara Mikulski" appears again in *The Sun,* this time as a National Institute of Mental Health-granted social worker providing testimony at City Hall on behalf of an anti-poverty bill put forward by then City Councilman William Donald Schaefer.

By 1967, the daughter of Polish corner grocers has risen to assistant chief of community relations at the city's Department of Social Services. She's also in charge of a new city program providing a housing subsidy that—at an average of $15 to $25—isn't much of a subsidy at all, she notes in one story. A year later, in the aftermath of the 1968 riots, she's highlighted among those teaching a class for a Johns Hopkins University "Freedom School" initiative.

The feisty, tell-it-like-it-is Barbara Mikulski that Baltimoreans have come to know, respect, occasionally fear, and often love? She first emerges in 1969—at least in print. (She's always joked that she considered becoming a nun before realizing, with the help of the sisters at the all-girls Institute of Notre Dame high school, that the "obedience" requirement might be a personal obstacle.) Still at her social services community relations position, Mikulski publicly calls out her own agency for allowing 55,000 city children to suffer from malnutrition.

The Sun characterized Mikulski and a welfare recipient who spoke up during the community meeting as taking "a healthy bite on the hand that feeds them."

The ambition, smarts, spunk, leadership, commitment to social justice, interest in bridging racial divides—the understanding that the ability to create fundamental change lies among those with political power—it's all taking shape. And the colorful personality, the self-effacing humor, the crackling quips, the bold strategic action—that's about to come into view, too. In August 1969, as her beloved Orioles are dominating the American League, Mikulski appears in the paper of record in the fight that will soon make her a rowhouse-hold name.

In a story headlined "Expressway Opponents Vilify Officials," a 33-year-old Mikulski goes after a 16-lane urban highway scheduled to cut through the heart of the city—her city, where she has lived her entire life—from West Baltimore to the Inner Harbor, Fells Point, Canton, and Highlandtown. At a coalition gathering with West Baltimore residents, Mikulski takes a poke at city and state leaders' promises of future development when, she snaps, "We haven't even had present-day development."

She was just getting started.

The Fells Point Fun Fest that fall drew 50,000 people to the base of Broadway for steamed crabs, raw oysters, Polish sausage, beer, live music, tugboats, and ethnic folk dancers. The third annual event attracted local politicos, including former Mayor Theodore McKeldin, Del. Julian Lapides, and Schaefer—who had become City Council president, as well as a strong proponent of the East-West Expressway, which was projected to raze a couple hundred of Southeast Baltimore's historic homes.

The Sun reporter assigned to the event noted that throughout the otherwise festive carnival atmosphere, a protest group identifying itself

229

as Radio Free Fells Point had blasted "SOS" messages condemning the city's Urban Design Concept Team, deriding it as the Urban Design "Concrete" Team.

One member of Radio Free Fells Point, the reporter quoted in the last line of the story, shouted her opposition as Schaefer tried to speak. "The British couldn't take Fells Point, the termites couldn't take Fells Point," the protestor railed. "And we don't think the State Roads Commission can take Fells Point either."

Could there be any doubt who those words belonged to?

In March of last year, Mikulski announced at Henderson's Wharf in Fells Point that she would not seek reelection after 30 years in the United States Senate. Although she's now 80, the news still came as something of a minor shock. She remains healthy and vigorous and the state's most popular elected official. By all indications, she would've handily won office again. The cobblestone street where she delivered her announcement could not have been a more fitting location. She noted it was not far from where her immigrant grandmother opened a bakery, where her parents ran a small grocery, and just a few short blocks from where she launched her political career.

"It's where I learned that we are all in this together," Mikulski said at the press conference, choking up briefly when speaking about her staff, upon which she is famously tough, and her close working relationship with fellow Maryland Sen. Ben Cardin. "And it's where I learned about service from my mother and father, who said, 'Good morning, can I help you?' every morning when they opened the small neighborhood grocery they owned and ran." (As a teenager, Mikulski spent a summer working nearby at Gibbs Preserving Co., one of the canning houses in Canton. "I came home every day smelling like ketchup," she says later.)

She had concluded, she explained, in her direct style that has lost little of its fire after four decades in Congress, that she didn't want to spend the next two years trying to finance another campaign run. Not when so much work remains to be done.

"Do I spend my time raising money or raising hell to meet your day-to-day needs?"

When Mikulski won election to the U.S. Senate in 1986, there had never been another Democratic woman elected to the upper house of Congress who wasn't appointed or succeeding a deceased husband. Her entrance into the quintessential "boys club" after a decade in the House of Representatives also distinguished her as the first Democratic woman to serve in both chambers. And by the time Barack Obama presented Mikulski with the Presidential Medal of Freedom last November, she had become the longest-serving female member of Congress ever.

Reflecting on her career a few months before the end of her final term in her Senate hideaway in the Capitol—furnished with her parents' restored dining room table and other Highlandtown mementos—Mikulski says former Kansas Senator Nancy Kassebaum was particularly helpful when she arrived. As were several male senators, notably Ted Kennedy, who quickly became friends as well as advisers. But it was Maryland's senior senator, Paul Sarbanes, who became her indispensable mentor. She gives him tremendous credit for showing her how to be successful in the "old-boy" network and get things accomplished.

The two became close over the years, commuting back and forth to Baltimore every day.

It may seem ironic that a man would've been in that mentoring role, but it shouldn't, Mikulski says. "My real shining light was Sen. Paul Sarbanes. And I want to make sure this gets mentioned. I've had the chance to serve with two of the best men in Maryland politics ever. First, with Sen. Sarbanes, and now with Sen. Ben Cardin.

"You know," she continues, "there is something else that I've learned over the years. Men of quality are never in fear of a woman who seeks equality."

109. Vaulting Ambition

At 4 years old, Donnell Whittenburg was already turning his mother's Northeast Baltimore duplex into his personal jungle gym. He'd learned to shimmy to the top of the home's interior doors. If he found a ceiling rod in the basement or a beam above the patio, he'd find a way to climb and swing himself off of those. He mastered jumps and flips from the stairs and living room cartwheels. He wasn't a boisterous or rebellious child. In fact, Whittenburg was, and remains, quite shy and soft-spoken, just extraordinarily active.

By 5, he was scaling up the side of the house and walking around the dining room table on his hands. His mom, Sheila Brown, remembers him once taking an accidental tumble down a full flight of stairs—in front of guests, no less—only to watch him land on his feet and shrug it off as if nothing happened.

Today, the 21-year-old is heading to the Olympics as a U.S. men's gymnastics team alternate. He has been featured in *Time* and a television commercial with Michael Phelps, promoting the games in Rio de Janeiro this month. Recently, *Sports Illustrated* ranked him one of the 50 "fittest" male athletes in the world. ("Oh, you can't find me when Donnell's turn comes," Brown says, sitting on her sofa while thumbing through a scrapbook of her son's career. "I can't stay in my seat. I'm up. I'm walking around the stadium." And if her son gets the opportunity to compete in Rio? "Those television cameras shouldn't even bother looking for me.")

But none of this was ever planned. Or even dreamt. His single mother, a career social worker, didn't know anything about gymnastics when Whittenburg was a little boy. She was simply looking, prodded by his older sister, who was in high school at the time, for somewhere safer than her house for him to practice his stunts when she enrolled him in youth classes.

"I was like, 'Mom, you have to do something with him,'" Latisha Smith, Whittenburg's sister, recalls with a laugh.

Postscript: Donnell Whittenburg won three bronze medals and a gold medal in the vault at the 2017 U.S. National Championships.

110. Love Shack

Behind the DJ booth, a pair of turntables, and stacks of metal record suitcases, Fred Schneider digs through his 45-rpm collection, handing old-school vinyl selections to host Rob Macy. It's cramped and hot, and the packed house inside the Lithuanian Hall is twisting and shouting to some of the best, and rarest, greasy rock 'n' roll, Motown, R&B, funk, and soul ever made.

Macy concentrates momentarily as he lowers the needle onto "You've Got My Soul on Fire," then nods and grins as he lifts off his headphones. "This is sick," he says, referring to Edwin Starr's 1973 single.

By midnight, the air is so heavy with perspiration that women are lifting the matted hair from their necks and pinning it atop their head even as they keep moving. It's mostly twenty- and thirty-somethings, but more than a few Gen Xers have come to see Schneider, the famous party-chasing frontman for the new wave B-52s, who broke out in the late '70s and early '80s with hits like "Rock Lobster" and "Private Idaho."

The vintage recordings behind the first-Friday-of-every-month Save Your Soul dance party, launched two decades ago, are both an homage to the music Schneider loved as a teenager and the organizing principle behind his retro, bouffant-sporting band.

"Word apparently got to Fred that Baltimore had one of the top soul dance parties on the East Coast," Macy says. "So we invited him, and he was game. He'd bought some records and he wanted a place to play 'em."

As the evening turned to the wee hours of the morning, the 65-year-old singer, who doesn't appear to have slowed down much, hit the dance floor more and more.

"I was showing them all how to boogaloo and shing-a-ling," says Schneider, who still manages to convey a certain intoxicating blend of Southern-influenced civility and randy mischievousness when he smiles. "It helped that I was a little bit tipsy."

111. Star Struck

"Now don't accuse me of putting in a slide," Heyn cracks, adjusting his telescope and tripod in front of the Chipotle in Charles Village as a middle-school girl peers in.

"Oh wow!" she squeals, which, after the half-million "looks" Heyn figures he's offered over the past three decades, still makes the 85-year-old, street-corner astronomy busker smile. "The rings are so bright!"

The "rings," billions of ice, dust, and rock particles circling Saturn, are so geometrically exquisite at 800 million miles away that it's hard to believe one's eyes. "I've been doing this for 29 years. Same number it takes Saturn [hurtling at 21,000 miles per hour] to go once around the sun," Heyn says. "And I've been accused of all kinds of tricks."

A few minutes later, a retired Indian-born biologist who lives nearby takes a peek. "They're perfect," he gasps.

Tonight, Mars is "near" Saturn. Jupiter, meanwhile, sits to the right of the moon, which is half-lit in its current phase, with craters resembling a pockmarked sidewalk. Later, two 20-something researchers from the Johns Hopkins-based Space Telescope Science Institute—home to the Hubble—walk by. "Scientists we work with stare at data being downloaded on their computer all day long," Joseph Long says. "They couldn't even tell you when the planet they're studying is visible."

"Herman introduces the beauty and scale, which is visceral, to people. You feel it in your gut," adds Brendan Hagan, who with Long has followed in Heyn's footsteps, bringing pop-up telescope events to the Inner Harbor and downtown.

"Years ago, a woman stopped by and told me she'd just submitted her master's thesis on Venus. And then admitted she'd never seen Venus directly," Heyn recalls. "I said, 'Would you like to?'"

Heyn discovered his calling at an age when most people consider retirement. He had initially tried teaching school. He worked sales gigs and a job as a lab tech. He also spent two years at the Pratt Library. His longest previous stretch of regular employment was the 12 years he worked as an office manager and delivery driver for a local construction company. Astronomy was never far away, however, always a passionate hobby.

"I got interested in astronomy at Garrison Junior High in Northwest Baltimore—Mrs. Wicker's eighth-grade general science class," Heyn says. "She drew the Big Dipper on the blackboard and told us that night to go look for it in the sky. And I did. I did my homework and I was hooked."

That was 1944.

Postscript: In November, after 2,857 nights on the street by his count, Heyn and his sidewalk telescope retired.

112. Death in Diorama

Frances Glessner Lee, considered the mother of forensic science, often wore all black and was nicknamed "the Tarantula" by her family.

"I would've loved to have met her," Bruce Goldfarb, spokesman for Maryland's Office of the Chief Medical Examiner, deadpans to the sold-out crowd at a presentation of Lee's famous miniature dioramas known as "The Nutshell Studies of Unexplained Death."

Goldfarb, in fact, is enthralled with Lee's story and legacy, which he's sharing tonight at The Maryland State Medical Society. Bright and born to a wealthy family, Lee was nonetheless discouraged from attending college. Instead, she became the first woman invited to join the International Association of Chiefs of Police in 1943. Through a brother's friend, she'd become intensely interested in early forensic science and eventually began the painstaking process of building intricate, true-to-life, dollhouse-size crime scenes where "unexplained" deaths—accidents, suicides, and murders—had taken place.

The purpose of the models, authentic down to hand-rolled cigarette butts that are half the size of a fingernail and filled with tobacco, is to teach real-world homicide detectives how to observe, record, and evaluate crime scenes. The whodunit answers remain a closely guarded secret to protect the learning process.

The 18 studies, along with actual witness statements taken by police at the time of the original murders, were given to the Baltimore office of the state medical examiner's office in 1966 after Lee's death. They continue to serve as a component of an acclaimed, national law enforcement seminar. From time to time, visitors, who have heard of the death-scene dioramas, come by for a look as well.

"The other day two women stopped me and wanted to know the answer to one scene," Goldfarb says. "I explained I wasn't allowed to say and that it wasn't really the point.

"As soon as I finished," Goldfarb continues, "one woman turns to the other and says, 'I think the husband did it.'"

Postscript: Goldfarb's book 18 Tiny Deaths, *about Glessner and the Nutshell Studies of Unexplained Death, was published in February 2020.*

113. Laugh Out Loud

"Whenever I go do shows in D.C. or in the county, and I tell people I live in Baltimore City, everyone's like, 'Oh my God, you must be so brave!'

"And, I'm like, 'Yo, look at me—I'm wearing skinny pants and black, thick-framed glasses," 27-year-old Umar Khan tells the LOL@ Artscape crowd as it breaks into laughter at the second of the festival's two nights of live comedy. "I live in a neighborhood with cupcake shops. I'm safe."

A Baltimore City schools' psychologist by day, and proud resident of gentrifying Hampden, which he notes by taking a gentle swipe at his neighborhood's charcuterie trend, the self-deprecating Khan is serving as host of Artscape's comedy shows for the first time this year.

"It was a really diverse crowd—young, old, Black, white—which actually makes for a lot better show for a comedian," Khan says afterward. "Telling jokes about white hipsters to white hipsters isn't funny. There's no tension."

Several performances fall flat, including an over-sharing 20-something female comic who's more uncomfortably awkward than funny, and an orange-jumpsuited ukulele singer-songwriter who sounds like country star Trace Adkins. But most of the comics effectively play off of their personas and the audience, cracking jokes about loved ones, race, drugs, and Baltimore—sometimes all at once.

Mike Smith, an animated, mid-30s newcomer to comedy, talks about urban life and family and, in particular, a close relative, an aunt, who's recently turned her life around.

"She used to be a crackhead, and now she's a vegan," Smith says, rolling his eyes. "Now she's a real pain in the ass."

114. Cross to Bear

In Europe, stained-glass windows have been associated with Christianity and appreciated for their beauty since the Middle Ages. There is also historic, if not quite as old, stained glass inside Bolton Hill's Brown Memorial Presbyterian Church. This Sunday morning, as part of Artscape's slew of events, congregation member James Shuman is leading a post-service Breakfast With Tiffany look at the Gothic-style, 1869-built church's exquisite windows, which a glass art expert once described as "the finest collection of Tiffany windows in the country and quite possibly the world."

Tiffany glass, Shuman notes, refers to the work of the prolific decorative artist Louis Comfort Tiffany, son of the founder of the famous luxury jewelry retailer Tiffany & Co. The two largest windows at Brown Memorial measure 16 feet wide and stand three stories tall. Facing each other, they depict the annunciation to the shepherds and the heavenly city of Jerusalem. "These were made when there was no TV, no radio, and people came to church twice on Sunday and once during the week," Shuman says. "They each preach a message."

From outside, however, the images in the church's 11 windows appear, at best, in shadowy outlines.

"There was a boy, 8 to 10 years old, who made his mother bring him in 10 years ago," Shuman recalls. "It gets a little rough a couple blocks west, and there had been some shootings in the neighborhood around that time. He said he wanted to see the picture of the man holding the gun.

"What the image was," Shuman explains, "was a seeker holding his arm outstretched with a cross."

115. Past Lives

"Look around, what do you see?" asks the top-hatted, cane-sporting guide of the 30 or so Charm City visitors gathered Friday evening at the foot of Broadway for The Original Fells Point Ghostwalk. "Friendly part of town, right? Pretzel place. Ice cream parlor. Young professionals. That's a new phenomenon, however," he adds, somewhat ominously. "This used to be a dangerous part of town. Pirates here would stick you in the gut for the coins in your pocket."

Among the ghosts said to reside nearby is a 10-year-old girl who has appeared in the second-floor stockroom above Bertha's restaurant across the street. The girl has been spotted over the years by restaurant employees, according to the guide, glancing from the window to where this crowd now stands, which is reputedly a mass burial site from a very real 18th-century yellow-fever outbreak that may have claimed her mother.

On Thames Street, the discussion turns to the former practice of shanghaiing young men into service aboard a ship—known as "crimping" in Baltimore.

One such young man, who apparently did not survive his initial kidnapping, is said to haunt Leadbetters Tavern around the corner.

The Ghostwalk also includes a visit to the family cemetery of Fells Point founder William Fell, whose long dead ne'er-do-well son is reportedly sighted from time to time, walking down narrow Shakespeare Street.

Naturally, the best tales blend fact and hard-to-fact-check anecdotes.

Melissa Rowell, a former Johns Hopkins medical illustrator who launched the Ghostwalk tours, admits to being skeptical as she did her initial research.

"Then something strange happened," she says. She'd bought a T-shirt from an older Cat's Eye Pub bartender and not long afterward found herself back there and asked another employee about him. "I described him to the woman working—that he kinda looked like Abraham Lincoln," Rowell continues. "And so she points to a photograph behind the bar. I said, 'Yes, that's the guy I bought the T-shirt from.'

"She says, 'Well, he worked here. Doesn't anymore. He's been dead eight years.'

"True story."

116. Leap of Faith

On a late summer morning, Isaac Schleifer is driving past the house where he grew up in a working- and middle-class section of Falstaff, which sits just inside the city line below Pikesville. He has to stop and share a story. Or two. He's married, the father of one, and soon, two. He's also sharp, confident, and remarkably even-tempered for his age. Any age, really. Schleifer, who is just 27 and goes by "Yitzi," becomes the 5th District's new city councilman this month. But he admits he bristled, ever so slightly, whenever it was implied during the campaign that being a young, successful Jewish businessman automatically meant that he came from money and was therefore out of touch with parts of his district.

Stretching from Howard Park to Pimlico and Park Heights to Mount Washington and Roland Park, the 5th District is one of the most diverse districts in the city. It's got a Muslim community and a Latino community. It has some of the wealthiest neighborhoods in the city, as well as some of the poorest. "I'm the youngest of five. I have four older sisters," Schleifer says, gesturing toward the modest, brick duplex of his childhood. "There were seven of us in that house—three bedrooms and one bathroom. Everything I've gotten I have worked very hard for by building a business that, thank God, has been very successful."

As he begins driving again, he talks about playing baseball and basketball with the mix of Black, Jewish, and Latino kids up and down the street. "Once a year, the maintenance guy at the school would go up on the roof and throw all the balls down," Schleifer recalls. "We celebrated like it was the biggest day of the year." It's also on this block where his interests in community service and politics were first encouraged. Schleifer's father, Barry, is a former Falstaff neighborhood association president.

After he turns past the school and continues on this swing through his district, he notes the new sold-out Bancroft Village townhome development on Park Heights Avenue—with SUVs and bicycles parked in front of nearly every doorstep—and the synagogue next door. He also highlights the imminent closing of Northwestern High School. "There was a fight over the closing of the school, but we have to look at the property as an opportunity now," Schleifer says. "It's not often that that many acres of land become available—whether it's for a park or recreation center or some other kind of redevelopment."

Looping past Pimlico, in the heart of the district, he says he'd like "to see 50 events a year, not one or two" at the historic racetrack. Not long afterward, he waves to a police officer standing on a corner and looks closely at another officer getting out of a car before again nodding hello. "If you're a cop in this neighborhood and I don't know you, it's because you're new here," Schleifer says.

"My family has been here for 40-plus years," he continues. "I was born at Sinai Hospital. You know the saying, 'It takes a village to raise a kid?' That's me."

Later, with lunchtime approaching, Schleifer pulls into Tov Pizza ("Baltimore's Best Kosher Pizza"), which is nearby in Northwest Baltimore. Owned by his older cousin, Ron Rosenbluth, a former Democratic State Central Committee official, the busy Reisterstown Road pizza, sub, and knish joint has been around since 1984, but it feels even more retro with its checked Formica floor and gumball machines. And it's here that Schleifer and Rosenbluth gamed out maybe the most surprising primary victory in this watershed election year. This isn't a pizza place where people talk politics," Schleifer jokes as he slides into a seat. "It's a political clubhouse that sells pizza."

The target, at least initially, was 39-years-in-office city council-woman Rikki Spector. (Three months before the primary, the 80-year-old Spector unexpectedly declined to seek re-election. Instead, she tapped Betsy Gardner, City Council President Jack Young's longtime 5th District aide and citywide Jewish liaison, to succeed her.)

A successful software entrepreneur, Schleifer had funded a poll that examined Spector's vulnerability in the Democratic primary, but the data coming back wasn't great. Schleifer and Rosenbluth figured they had to convince about 800 registered Republicans and independents to switch party affiliation if they were going to win. Still, given the size of the politically conservative Orthodox community in the 5th District, Schleifer, an observant Jew, calculated it was worth a shot. (Spector is also Jewish but less observant.)

"We never said it publicly," Rosenbluth, 53, says, "but on the campaign, our theme going in was that line Reagan used—you know, 'Are you better off than you were 40 years ago?'"

117. Sisters in Arms

Beyond the Ferris wheel and funnel cake, there's a compelling array of events on the outskirts of the Maryland State Fair's midway. For example, a newborn calf is being gently pulled from its mother's womb at the appropriately named Cow Palace birthing center this afternoon. ("I'm not licking my baby," a pregnant woman warily quips, as the calf falls to the ground and its mother begins the natural cleaning process.)

There's also a variety of country-strong contests, including chain saw carving, mechanical bull riding, and the annual state arm-wrestling championships.

A variation of a game with hard to discern roots (some say Native American; others say ancient Greece), modern arm wrestling gained popularity in barrooms before becoming a popular televised sport in the '70s and '80s. In fact, Steve Simons, the organizer of today's tournament, quit his investment-banking job to launch a professional circuit in those renaissance years.

"I've known a few of these guys for 30 years," Simons says, gesturing toward the still buff, 63-year-old J.R. Hostler, a former horse trainer, who wins the men's light-heavyweight division.

In the women's open division, a pair of blond, solidly built sisters from Bel Air—Jessica Coleman, 33, and Christy Coleman, 32—meet in the finals for the second year in a row. "I usually don't tell people my secret, but I've been an auto mechanic for 13 years," says Jessica, who outmuscles her younger sis. "Lifting heavy things, turning wrenches—that's every day."

Christy, she adds with a smile, does body repair.

The sibling rivalry between the "Irish twins," as the women describe themselves, makes for an unexpected and entertaining match, but they are not Simons's favorite pairing ever.

"The all-time dream finals was a Hell's Angel versus a Methodist minister, our first year in the Deep South after taking the sport out of California," Simons recalls. "The preacher won, too."

118. A Tall Tale

"Two towns formed to make Baltimore," guide Marsha Wight Wise notes, as Baltimore Heritage's tour of Jonestown, one of those towns, gets underway at the Baltimore Farmers' Market.

"Mr. David Jones, a Quaker, was the first settler in 1661 and built a mill. In 1745, Jonestown merged with Baltimore Town—then just a village near the Inner Harbor. But since it was named after Lord Baltimore, and because royalty always gets its way, the Baltimore name won out."

This morning's walking tour, highlighting Jonestown's often overlooked treasures, passes several of the city's prominent examples of cast-iron-fronted buildings, including an old food emporium that's been readapted into a 7-Eleven. It also visits St. Vincent de Paul, celebrating its 175th anniversary, and Zion Lutheran Church, whose congregation predates the Revolutionary War. The highlight, however, is the trip inside and up the iconic Shot Tower, a Baltimore landmark since 1828.

In fact, the 215-foot edifice and its estimated 1.1 million bricks remained the tallest structure in the U.S. for almost two decades.

Shot was made by pouring molten lead through a colander and letting it drop straight down the open-air shaft. As the droplets fell, gravity spun the lead into spheres before they splashed into a water-filled barrel, where they cooled and solidified. Musket balls from the tower were likely used by Union soldiers during the Civil War and were sold to local hunters until 1892, when new methods and the price of lead made the operation obsolete.

Forty years ago, in one of the city's first acts of preservation, the tower opened to the public.

"The world's only remaining working shot tower is in Riga, Latvia," says Matt Hood, program assistant with Carroll Museums, which oversees Baltimore's iconic tower. "I don't speak Russian or Latvian, but basically what they told me was, 'Shot still flies in the Third World.' That, and they get the occasional call from a Saudi prince who wants to go hunting in Pakistan and doesn't mind paying a 3,000-percent markup."

119. Godspeed

"Let's do it again," shouts fitness instructor Roxana Feenster, as '80s new wave blares from the steps of the Cathedral of Mary Our Queen. She's warming up 800 joggers and power walkers—including a goodly number of priests, seminarians, and Catholic sisters in full habit and running shoes—for this morning's 5K and 1-mile fun walk.

"Easy to start," Feenster shouts again. 'Easy, easy. Four . . . three . . . two . . . one."

The Oriole Bird and Archbishop William Lori are on hand, also pumping up participants for the third annual Nun Run, which supports Catonsville's Little Sisters of the Poor and St. Martin's Home, where the women serve seniors with limited resources.

Founded in Baltimore in 1869, Little Sisters—in the midst of a $25 million overhaul of St. Martin's—provides 24/7 care, including skilled nursing. While the nuns haven't specifically trained for the run, they all do quite a bit of walking on the campus grounds as part of their daily duties, Sister Lawrence Mary assures. The long-sleeve habits are not as hot as they appear, she adds. "They're white; they reflect the sun. And we're used to them, of course."

After completing her 1-mile power walk, Sister Cecilia Mary grabs a bottle of water and happily collapses into a chair beneath a shade tree.

"This is the first time I've been able to do this," she says. "I had a knee replacement last year." She politely declines to give her age—"Oh, we're ageless," she says—but mentions she recently cele-brated 50 years with her order after growing up in Detroit.

"I'm a big baseball fan," she adds, needling another participant who's sitting next to her in a bright orange O's T-shirt. "You do know that the Tigers beat the Orioles last night, right?"

120. Going the Distance

"I counted on the first 60 miles wearing her down, but it didn't help," says Erek Barron, a Prince George's County state delegate, as he jogs into the Greenmount Avenue offices of Community Mediation Maryland behind a surprisingly fresh Lorig Charkoudian. "She can run."

Charkoudian, co-founder of the nonprofit, which offers free mediation services to prison inmates, their families, and others, had just completed a two-day, 70-mile run from Hagerstown to Baltimore to raise awareness about the benefits of reentry services. Supporters joined her along the trek—symbolic of the journey thousands make each year as they return from Hagerstown's penitentiaries—including Barron, a key legislator behind Maryland's recent Justice Reinvestment Act, who ran the final 10 miles with her.

As she reached the Baltimore Museum of Art, Charkoudian picked up a gaggle of runners and then was greeted by balloons and cheers as she led the way across 33rd Street. Later, glancing at a 10-foot map hung in the nonprofit's hallway to chart her progress, she notes her southeastern route appears misleading.

"It looks downhill, but I can assure you it wasn't," she says, running her finger toward the Appalachian Mountains range between Hagerstown and Baltimore.

Among those meeting Charkoudian were Barbara Doran and her daughter, Rita, who went through multiple family mediation sessions with Doran's son, Ricky. He's been incarcerated for much of the past

13 years. "I didn't know what we were going to do with him when he got out," says Barbara, choking up. "We had lost trust."

Rita, 22, grew up without her brother around. "Basically, we didn't have a relationship," she says.

"The sessions were his idea. He learned about them [while incarcerated]," Barbara says. "They've made a big impact on all our lives. And my son isn't even home yet."

Postscript: Erricka Bridgeford, director of training at the Community Mediation Center, founded Baltimore's Ceasefire weekends movement in 2017.

121. Time Out of Mind

The metal letters nailed on the wooden door simply read "HANS SCHULER—SCULPTOR."

"I've walked past it so many times and have always been curious about what's inside," says a visitor, ducking into the 110-year-old, ivy-covered brick and sky-lit atelier.

"We get that a lot," chuckles Francesca Schuler Guerin, the granddaughter of Hans Schuler, an Alsace-Lorraine immigrant known as Baltimore's "monument maker" for his classical works across the city. An accomplished sculptor in her own right, Guerin is leading a rare tour of the Schuler School of Fine Arts, founded here in 1959 by her parents—Schuler's son, also named Hans, and her mother, Ann Didusch Schuler.

Schuler's works include five pieces in the Walters Art Museum collection, most notably a sculpture of Ariadne, the distraught daughter of the mythological Greek king Minos, which won him a gold medal at the Paris Salon in 1901.

His outdoor works in Baltimore include the renowned Meditation and Memory pieces at Green Mount Cemetery, the 18-foot statue of Martin Luther at Lake Montebello, and the giant relief of Gen. Casimir Pulaski at the entrance to Patterson Park.

At the moment, a half-dozen students, surrounded by original scale models of Schuler's sculptures, are quietly painting and sculpting clay in the day-lit studio, as others practice the basic drawing techniques that serve as the foundation of the school's traditional curriculum. Students here learn to grind their own pigments in the manner of the old masters. In fact, the school was started as a protest against the modernist movement sweeping the nearby Maryland Institute College of Art, where Hans and Ann taught and the elder Schuler served as director from 1925 to 1951.

Despite the changing times, the school survives, buoyed by a commitment to what Schuler once described as "pure art" that has remained steadfast through succeeding generations.

"I read an art magazine story about how the practice of teaching 'cast' drawing [charcoal studies of plaster busts] has been recently 'rediscovered,'" Guerin says. "We've always taught cast drawing. It's not like somebody's discovered the Incas or something."

122. Visiting Hours

Charlie Murphy taps the brakes of his road bike as he heads down St. Paul Street, slowing to allow the three-dozen bicyclists trailing behind to keep pace during the blustery morning start of the Doors Open Baltimore Bike Tour. With more than 50 distinctive buildings accessible to the public today, the third annual Doors Open project (organized by the Baltimore Architecture Foundation and the Baltimore branch of the American Institute of Architects) offers a free opportunity to peek inside some of the most historic structures in the city.

Led by Murphy, a board member of Bikemore, the city's nonprofit bicycling advocacy organization, and Zach Chissel, founder of Two Wheel Tuesday, a weekly bike-to-work event, the ride includes stops such as the Arabber Preservation Society in Sandtown, the new Lillie Carroll Jackson Civil Rights Museum in Bolton Hill, the Eubie Blake Cultural Center on Howard Street, Open Works in Greenmount West, and Lovely Lane United Methodist Church on St. Paul Street. Eventually, it wraps up at the Peabody Heights Brewery, which is situated at the former home of old Oriole Park in Waverly.

The oldest building on the cue sheet is the first, the Lovely Lane church. This historic congregation, known as "the Mother Church" of American Methodism, broke ground here in the late 1800s, almost a century after its original meeting house hosted the famous Christmas Conference that established the first Methodist denomination in the U.S.

Designed with an oval sanctuary for better acoustics, the church still has its original organ and oak seats. But it is best known for its nearly 200-foot stone tower, with massive windows that are lit in the shape of a beacon cross each evening, and in the dome above the pulpit, a heavenly fresco depicting the stars in their exact position on the night of the church's dedication on Nov. 6, 1887.

"It's a great place to preach, but if you're boring, you'll know right away," says Rev. Travis Knoll. "Everybody starts looking up."

123. Mourning After

Inside the tiny Hollins Market rowhouse once owned by James and Sarah Feeley, an opened bottle of Jameson whiskey, playing cards, and a pipe and loose tobacco sit on the table next to the door. Standing against the living room wall, there's a Catholic priest in a black cassock. Well, at least a mannequin in a priest's cassock.

And, laying on a wooden slab alongside the living room wall, there's another, smaller mannequin, covered in lace, rosary beads in hand, and surrounded by candles. The figure represents the body of the Feeleys' son, William, who died just before St. Patrick's Day in 1876.

"It wasn't unusual for people to have 10 or 11 children and five that died," says Cecilia Wright, an Irish wake expert, presenting this morning at the Feeleys' restored home, which today serves as part of the Irish Shrine and Railroad Workers Museum. "Several of the Feeley children died."

Later today, the museum will host an informal gathering at tucked-away St. Peter's Cemetery in West Baltimore, the 22-acre resting place of many early Irish immigrants, including the ancestors of some of those in attendance today. (Philip Berrigan, a World War II veteran and priest who famously protested the Vietnam War, is one of the more well-known Irish Catholics buried at St. Peter's.) But at the moment, Wright is explaining the traditions and superstitions of wakes brought by the Irish to the U.S. and Baltimore, where so many worked for the nearby B&O Railroad, as James Feeley did.

Someone had to sit with the body for three days, for example, literally on watch to see if the deceased "awakened," which is how the term wake originated. Candles were placed at the head, feet, and sides of the body, Wright notes, to ward off evil spirits. Windows were opened to allow the soul to depart for heaven and then closed to prevent the spirit from returning.

Not all Irish wakes were the same, however. The death of a child was a much more somber occasion than the passing of a beloved older relative who had lived a full life—one worth celebrating with three days of song, food, games, contests of strength, and serious drinking. "It wasn't considered a good wake if at least one fight didn't break out," says Wright.

A few people at the small but packed museum recall the authentic Irish wakes of their own Baltimore neighborhoods, which admittedly seem somewhat surreal in hindsight. "I don't remember any funeral homes in those days. The living room was the funeral parlor, and the body was carried straight to the cemetery," says Jackie Waltemeyer. Her cousin, Thelma Graziano, whose parents were Irish, remembers that families with Emerald Isle roots put funeral wreaths on their door when someone in the house died. "Even when I got married and moved into my own home, my Irish mother would never allow me to put even a Christmas wreath on the front door," says Graziano, who grew up in Northeast Baltimore. "She hated seeing any kind of wreath on a door her whole life."

Luke McCusker, director of the museum, heard tales of his family's Irish wakes from his father.

"He still tells the story of playing and hiding beneath the sawhorses in the living room as a boy," McCusker shares with a wry smile, shaking his head. "While my great-grandmother was laying on a board above his head."

124. Star Fighters

"How many people know who Benny Leonard was?" Mike Silver asks the crowd gathered at the Jewish Museum of Maryland. "Benny Leonard was the most famous Jewish person in America in the 1920s. Not Albert Einstein. Not Justice Louis Brandeis."

Leonard, explains Silver, author of *Stars in the Ring: Jewish Champions in the Golden Age of Boxing*, fought his way out of Manhattan's East Side ghetto to become one of the great boxers of all time during the Roaring '20s, holding the lightweight title for nearly seven years. "He quit to take care of his sick mother. How Jewish is that?"

In his book, Silver chronicles 29 Jewish, world-champion boxers and more than 160 contenders from the 1890s to 1950s, including a half-dozen Baltimore brawlers—welterweights Jacob "Jack" Portney and Benny Goldstein, flyweight Benny Schwartz, middleweight Sylvan Bass, and lightweights Charley Gomer and Isadore "Izzy" Rainess. Silver also gives a shout-out to legendary local trainer Heine Blaustein. "Baltimore was a great fight town," Silver says.

It wasn't unusual in those days, he continues, for Jewish boxers to change their name. Not because of anti-Semitism but family (read: mother's) disapproval of the sport. Leonard was really Leiner, for example. Often, Jewish fighters switched ethnic identities altogether, killing two birds with one stone by trying to appeal to the sport's huge Irish fan base.

"My uncle was Baltimore welterweight Patsy Lewis—that's pretty Irish. His real name was Julius Rosenbloom," volunteers Jerry Russ, 81, who went to the fights with his father at the old Baltimore Coliseum. Carlin's Park was another popular venue.

At a time when boxing and baseball were the country's biggest draws, fighting wasn't just a means to make money for working-class immigrants (a four-round bout could pull in the same pay as a week in a sweatshop); it was also a means of assimilation and pride for Jews.

"Einstein, brilliant scientist, but who understands the theory of relativity? Brandeis, brilliant justice, but how many people read Supreme Court decisions?" Silver asks. "A punch in the nose? That, everybody understands."

125. Paper Dreams

Katherine Fahey begins to unravel a long, illustrated scroll at the Creative Alliance as an arabber just off center stage sings out:

Yeah, bananas, cantaloupes, and watermelons
Sweet potatoes and collard greens

Nearby, a musician clapping coconut shells and jingling bells mimics the jangled beat of a workhorse plodding through a narrow rowhouse street.

"Each door on the block was a different color," Fahey says, telling the story of "From Monument to Montford," her paper cutout fable of an East Baltimore childhood when arabbers and their decorated horses and carts "seemed like a fairy tale."

Fahey's narrative, hand-cranked scroll and musical accompaniment is based on a 19th-century visual storytelling form once known as moving panoramas and now called, with some endearment, "crankies."

In fact, the fourth annual Baltimore Crankie Fest this weekend, the largest of its kind in the U.S., sold out all three shows in advance.

"There is something really magical about it," says Fahey, an award-winning artist who combines shadow puppetry with her exquisite backlit scrolls and has collaborated on crankie music videos with the likes of Wye Oak and Ellen Cherry. "I remember at the first Crankie Fest being blown away by how entranced the audience becomes."

Other crankies tonight revolve around a Syrian folktale, a girl from Nova Scotia, and a cosmic country ballad with roots in Alabama and Babylon. Musical pieces include performances by the Gospel Peacemakers, Caleb Stine, Liz Downing, and young old-time artists Anna & Elizabeth.

The most autobiographical crankie comes via a hand-held scroll sewn by 75-year-old German immigrant Ursula Populoh, who graduated with a degree in fiber art two years ago from the Maryland Institute College of Art.

In a series of stitched images, Populoh recounts her story as a young widowed mother, her subsequent and nearly fatal bout with alcoholism, and her desperate hope of moving to America during her long stay in a German hospital.

"I was living in a small town with no money, shunned by my neighbors, and the dream of going to America kept me alive," Populoh says. "I sold everything, and I saw New York, Philadelphia, Washington, D.C., St. Louis, and New Orleans. When I got to Denver, someone took me to a square dance," she continues. "And I was in heaven."

126. Mangiamo!

"He flew in from Chicago, carrying 30 pounds of frozen meat, spatulas, a cutting board, knives, spoons, the works," explains Marcella Volini, as her dad dishes meatballs at the sold-out Sons of Italy lodge. "He's gone to the same butcher for 30 years, since before I was born, and doesn't trust anyone else."

Tom Volini, father of 12, made the trip to enter—along with his daughter, a Baltimore artist—the family meatballs into the Little Italy Meatball Fest "best recipe" contest.

"Of course, his youngest daughter couldn't possibly have a well-stocked kitchen," Volini adds, glancing toward her father.

Naturally, there's also plenty of baked ziti, rosemary bread, and Chianti.

"The meatball is a part of every Sunday dinner," says Joe Gardella, owner of Joe Benny's Focacceria and organizer of the event, a benefit for the nearby Rev. Oreste Pandola Adult Learning Center, which offers classes in Italian language, culture, and cooking. "Everybody has their own recipe, and each family recipe has its own story."

The winning meatball recipe (as judged by taste-testing attendees) eventually goes to Margaret Miller, née Occhiogrosso, who works as an event planner at Aldo's restaurant. "The veal and pork have a lot of flavor, and then I substitute 10 percent beef brisket with regular beef. That's the slight change," she says, with a smile. "Just a little more flavor."

The other contest this afternoon is a meatball-eating contest, which is won by Phil "the Fury" Fiore, who downs 31 meatballs made by Gardella himself.

Angelo Perri, who took third, came with nine family members, including his Italian immigrant mother, with whom he promises to enter the recipe contest next year. He ate 26 meatballs. "Honestly, I thought those were the best meatballs I had all day," Perri says. "I grabbed a few more to take home."

127. Who Wants to be a Cop Now?

On the Saturday morning after Thanksgiving, Maj. Richard Gibson arrived at the Northern District police station expecting a long shift. The previous day, Black Friday, two of Gibson's officers had shot, multiple times, a 48-year-old man who was wielding a pair of knives near the busy, commercial intersection of 33rd Street and Greenmount Avenue.

The 911 call had come from a woman working at a nearby salon, who had reported that someone beating a cane into the sidewalk and waving two knives was terrifying passersby. Body camera footage released a few days later would show that police officers told the man 10 times to drop the green knives with the word "MARINE" painted on the blades. The man can be heard saying, "I have one life to live, and I'm ready to give it."

But several witnesses believed that arriving officers fired too quickly on the man, who was clearly in the throes of a mental health crisis and never lunged at police.

The next day, activists from the People's Power Assembly and West Coalition mobilized a protest at the intersection, as the man, who survived the shooting, recovered in a hospital. Not wanting to escalate tensions, Gibson decided against send-ing any officers to the Saturday protest. He drove over himself, met with organizers, and simply requested that demonstrators not block the intersection. He parked his unmarked car at a gas station across the street and watched as the rhetoric from the 60 or so protestors grew increasingly loud, vehement, and anti-police. Tawanda Jones, the activist sister of Tyrone West, an unarmed man who died in a controversial police custody incident four years ago, questioned why law enforcement officers refer to shooters in the community as "cowards" but never apply that description to other cops.

"What about the cowards who killed my brother?" she asked. Another protestor blasted Lil Boosie's "F--k tha Police," according to *City Paper* coverage of the demonstration. At one point, protestors spotted Gibson in his uniformed white shirt and began harassing him as he sat in his vehicle. He rolled up his window and drove around the block. Then, not long after, he returned, and several demonstrators spotted him again and began running toward his car.

This time for a different reason.

A protestor who brought her weeks-old daughter to the demonstration had stepped into Mama Lucia Italian Eatery to feed the baby, and now it had stopped breathing and was bleeding from its mouth and nose. Gibson called for an ambulance as he rushed across the street and began performing CPR immediately. "I blew breath after breath into that little girl's mouth, and her chest would fill with air and heave," the beefy Gibson recalls. "I did a couple of compressions but was very careful. Her chest was so tiny. I thought she was going to make it."

Gibson learned later that she did not. Many at the scene had tears in their eyes as the child was rushed to Johns Hopkins Hospital. A father of three daughters, Gibson was distraught afterward, with blood visible around his mouth. Local residents and some protestors applauded Gibson, who, with other officers, hung around the pizza shop and bought slices for the crowd. "Other protestors still didn't want anything to do with me," Gibson says. The 20-year veteran recounts the story in his office, where the threaded brass fitting that knocked out two of his teeth during the

April 27, 2015, riot, sits on his desk as a grim reminder of that hellish day. Coincidentally, that date is also Gibson's wedding anniversary. "My wife and the kids watched everything that was happening on TV at home," he says.

Asked what it's been like as a Baltimore cop in the two years following the death of Freddie Gray, Gibson, an earnest, outgoing, lead-from-the-front optimist, pauses. He leans back in his chair and reaches to find the words. He considers the riot, the intense scrutiny of police officers, the indictments of the six cops involved in the arrest and transportation of Gray, the scathing Department of Justice investigation into the department, the continuing attrition in the police ranks, and most unnerving, an unparalleled spike in violence that shows no signs of abating. "I'd say it's been a challenge."

Since the April 2015 riot, the ongoing surge in gun violence in Baltimore is, as best as anyone can tell, without precedent in modern U.S. policing history.

When the city recorded its 50th homicide of this year on Feb. 23— an otherwise ordinary weekday when nine people were shot across the city—it put Baltimore nearly a month ahead of 2016's murder rate, which was the worst on record, other than 2015.

Street robberies and aggravated assaults are also surging, with each up nearly 40 percent year-to-date over 2016. And recent carjackings, which included the high-profile assault of 80-year-old former City Councilwoman Rikki Spector in her Federal Hill garage, have nearly doubled. Meanwhile, with court-enforceable federal mandates now hanging over the department, the BPD faces an uphill battle of rebuilding trust in the community, recruiting more cadets, and putting additional uniformed bodies on the street.

It's a huge climb that only got steeper last month after the stunning federal indictments of seven police officers, who served on a specialized gun unit, on racketeering and extortion charges. (The allegations of brazen thuggery include robbing a driver after a routine traffic stop and stealing $1,500 from a nursing home maintenance man who needed the cash to pay his rent.)

"Look around at everything that's been going on," says Lt. Victor Comegna, a shift commander serving underneath Gibson in the Northern District with 17-plus years on the force. "Who would want to be a Baltimore cop today?"

128. Day Shift

Twenty-eight-year-old Northern District police officer Darius Carter is from the Sandtown neighborhood of West Baltimore and still has family on Gilmor Street, down the block from where Freddie Gray was arrested and detained. He and his buddies were into sports as kids, playing ball at the local Police Athletic League center, which, notably, has since been closed. Carter played basketball and baseball, swam at Southwestern High School, and played trumpet in the band. He's also always been something of a tech geek and avoided any serious trouble growing up.

He joined the Army National Guard after high school and hadn't considered becoming a cop until another military buddy from Baltimore said he was joining. Personable, approachable, a Baltimore City native and resident with military experience, Carter checks a lot of boxes in terms of the ideal recruit.

During a recent afternoon ride-along, which included an investigation of a stabbing in which a woman was rushed into surgery at Sinai Hospital, Carter admits, military and academy training notwithstanding, that he was nervous answering calls at first. "I think everyone is. It's the unknown," he says. "It takes a couple of months, maybe two to three months, to get your bearings in your district. Once you know your way around and get to know people, the business owners, then you don't want to go anywhere else."

After the unrest began, Carter was actually called back into Maryland Army National Guard reserve duty to protect the city. "It's a strange feeling, knowing that the same people who are throwing rocks at you, if something would happen to them, you'd run over there to help them and not think twice," Carter says, his voice swelling slightly with emotion.

What he learned from his military service, he says, is that the stress of that job—and his current job—cannot be ignored. As young as he is, he says he recognizes that healthy coping mechanisms are required, as is counseling, in some situations. Carter rides a motorcycle to relax and has begun to fool around with drone photography, which among his other tech pursuits, he says, helps him leave work at work. "One of the guys I was stationed with in Egypt, who had been deployed in Iraq, killed himself while we were over there together," he recalls. "No one would've guessed there was anything wrong. He came to work every day with a smile on his face. You can't keep that stuff inside, but some guys do."

His biggest surprise after becoming a Baltimore police officer—keeping in mind he grew up in what is considered a high-crime neighborhood—was how hectic it is.

"I couldn't believe how many calls were coming in," he says. "It's just kind of shocking that people are committing crimes hour after hour, day after day. Not even citywide, but in your district. Your sector."

129. Portraits in Courage

"Frederick Douglass was the most photographed American figure in the 19th century," Harvard professor John Stauffer tells the audience in the packed auditorium at the Reginald F. Lewis Museum. "It wasn't Lincoln, Grant, or even Walt Whitman. It was a Black man. Douglass understood how photography could be used to shape public opinion, not unlike the way the Black Lives Matter movement has utilized cellphone videos."

Born into slavery in Talbot County, Douglass learned to read in Baltimore as a child and worked as a ship's caulker only a few blocks from the museum. He later returned to Fells Point after the Civil War to build a block of rowhouses on nearby Dallas Street.

Part of the museum's Black History Month series of events, Stauffer's presentation, based on his book *Picturing Frederick Douglass*, is almost as much about the early, silver-nitrate photographic technology as it is about Douglass. The exposure times required long sits for portraits, during which, Stauffer says, the abolitionist actively participated in the artistry of his photographs, perfecting the image of "majestic wrath" that he wanted to project, hoping to stir viewers from their moral slumber.

Pointing to Douglass' significance as a historical figure but also to how ill-informed many people are about him, Stauffer notes that Douglass has been in the headlines again recently with President Donald Trump's remarks that seemed to imply that Douglass is alive. By coincidence, one compelling photo in the presentation is of

Douglass during President Lincoln's overflowing second inauguration (with John Wilkes Booth also in attendance) at the Capitol.

"The next time Trump claims the crowd at his inauguration was as big as the crowd at President Obama's inauguration, please post that photo," a museum visitor suggests during the Q&A. "Remind him Lincoln drew a bigger crowd than he did, too."

130. Winds of Change

On the Sunday morning of Feb. 7, 1904, a fire was reported at the John E. Hurst Building, across the street from where Royal Farms Arena now sits. It's suspected, local historian Wayne Schaumburg tells a Fire Museum of Maryland-organized tour group gathered at that location this afternoon, that a cigarette butt or cigar, discarded by a Saturday night reveler, fell by chance through a broken glass opening in the sidewalk into the building's basement.

First responders initially missed the smoldering in the cellar, however, and by the time they returned an hour later, the blaze had raced upward, soon exploding through the six-story building's ceiling. Embers quickly began blowing "rooftop to rooftop," Schaumburg explains. "Like a forest fire. It's not the base of trees that catch and burn first, but the highest branches. Seven buildings were suddenly on fire in the next 10 to 15 minutes."

By the following morning, *The Sun*, with its offices in the path of the blaze, hurried to Washington, D.C., to produce an extra edition and reported, "To all appearance, Baltimore's business section is doomed." Which proved accurate. The Great Baltimore Fire would turn 140 acres of the downtown district to ash, including 1,526 buildings.

The fire missed City Hall by the width of Fayette Street as it headed east, turning south at St. Paul Street because of a quirky shift of the wind, according to Schaumburg, retracing the fire's route by foot. Essentially, everything north of Fayette Street survived; everything south of Fayette burned, other than a handful of structures, including the Alex. Brown & Sons Company Building on East Baltimore Street. That iconic building's domed, stained-glass ceiling, which attracts visitors to this day, didn't catch because of its small stature. The inferno's flames literally flew over the top of its roof.

"The heat was an estimated 2,000 degrees at this corner, and it cracked the brownstone facade around the Brown building steps," Schaumburg says, pointing. "That's the only remaining visible damage from the fire."

On a positive note, Thomas O'Neill, owner of the once giant O'Neill & Co. department store on Charles Street and a devout, Irish Catholic immigrant, bequeathed $7 million to the Archdiocese of Baltimore after his business was spared by the same shift of wind that saved City Hall.

O'Neill's generosity helped build the Cathedral of Mary Our Queen and Good Samaritan Hospital. "He believed a miracle, the work of God, saved his store," Schaumburg says of O'Neill.

"Which also means, I guess," chimes in a tourgoer, "that there weren't any devout Catholics south of Fayette Street."

131. Last Meal

Bel-Loc Diner owner Bill Doxanas will be serving his last omelet and coffee later today. But he isn't really sad to close the iconic Parkville diner's doors.

"I'm 66. I started working here in 1964 for my dad," he says, as he manages the long line that began forming before the sun rose. "I can't keep up the pace any longer. It's time to go."

Over the decades, regulars at the Bel-Loc included Colts and Orioles legends like Johnny Unitas and Luis Aparicio. Former Colt star Tom Matte stopped by Friday to say goodbye. Other next-generation Colts, like Marty Domres and Bruce Laird, remain longtime friends of the Bel-Loc—one of the last of diners of a bygone Baltimore era. The name of the diner, as Baltimoreans no doubt can guess, is a reference to its location near the intersection of the Baltimore beltway ("Bel")—which was completed a few years before the diner opened—and Loch Raven Boulevard ("Loc").

"Anyone here that isn't part of a party of six or seven?" a hostess asks as she ducks her head into the jam-packed waiting area.

The diner is set to become a Starbucks. Doxanas says he contacted the multinational giant, which he believes is a good company, after concluding he wanted a buyer. He says they plan to build a handsome new coffeehouse on the spot.

Once word got out that the Bel-Loc was closing, its iconic coffee mugs, featuring the image of a retro-uniformed waitress kicking up a heel as she handles a serving tray, have been at a premium. Normally available for purchase, the diner only has enough left for serving coffee this morning.

"I wanted to buy a mug," a visitor, getting up from his counter stool, tells Doxanas.

"Just steal one," the retiring owner responds.

For decades, the Bel-Loc was open 24/7. Doxanas says he's going to spend more time playing golf.

"It's been a great run," he says. "I went to college thinking I'd never return. But rather than spend a few weeks tending bar in Ocean City before a college lacrosse all-star game after my senior year, I decided to work my last couple of weeks here. And then I never left."

Doxanas adds that it was the best decision he ever made because of the Bel-Loc's customers, who he says are the best around. (He would know, too: his family's diner legacy proceeds the Bel-Loc. His father, Tom Doxanas, also co-founded the Double-T Diner—the "T" in Tom serving as one-half of the "Double-T"—with fellow Greek-American partner Tony Papadis.)

Many Bel-Loc customers, not to mention longtime employees, still seem a bit disoriented, wondering where they'll meet for coffee, eggs, pancakes, pie, and conversation after this weekend.

"We're like a lot of the waitresses," one man says, sharing a booth and final breakfast with his wife and sister-in-law, both of whom grew up down the street from the Bel-Loc. "We don't know where we are going to go now."

132. Almost Famous

On the packed deck outside the Hard Rock Cafe, the original members of Baltimore's popular one-hit rockers The Ravyns are playing their single "Raised on the Radio," which found its way onto the soundtrack of the 1980s teenage classic Fast Times at Ridgemont High. (The enthusiastic jeans and T-shirt crowd appears just old enough to recall all of the above.)

"Everybody remembers that movie and that song," says Tim Tilghman, 54, host of Radio RockOnTour on WLOY. "And everybody remembers Phoebe Cates"—the young actress who had a memorable bathing suit scene in the film.

The Ravyns' six-song set is meant as a kickoff for a bigger reunion show in 12 days in Annapolis. But the band is clearly happy to be together again this evening. Guitarist and singer Rob Fahey, who wrote their signature song, explains he was simply transcribing his own teenage years when he discovered rock 'n' roll, which became his lifelong obsession, lasting stardom or not.

Raised on the radio
Just an all-American boy
I found my favorite toy

"Being a musician, I'm just still trying to get better," says Fahey.

In their heyday, the band opened for Billy Idol, the B-52s, and, on their biggest night, Styx at the Baltimore Civic Center. "The phone rang at 10:30 in the morning, and I was the one who woke up and answered it," recalls keyboardist Kyf Brewer. "It's Styx's promoter, and he says their opening act can't make it; is there a chance that we can play? I tell him we're booked for a late gig at the Dulaney Inn, which was true.

"Anyhow, we open, and we've never been on a stage anywhere near that size. After we finish playing, the event staff tells us to throw some guitar picks and drumsticks into the front row—which we can't even see because it's so dark and the stage is so big. Long story short, the picks and drumsticks barely roll off the end of the stage and end up landing on the security team.

"Then we went and played the Dulaney Inn."

133. The Two Dominics

On a warm Sunday, in the street alongside Our Lady of Pompei, the annual Highlandtown Wine Festival is well underway when someone refers to the neighborhood here as "little" Little Italy.

Joe DiPasquale, whose grandfather opened the original DiPasquale's Marketplace on this block more than a century ago, gently corrects the visitor. "Oh no, this is big Little Italy. Not the other one," DiPasquale says, referring to the popular Italian restaurant destination near the Inner Harbor. "Always was."

For decades, Rev. Robert Petti of Our Lady of Pompei organized a local wine and food get-together, which the festival has supplanted as a community fundraiser. Petti used to collect grape orders, trucking them in from California, for those in his congregation who toiled as basement vintners, similar to those in the festival's competition this afternoon. DiPasquale assumed that task after the beloved priest passed away in 1984.

"We get a tractor-trailer delivery every October," DiPasquale explains. "There's still about three-dozen basement winemakers in this neighborhood."

For the first time ever this year, the same basement winemaker, Dominic Petrucci, sweeps first-place honors in the red and white categories. Petrucci's chief competitor, Dominic Parravano, won top honors in the festival's first year and ever since, the two men—both stonemasons, both immigrants from the same small town south of

Rome—have become rivals not just in business but in winemaking, after arriving separately in Highlandtown in the 1970s.

Parravano, who still lives on this street, dug his basement down an extra 7 feet to make room for larger fermentation tanks years ago. Petrucci eventually moved his operation to a bigger cellar in Cockeysville.

Although the guest judges choose Petrucci's wines in both categories this year, it's not as if it settles the issue of which stonemason is the better winemaker once and for all.

"We usually have about 30 entries," says DiPasquale. "But it's pretty much the battle of the Dominics every year."

134. Cake and a Snake

Since 2014, Mr. Trash Wheel, the Inner Harbor's water-and-solar-powered, garbage-devouring device, has pulled 1.1 million pounds of debris from the harbor, including nearly a half-million polystyrene containers, more than 650,000 snack and grocery bags, nearly 400,000 plastic bottles, and more than 9 million cigarette butts.

"He also gets a lot of baseballs and soccer balls and random stuff, including beer koozies, a beer keg, a motorcycle helmet, pink flamingos—once a lost, 5-foot python," says Cy Kellett, who helped build the prototype with his uncle John Kellett, Mr. Trash Wheel's inventor.

Situated near where the Jones Falls flows into the Inner Harbor, the beloved Mr. Trash Wheel (a viral video showing him in action garnered nearly 1.5 million views, and he's been profiled by the likes of CNN, NBC News, and *National Geographic*) is celebrating his birthday today. Along with staff from the Waterfront Partnership's Healthy Harbor Initiative and a dozen or so local fans, the party this afternoon includes students from Commodore John Rodgers Elementary School, who have brought a "cake" (a used tire filled with plastic bottles and junk) to feed to Mr. Trash Wheel.

After the desserts are served, including actual cupcakes for the kids, Adam Lundquist, director of the Healthy Harbor Initiative, and Jonathan Jensen, on guitar and ukulele, respectively, lead the students and crowd in song. First there's a rendition of "Happy Birthday" and then an homage to Mr. Trash Wheel, penned by Jensen, who normally works evenings as a bassist with the Baltimore Symphony Orchestra.

Scooping up the yutz and the cigarette butts
Up to 25 tons a day
Mr. Trash Wheel, Mr. Trash Wheel, Mr. Trash Wheel
He's the hero of the harbor

"The world premiere of 'Hero of the Harbor' was last month at Peabody Heights Brewery," Jensen says. "For their launch of Mr. Trash Wheel's Lost Python Ale."

135. Statue of Liberty

On May 17, 1917, nearly a century after the Marquis de Lafayette's last visit to Baltimore, city leaders and a French delegation broke ground for a statue of the American Revolutionary War hero in Mount Vernon Square. The effort to memorialize the wildly popular Lafayette in Baltimore (a major downtown thoroughfare had already been named in his honor) was meant to symbolize the important bond between the two countries as the U.S. entered World War I.

"Fifty-thousand residents of Baltimore turned out for the ground-breaking," Robert Dalessandro, chairman of the U.S. World War I Centennial Commission, reminds a smaller but enthusiastic crowd gathered in Mount Vernon Square to mark the 100th anniversary of the groundbreaking. Behind Dalessandro and the statue—and in front of Baltimore's towering monument to George Washington—two 30-foot American and French flags blow in the wind.

Lafayette's first visit to Baltimore came in 1781, when the dashing officer and his soldiers camped near here before heading further south. His second visit came in 1784 and his third in 1824, according to *Baltimore Sun* archives, when the 67-year-old was greeted by celebratory cannon fire at Fort McHenry and a parade of ships.

It's hard to overstate Lafayette's courageous, freedom-fighting hold on the American imagination, which continued long after his death.

Dalessandro notes that when American troops first arrived in France in 1917, Col. C.E. Stanton, an aide to Gen. John J. Pershing, was said to have uttered, "Lafayette, we are here!"

After the ceremony, Michel Charbonnier, consul general of France at the French Embassy in Washington, is asked by an attendee about the French reaction to the election of President Donald Trump amid the administration's early controversies.

"The French people have been interested in American politics for more than two centuries," Charbonnier says with a diplomatic smile, alluding to Lafayette's mission. "Not that we have always understood it."

136. Back to the Future

Kurt Schmoke tore up the speech that had been written for him. It was April 1988, and just months before, the 38-year-old former City College quarterback and Yale-, Oxford-, and Harvard-educated lawyer had become the first elected Black mayor of Baltimore. The next morning, he was scheduled to address a joint gathering of big-city mayors and police chiefs at the U.S. Conference of Mayors in Washington, D.C. Organizers had asked him to comment on the impact of the War on Drugs on cities and to focus on Baltimore.

"I had two speech writers, and Howard Lavine wrote a pretty good overview of the city and some of the issues we were facing related to substance abuse," recalls Schmoke. "But I thought, 'No, this is a unique opportunity with the police chiefs and mayors in the same room.' I had one night to rewrite it, and I didn't show it to anyone, including my chief of staff, because I did not want to be talked out of it." Only Schmoke's secretary, who typed it up before he left for Washington, saw the speech.

By the time Schmoke returned to City Hall that afternoon, his political future was an open question.

"I walked through the door, and the first thing I heard from my staff was, 'What did you say?'" recalls Schmoke, in his office at the University of Baltimore, where he serves as president. "The Associated Press was already working on a story about the speech, saying I was in favor of legalizing drugs."

The first draft of history does not always get the facts straight. Schmoke had not proposed legalization. He suggested, 30 years ago this month, in what would become a landmark address, that the U.S. ought to seriously consider and debate an alternative approach to the War on Drugs. He also used the term decriminalization, not legalization. Schmoke had been thinking about national drug-control policies and the historical similarities to Prohibition—"the war on alcohol," in his words—for some time.

The issue had become more urgent and personal for Schmoke when an undercover detective was shot and killed during a drug buy three years earlier while he was the city state's attorney.

"Marty Ward," Schmoke says, the name of the fallen officer and circumstances still fresh, three decades later. "He was married and a father. He was wearing a body wire, and I had to listen to the recording several times, because if there was intent to [knowingly] kill a police officer, then the death penalty would come into play. You could hear everything that happened."

Schmoke had also begun reading critiques of the drug war by then-Princeton professor Ethan Nadelmann, who advocated a European-style, harm-reduction approach to drug use. "How could we improve communities without a war on drugs?" Schmoke says. "We didn't seem to be getting anywhere. Law enforcement would make a show of the drugs and money they seized, but the problem persisted. Marty Ward and all that was floating around in my head before the mayors' meeting in D.C. This group will be engaged, I thought. Hopefully, it will start a discussion."

How was the speech received in the room?

"Deafening silence."

137. Pulp Nonfiction

As the packed bus pulls away from the Howard Peters Rawlings Conservatory and Botanical Gardens at Druid Hill Park, arborist Gary Letteron points out a state champion bur oak and a city champion white ash. He also notes the city's little known Grove of Remembrance—pin oak trees, one for each state, planted 25 feet apart—representing the first living memorial to the veterans of World War I.

Letteron, along with Ted Martello, is leading the morning bus portion of TreeBaltimore's "Notable Tree" trek, which is headed next to Cylburn Arboretum but not before passing several massive English oaks near the park's disc golf course.

"We don't know how old those trees are," Letteron says. "But there are pictures of Civil War soldiers sitting underneath them. That's how big they already were then."

Entering Cylburn, the tour bus passes a showy magnolia in full bloom.

Walking the 200-acre arboretum, and now led by Glenda Weber, a naturalist with Baltimore City, attendees get up-close looks at a silver maple, a Himalayan pine, a Chinese chestnut, and a 1970 progeny of the iconic, now-deceased Wye Oak tree, an Eastern Shore specimen once recognized as the nation's largest white oak.

Later, the three-hour tour heads to Chinquapin Run Park, passing by a weeping cherry on the way, donated by Al Capone to Union Memorial Hospital (Johns Hopkins refused to treat the Chicago gangster's syphilis). Approaching Evesham Park, the tours stops at the city champion male ginkgo biloba—a species that dates back 2.5 million years.

Beneath a giant bald cypress at Evesham Park, Weber explains that many trees have a single gender: male trees with flowers that produce pollen, or female trees with "ovaries" that produce fruit. Other trees have both characteristics, while others can switch genders during their lifetimes.

"They are all different, and they are all my friends," Weber says while discussing the nuanced gender and reproductive systems of trees. "Look closely and take notice of each one."

138. Irish Eyes

With the game still scoreless after a dozen minutes, Fiona Guinan snatches the baseball-sized white sphere skittering across the grassy field with a bare hand. She quickly tosses it a few inches above her waist, and then, in a single motion, like a right-handed Chris Davis, but on the run, swings her open-faced wooden stick and bashes a long, rising fly ball through the uprights for the game's first tally.

Minutes later, Guinan does it again, this time from 35 yards away, and suddenly, the Baltimore Gaelic Athletic Association's camogie team and their Irish-born and raised ringer are on their way to an easy win over their Washington, D.C., rivals. "I've been playing since I was 6," says Guinan, a visiting 21-year-old Dublin college intern, after the game.

The women's version of the ancient Emerald Island game known as hurling, camogie is akin to a smash-up of lacrosse and field hockey, but with both soccer-like goals and American football uprights for scoring.

The game's roots, explains Isadore Beattie, the sixty-something Irish coach of the Baltimore squad, date back several thousand years to when villages settled scores with daylong matches. "The annual All-Ireland Hurling Championship is bigger than the Super Bowl," he explains. "The whole county goes to watch if their team makes the final. You won't find a dog in the street that day."

The Baltimore Gaelic Athletic Association, which also includes men's hurling and Gaelic football teams, was formed in 2003 by Lucy

Prendeville, who was inspired to take up the camogie after visiting her ailing Irish grandmother in the old country.

"She told me to forget field hockey and start playing camogie," Prendeville says. "So I did. I guess I was anxious to connect to my Irish heritage."

"She's 40 and runs around like a teenager out there," marvels Prendeville's Ireland-born husband, Tadgh, who has since retired to the sidelines. "She hasn't said it as such, but I think she intends to keep playing until our 7-year-old, Patricia, is ready to carry on."

Prendeville's daughter will likely have help keeping the Gaelic sporting tradition alive here for another generation.

"So far, there have been four marriages, another is in the works, between the men's and women's teams, with nine children altogether," Prendeville says. "That would definitely make my grandmother happy."

139. Kill Joy

"Who would like this game?" a twenty-something man with dyed blond hair asks Cole Pritchard, co-inventor of Mister Mart, a virtual reality game in which a retail clerk at a badly run store punches annoying customers, trying to return their purchases. (Players rack up points by successfully refunding merchandise and "relieve stress" by smacking customers and hitting them with store items.) "Anybody who likes violence," Pritchard shrugs.

In fact, since the opening of the Gamescape pavilion at Artscape, there has been a line to play Mister Mart, which began as Pritchard and Karen Chang's thesis project at the Maryland Institute College of Art three years ago.

Set to launch via the online gaming platform Steam, Mister Mart is one of two-dozen indie, professional, and throwback games available for play at Gamescape.

"The old-school Nintendo games like Mario Kart and Super Smash Bros. are popular," says Ben Walsh, who founded Gamescape in 2010 and is the owner of the Highlandtown-based company Pure Bang Games. "But it's great to see independent games getting so much interest."

Another popular, still-in-development indie game is Rock, Paper, Scissors, which brings the basics of the classic contest into a fast-paced, multi-player gaming space where all three competitors try at once to "prey" upon their various targets—paper for scissors, for example—while scurrying away from their own predator.

For game makers, the tweaking process takes years, with Gamescape providing valuable, real-time user feedback. Some, like Pritchard and Chang, have brought their games back more than once for public pleasure and scrutiny.

"I love it," says 8-year-old Jackson Limmer after pulling his Oculus virtual reality headgear off, following a long, successful turn bashing Mister Mart virtual customers. "It's better since last year, too. You can see everything better," he says. "Last year, I punched a real person by mistake."

140. Lot of Music

The giant inflatable guitar at the entrance to the Putty Hill Shopping Center is hard to miss, as is the sea of baby boomers, in a mix of Ravens gear and throwback concert T-shirts, dancing in the parking lot to a cover of "Something in the Air" by 1969 one-hit wonder Thunderclap Newman.

We've got to get together sooner or later
Because the revolution's here
And you know it's right.

Welcome to Parkville's annual Stanstock, the brainchild of 62-year-old former saxophone player Stan Gibson, whose previous claim to fame was sharing a stage with John Denver in 1971 on WBAL's Kerby Scott Show.

For the past two days and nights, hundreds of middle-aged Baltimore rockers have been partying and reminiscing inside McAvoy's Sports Bar & Grill—and outside in the parking lot-turned-concert-venue—to tunes from popular local bands of decades past. "Stan could play the sax like you never heard before in your life," says former bandmate Ronnie Malvaso, standing next to Gibson during a break. "When he kicked in, we wanted to stop and listen."

Because of a neurological birth defect that eventually forced him into a wheelchair, Gibson had to give up playing as a relatively young man. Struggling in recent years simply to attend live music events and nearly paralyzed today, Gibson started a Facebook page—Baltimore Bands from the 70's 80's 90's—to keep in touch with his musician pals and friends. That effort morphed into Stanstock, which has hosted, among others, old-school Baltimore favorites such as Crack the Sky, Face Dancer, and the Rayvns.

Not that everyone here was a hard-rock fan back in the day. "We were disco queens," says Debbie Mowry, swaying alongside sixty-something girlfriends.

The groups play for free, Gibson notes, with net proceeds—more than $55,000 over the first four years—going to charity.

"My family told me doing this would kill me," says Gibson, struggling to speak audibly. "But it's what keeps me going."

141. Spinning Wheel

Two years after graduating from the Maryland Institute of College of Art in 2011, Cary Gray hopped on a unicycle and took off for South America, attempting to break the world record for the longest trip ever on a single-wheel, pedal machine. "I did, too," Gray recalls before his talk this afternoon at Baltimore Bicycle Works. "I'd broken the record when I got to Columbia [with the help of a kayak] and was going to double it by reaching Argentina, when my bag—with my GoPro, GPS, passport, and witness signatures to prove to Guinness I'd set a new record—were stolen. I couldn't document what I'd done.

"I flew home. I had to let it go."

Along the way, he tells the small crowd of soon-to-be bike-campers, the Mexican people, in particular, were hospitable. "So friendly, I was overwhelmed. Aggressively friendly." He adds, however, that he briefly feared for his life once in Mexico, when an armed farmer approached him while he was camping. "He was protecting his property; it was an area with a lot of drug trafficking," he says. "The unicycle diffused a couple of situations."

Since those initial 11,000-plus miles, he's ridden an additional 10,000 miles through 30 states and 11 countries, planning to tackle other unicycling records now.

At 28, he admits his parents wonder when he will begin a "real" career. Gray insists he already has, self-publishing a children's book, *Luno!*, which he illustrated with his feet for fun, and a nonfiction ebook for adults called *The Naked Unicyclist*, which chronicles his tire punctures, bouts of extreme dehydration, and food poisoning, along with other mishaps and joys. "The title is a metaphor," Gray says. "It's about being vulnerable and open to the world."

Someone asks if he felt like quitting during his one-man, one-wheel trek to South America.

"Yeah. And I did. Several times," Gray responds. "Usually when I was cold, wet, tired, and hungry in the middle of nowhere. The problem was that I still had to get somewhere dry, get somewhere to eat. Then I'd feel better and forget I had quit."

142. Tomorrowland

As Mark Rice steps onto one of the city's new, sleek, black water taxis at the dock outside his company's manufacturing plant in South Baltimore, he can't help but gush about the cutting-edge vessel. The 55-foot boat—two similar models are currently in operation, with seven more to follow—comes equipped with WiFi, USB ports beneath every third seat, PowerPoint capability, a weatherproof, flatscreen TV, and cabin lights that can be changed to purple on Ravens game days.

With a cool, all-aluminum hull modeled after the classic Chesapeake Bay deadrise fishing boats, the "taxi" is so deluxe that it is regularly chartered for corporate outings.

The new shuttles—the prototype ran more than $1 million—reach a top speed of 8.5 knots, which is significantly faster than the current 6-knot limit. They stow up to eight bicycles and have a built-in maritime GPS tracking. (Need a lift from Canton to Locust Point on some future Saturday night? Imagine an Uber-like service on the water with an on-demand network of smaller boats.) They deploy fold-down windows for inclement weather and heaters for winter commutes and carry up to 49 passengers and two crewmembers, although a crew may not be required for long.

"The capability for an unmanned fleet is there," says Rice, who is leading this little expedition with Plank Industries executive creative director Marcus Stephens. "The barriers are regulatory, not technical," adds Rice, whose Maritime Applied Physics Corporation makes both manned and unmanned watercraft for the Navy. "We'd want six months of testing, but that's about it. These water taxis have a lot of technology."

In the midst of City Council deliberations last year over the unprecedented $660 million Port Covington tax-incremental financing request by Sagamore Development—the real estate arm of Plank's Under Armour empire—another Plank firm, this one called Sagamore Ventures, bought the city's entire water-taxi operation. Then they announced plans to turn the taxis, previously a tourist attraction, into a state-of-the-art transportation option, inking a 20-year contract with Baltimore officials.

"We had never made a commercial product of this scope," Rice continues, as the high-tech boat pushes up the Patapsco River toward Fort McHenry, leaving much of old industrial Baltimore in its wake. "Until Kevin Plank called."

Later, the vessel turns toward Port Covington, which the taxi will soon start servicing. A massive railroad hub in its heyday, the 266-acre site still looks mostly abandoned from the river. Stephens (the guy who designed Under Armour's famous interlocking "UA" logo years ago) highlights the once-in-a-lifetime opportunity on the self-contained urban peninsula. He talks excitedly about the possibilities of creating a "live, work, and play" city-within-a-city from scratch, connecting the transformation of the city's water-taxi system to Sagamore's aspirations for Port Covington. Like everyone at Plank Industries and Sagamore Development, Stephens is completely taken with the potential of deploying the latest forward-thinking infrastructure—omnipresent wireless connectivity, super-speed fiber-optic lines, multi-modal streets, green architecture, sensor rich buildings, soft-shore landscaping—all of which can be installed unhindered by awkward retrofitting.

Stephens, who plans to visit Songdo, South Korea, soon, a city built from scratch and coined The World's Smartest City, says there will be ubiquitous connectivity at every interface in Port Covington. Data is everything, he says.

He talks about bringing other concepts to Port Covington, too—concepts with alien-sounding names, like "augmented reality" way-finding, "frictionless" consumption, and "virtual valet" parking—the likes of which Baltimore has never seen. Baltimoreans tend to think of the city in terms of home or community or workplace, or quirky, historical neighborhoods, such as Hampden, Fells Point, Waverly, and Reservoir Hill. But Sagamore's digital master plan is designed to create a sparkling, smart, tech utopia built around the "city as a service" concept, which takes its cues from the on-demand model behind Google apps, Amazon web services, and digitized customer relationship management.

Company officials envision a Port Covington where a water-taxi trip, bike-share rental (they plan to launch their own bike-share system, too), visit to Sagamore's distillery or Rye Street Tavern, movie, concert, or shopping trip is curated and integrated into a single experience. Like on a cruise ship. Or at Disney's Magic Kingdom, as one Sagamore consultant along for the ride puts it—a place where transactions can simply be charged by touching a wristband or card against a touchpoint and are billed to a customer's account.

"I love Disneyland," Plank told *Bloomberg Businessweek* last year.

"Port Covington will be nothing like downtown Baltimore," says Stephens.

143. Homeland

Inside the Baltimore American Indian Center, a sign touts the cultural classes held every Tuesday night, while noting the remarkable resiliency of the native people of the Americas:

> *We are still here*
> *We are not going away*
> *We have pow wows*
> *We have parts of our culture*
> *It is still here*
> *We still make our jewelry*
> *We still make our leather*

Tonight, however, the center, which has served the metro area's indigenous population (more than 8,300, according to the last census) since the late 1960s, is filled for a rally and petition-signing drive in support of renaming Christopher Columbus Day to Indigenous Peoples' Day.

Last year, notes organizer Rebecca Nagle, whose family includes Cherokee ancestors, City Councilman Brandon Scott introduced legislation that would've placed Baltimore among other cities, including Los Angeles, Denver, Seattle, and Albuquerque, which have renamed the holiday. But the Indigenous Peoples'/Italian Americans Day bill did not pass.

Jennifer Hunt, a Baltimore County mother of two, begins the evening with an emotional reading of Columbus and his men's well-documented cruelty against native peoples, including execution, rape, dismemberment, forced work, and sale into European slavery.

"I wasn't sure that I'd be able to get through it," says Hunt, who is Choctaw, referring to her text, which includes entries from Columbus' own journal and testimony from a contemporary Spanish witness to the atrocities. "I knew children would be here. But my husband, who is African American, said people need to know the truth. All I learned in school was the same thing as everyone else: 'In 1492, Columbus sailed the ocean blue.'"

Later, she notes that it was her Choctaw grandfather who came to Baltimore after joining the Coast Guard. She says that despite brutal federal policies that removed Native Americans from their land and pushed them onto reservations, "joining the military is often how you try to get out of poverty."

In fact, Hunt adds, a higher proportion of Native Americans serve in the U.S. military than any other ethnic group.

She also adds that she certainly doesn't hold any animosity toward Italian Americans, particularly those in nearby Little Italy—she just takes issue with the veneration of Columbus. "I love Sabitino's and their Bookmaker Salad," Hunt says with sincerity. "We go there all the time."

144. Found Art

"There's no such thing as a bad home movie."
—John Waters

The home movies screened at Normal's Books & Records tonight include the expected clips of a 1950s-era Ocean City vacation and an Irish-Catholic wedding reception of the same vintage. There's footage of a crammed 1983 East Baltimore rowhouse Christmas and a swinging sermon from a local Black church. And also shots of a sister and brother playing in their Rodgers Forge backyard, which begins in rather pedestrian fashion until the boy dons a Fidel Castro-inspired beard and Cuban military-style cap, picks up a toy rifle, and chases after his sister.

Some of the footage screened is from professionally archived sources, others are found on eBay and the like, and some are courtesy of audience members who have brought along their own home movies.

"Hey, it was 1959," the grown-up, would-be revolutionary explains from the back of the crowd amid raucous laughter. "Castro was a hero in the U.S."

Hosted locally by the Mid-Atlantic Regional Moving Image Archive (MARMIA), Home Movie Day is an annual event that's been held around the world since 2002. Among other efforts, the preservation nonprofit recently began digitizing historic footage from WJZ-TV.

Also on hand is Jasmyn Castro (no relation to Fidel, needless to say), media conservation and digitalization specialist with the National Museum of African American History & Culture, who is screening home movies shot by Black families in Washington, D.C., and Baltimore. Those films, mostly from the 1960s and 1970s, capture everyday African-American family life—at home, at their local schools, at wedding receptions—that simply was not represented on television or by Hollywood at the time.

"Home movies hold all kinds of finds and provide context that documents life in the region the way it was lived by everyday people," says MARMIA president Siobhan Hagan, before a lively crab feast/day-camping adventure on the Chesapeake Bay from the early 1960s appears onscreen. "You can practically smell the Natty Boh, cigarettes, and hairspray," someone comments.

Not all home movies are fun. There is also amateur footage shot during the 1968 Baltimore riot.

One of the truly gorgeous films is 16mm color footage from The Johns Hopkins University Medical Archive of a physician's fishing expedition on the Chesapeake in the early 1940s.

The wooden boats and crisp, white sails—not to mention the well-attired men sporting fedoras as they cast their lines—appear to be from another epoch altogether, as does the sterling blue bay, with its then-plentiful rockfish seemingly jumping into the boat. "Otherwise," says JHU visual projects archivist Tim Wisniewski of the school's medical film archive, "our footage is mostly surgeries."

One of the first home movies of the evening includes upper-deck footage from the last Opening Day at Memorial Stadium in 1991, a potentially auspicious afternoon that proved anything but. One-term vice president Dan Quayle threw out the first pitch that afternoon before the O's lost 9-1—the first of 95 defeats that season.

"My mom had two rules when we went to Memorial Stadium," Hagan says, narrating the clip, as her 6-year-old self eyes a vendor's trayful of pink cotton candy passing onscreen. "You can't go to the bathroom while the Orioles are at bat, and no cotton candy. Ever."

145. City by the Bay

It is hard to picture East Baltimore as rural, Italian-like country-side, but you can get a sense of the rolling hills and long-gone trees from Clifton Mansion, the former summer home of Johns Hopkins. Built atop 266 acres, the panoramic views of the Inner Harbor, the downtown business district, TV Hill, and City College High School make the busy thoroughfares of Harford and Belair roads below disappear. The undulating natural topography—buried beneath dense, century-old rowhouse-laden streets—suddenly becomes visible.

"It is one of the highest peaks in the city," says John Ciekot, special projects director for the Clifton Mansion rehabilitation project, as he heads a mini-tour of the home, which includes an ongoing restoration of an 1851 Bay of Naples mural. "Horses and carriages would've rolled up the toll roads here to the private entrance."

Hopkins acquired the property, originally owned by Captain Henry Thompson, in 1841, several years after the horse artillery and militia commander, who served in the War of 1812, passed away. Baltimore's most famous benefactor recognized its potential for a grand summer escape. He soon transformed the captain's stately Georgian mansion into an Italianate villa, complete with a new *porte cochère* (a covered entrance large enough for carriages to discharge their passengers) and an 80-foot tower. The entrance hall features richly stained arch window frames, a marble floor, ornate hand-painted walls and ceilings, a black walnut staircase, and the centerpiece, a mural of Naples, its great bay, nearby countryside, and Mount Vesuvius.

The painting was discovered in 1993, Ciekot explains, when Civic Works, the nonprofit job training and community service organization, began leasing the long-neglected property.

"The mural was painted over probably a dozen times," Ciekot says with a wry smile. "Whatever bureaucratic beige, yellow, brown, or green was in that year."

Gillian Quinn, who is overseeing the restoration of the mural, could not help but make a side trip to the Southern Italy city on a family vacation to the country this summer. "It's a very popular location, on a hillside overlooking Naples and the bay, where the painting gets its perspective," says Quinn. "A lot of artists liked to paint [the scene] after Vesuvius erupted—there's really a beautiful glow—but I think the mural's backdrop is a sunset."

The artist who painted the mural remains unknown. However, a signature is beginning to be uncovered. This very afternoon, conservators Ewa Pohl and Sue Crawford are literally scraping back the layers of paint with scalpels, further revealing the blue-green bay hues and pink-rose sky. It's tedious work that likely will take a year to complete but not necessarily unpleasant.

"It's meditative," Pohl says. "We're like monks."

"You have to like each other," she adds.

The work, Crawford says, has been one of many small discoveries. What she initially thought was decades-old spackling eventually turned out to be sailboats on the bay. The mural faces, she notes, a large window whose golden light would have—and will again soon—made the painting look different in the morning, at noon, and dusk.

Generally, the conservators work with knives in one hand and cloths in the other—dampened not by some high-tech chemical solution but something readily available when the painting was made.

"Spit," Pohl says, dabbing the mural wall. "It still works best."

146. Well Suited

"I was walking past and, by chance, saw they were giving away free suits," says Veronica Lewis, as she thumbs through a rack of free jackets and slacks outside Sharp Dressed Man, a nonprofit clothing outlet founded by designer Christopher Schafer, the Baltimore Fashion Alliance, and Living Classrooms to support men re-entering the workforce. "My son just got out of the military. He's working but looking for another job, and he could use a suit."

Inside the cavernous store, which is hosting its annual Holiday Suit Giveaway—an all-day affair of measuring, fitting, and dressing that includes shoes, shirts, and ties, not to mention free haircuts and lunch—Fred Barksdale, 61, has two suits, a sports jacket, two shirts, and a tie slung over his shoulder. "I've lost 57 pounds since June when my sister died," the 6-foot Barksdale says. "We were in the hospital at the same time, and I got depressed and stopped eating. Nothing fits me anymore, just lost my appetite. But I feel better today. I've got something to wear for New Year's Eve with my wife."

Seth Schafer, who joined his father's eponymous haberdashery in 2013, looks like he's slightly worn down near the end of the afternoon, albeit for good reason. Everyone who comes through the door receives individual attention from the battery of 50 volunteers. By 4:45 p.m., some 448 men have been served, pushing the year-to-date number for the nonprofit over the 2,100 mark. (Normally, the storefront, including the barbershop, is open on Wednesdays only, receiving appointments by various agencies working with men re-entering the workforce.)

The suits shirts, ties, and shoes typically come from individual donors but also partnerships with retailers, which have included Men's Warehouse and J Shoes. "Brands include everything from JoS. A. Bank to Neiman Marcus and Armani. This is nice stuff," Seth Schafer says. "Everyone has their own individual style and can find something they like. You can't put into words how transformed people look—and how they feel about themselves—after a haircut and seeing themselves in the mirror in a nice suit. They are ready to take on the world."

One of the volunteers here, Dr. Gerard Burns, says the annual event has become increasingly important to him.

"I was a trauma surgeon at Yale, and then I began losing my eyesight to macular degeneration," the tall, nattily attired 57-year-old Burns says. "So I went back to school and earned an MBA and went to work in health care informatics, but then I couldn't even do that anymore—I couldn't even read email. Now, I only have peripheral vision."

Burns explains that his life has changed in unanticipated ways since as he lost his vision. He lives in a spare, 600-square-foot Fells Point apartment. He doesn't have a smartphone or computer. He has given away all his books and art—and most of his clothes. "I have four jackets, four shirts, four ties, and four pairs of pants," he says with a smile. "Life becomes simplified. You live in the moment, because you have to. I'm grateful for that.

"Still, I have all this education and all these skills that I can't use, which is frustrating. I want to help people, which is why I became a surgeon," he continues. "Obviously I can't pick out suits and ties for people, or even do the measuring and fitting. So my role here is placing everything in a bag when they are finished and asking them how their experience was, and if there is anything we can do better. I am the last person they see before they leave."

147. Sing It Now

Shortly after William Donald's death in 2011, Jonathan Jensen, a bassist by day with the Baltimore Symphony Orchestra, had an epiphany. "I couldn't help it," he says after the first staged reading of the first musical he's ever written, *Do It Now! The Mayor Schaefer Musical.* "There were so many testimonials, so many funny anecdotes, so many stories. I'm at a time in my career where I've begun writing some songs and I thought, 'What a perfect character to put on stage.'"

If you'd like to know my personal philosophy
On the way I think our city should be run,
There's a simple little phrase that means a lot to me,
And it's got to be the way we get things done:
Do it now! Do it now! Do it now!'

Inside the packed auditorium at Stevenson University's Greenspring Campus, Mark McGrath, financial advisor by vocation, baritone by avocation, does his best to channel the forever disheveled Schaefer, capturing the former mayor's earnestness, if not quite his odd physical bearing.

"I don't know if you could find someone with the size head that he possessed—who can also sing," McGrath says with a laugh.

The play follows Schaefer's rise from the city council chamber to the mayor's office, which came on the heels of the Baltimore riots a half-century ago. Jensen, who read C. Fraser Smith's book *William*

Donald Schaefer: A Political Biography and interviewed others who worked in, or covered, the Schaefer administration, melds the city's trajectory with Schaefer's career over two acts. The second act, fittingly, begins with the birth of the Inner Harbor and costume-loving Schaefer taking to the water outside the National Aquarium in a 1920s-style bathing suit and straw hat, oversized rubber duck in tow.

Jensen says he hopes to see to the play fully staged at one of Baltimore's downtown theaters for a weekend or, perhaps, longer run. He doesn't know if the play would have legs outside of Baltimore and doesn't care too much either way. "I just offer it as my gift to Baltimore, in memory of Schaefer, and the city that has been through so much. We have real problems. But we still have a great city, and he was a great leader."

From the get-go, the inside jokes, only-in Bawlmer references, and prescient, occasionally dark humor of the play resonate with the audience, clearly made up of longtime residents who remember the colorful and demanding Schaefer.

From Act I, for example:

Schaefer (to an assistant): I saw an abandoned car yesterday. I want it removed.

Bonnie (his assistant): I'll get right on that. Where is it?

Schaefer: That's for you to find out!

The play, which turned into a collaboration between Jensen and co-writer Rich Epsey, hits a number of memorable Schaefer public relation efforts from the '70s and '80s, including a "trashball" campaign to help clean up the city and a "pink positive day" to rejuvenate the city's spirits. But it also recalls more serious efforts, like the $1 homes program to rebuild blighted blocks.

Am I the only one still dreaming of better days ahead?
Am I a fool to think a city can rise from the dead?
I can't foresee how life will be or what the future has in store,
But I believe in Baltimore.
Yes, I believe in Baltimore.

Eventually, the play slides into the chaos surrounding former Baltimore Colts owner Bob Irsay's threats to move the team and his midnight run to Indianapolis.

McGrath actually began his career in Baltimore as a photojournalist for WBAL-TV. One of the lowlights was covering the infamous press conference at BWI Airport when Schaefer and reporters greeted an obviously intoxicated Irsay returning from Indianapolis.

"Schaefer, in terms of his [volatile] personality, was not always an easy guy to love," McGrath says of the mayor. No one, however, as the play makes clear, questioned his dedication to his beloved hometown. When friends fled to the Milford Mill suburbs, Schaefer stayed and fought on. "He could be gruff and short with people. I tried to capture a little of his vulnerability," McGrath says. "That night the Colts left, he did an interview that next morning on the steps of the Edmondson Village rowhouse where he lived with his mother. Snow was still coming down. His eyes were red. You could see he hadn't slept all night."

148. Water, Water Everywhere

"The only thing left behind was a 55-foot wooden flagpole, a marker that took 25 years to rust and fall apart and disappear, too," Sally Riley, of the Historical Society of Baltimore County, says of the long gone Warren, Maryland. For decades after the town of Warren was buried beneath 23 million gallons of water, Riley adds, boaters would search for the lost flagpole and tell stories of the old sunken mill village.

By the late 19th century, Baltimore's clean drinking water was in short supply. The polluted and sometimes depleted Jones Falls could not fill the needs of the city's growing number of citizens, so, in 1881, the first Loch Raven dam, the lower dam, was built, forming a reservoir. But it still wasn't enough to meet demand.

Plans for the massive 2,400-acre Loch Raven Reservoir as we know it today started as Baltimore City Council ordinance 141 in 1908. "GIGANTIC TASK AT HAND" read the headline in *The Sun* when the project, part of a $5-million water improvement effort, was approved that year. (The reservoir's name was coined for Luke Raven, one of the first settlers in the area, along with the Scottish word for lake.)

Construction of a new 51-foot upper dam, eventually containing 1.5 billion gallons of water, began in 1914. But it also was a stopgap, failing to meet the demands of the city's 600,000 residents and expanding industrial base, and plans were in the works to build the dam up to its current 240-foot height. The problem, however, was that a thriving mill town sat on the banks of Gunpowder, directly in the hollow just north of the dam.

At the time, Warren was home to cotton, flour, and grist mills, three churches—St. Paul's Protestant Church, Warren Methodist Episcopal Church, and Warren Baptist Church—a public school, general store, post office, and more than 900 residents.

After the project was approved, it was learned that city officials had been quietly—or secretly, some say—in negotiations with Warren Manufacturing Co. to buy out the mills and the town, in order to level them. In 1922, after several years of legal haggling, the citizens were given the boot, the mills and town dismantled, and eventually the whole of Warren disappeared under 23 billion gallons of Gunpowder water.

Today, the only intact remains of the town are four bungalows, residences of company management at the time, that were relocated out of harm's way to Old Bosley Road. Otherwise, there are only a handful of telltale remnants of Warren gravestones and stone fences around the reservoir's edges.

Fortunately, the city water department, for reasons still unknown, sent photographers to document life in Warren in a series of gorgeous, if depressing, pictures (more than 70 are included in Riley's presentation) before the town was dismembered. The black and white photos show girls walking across the original Gunpowder bridge, the company story and men gathered on a porch across the street, company houses on Main Street, and children playing in the schoolyard near the lost flagpole.

Riley adds that she occasionally still meets people, like local writer Ann Kolakowski, who will tell her that their grandparents or great-grandparents grew up in Warren.

"My grandmother lived to be almost 104, and when she was 99, when my brother and I were clearing out her house—she was moving to an assisted living facility—I came across an old school notebook that read 'Marian Brown, Domestic Science/Warren School, Maryland.' I was like, 'What the hell is Warren School?'" says Kolakowski.

Then, Kolakowski recalled that as a child she used to go fishing with her family in a section of the reservoir they referred to as Schoolhouse Cove. "I can remember my parents asking me to look for the flagpole there, but I never knew why."

Warren reminds Riley of Sparrows Point, the old Bethlehem Steel town where her grandparents lived when she was growing up. "One of my favorite childhood memories was driving there for Sunday dinner with my parents," she recalls. "There were a lot of kids who lived in Sparrows Point then and it was wonderful. I loved their old house. Of course, that's gone, too. Another ghost town, I suppose."

149. Spontaneous Beauty

"Believe it or not, Joe and I were co-workers at the Pizza Hut in Glen Burnie," Cindy France says in a mini-documentary that's part of the retrospective of former Baltimore photojournalist Joe Kohl's work at the Maryland Historical Society. "Where you'd expect to meet an artist."

Kohl, who died in 2002 at the age of 44 from leukemia, earned a degree in fine arts from the University of Maryland, Baltimore County and served on the staffs of *The Baltimore News-American* and *Baltimore Business Journal*. But it is his personal and freelance efforts for a diverse number of publications—including the *City Paper, Afro American, Village Voice, Easy Rider, Catholic Review,* and *Mid-Atlantic Gay Life*—that set his work apart.

Outside his daily journalism beat, the prolific Kohl recorded Baltimore's underground culture, which coincided with his own social interests and curiosities, as the Maryland Historical Society notes in a statement accompanying the exhibition. Those included "the city's erotic sub-communities, small-venue rock concerts, and queer night life."

"I don't think he was really interested in who was the prettiest," adds Donna Sherman, another friend of Kohl's, in the short film. "I think he was interested in personality and [people] who had some kind of crazy thing going on with them that he would love to put on to film."

The mostly black-and-white images in the show, titled *Unscripted Moments: The Life & Photography of Joseph Kohl*, are, as Sherman suggests, spontaneous and beautiful, but in a gritty, off-kilter, blue-collar Baltimore kind of way. They also feel like surprising material for a Maryland Historical Society exhibition, given their occasionally provocative nature and documenting the city's underground scene but also that the 1980s and 1990s are now considered historical.

Joe Tropea, Maryland Historical Society curator of films and photographs, describes Kohl's shooting of early marches for AIDS funding, protests demanding divestment from apartheid South Africa, Baltimore bar and street scenes, John Waters and Divine on the red carpet outside the Senator Theatre, the world of sex workers, BDSM play, and the underground music scene as "a time capsule from the end of the last century."

In other words, this is not the picture-perfect world of renowned former *Baltimore Sun* photographer A. Aubrey Bodine.

Tropea curated *Unscripted Moments* with Linda Day Clark, a professor of fine arts at Coppin State University, and former *City Paper* photo editor J.M. Giordano, and award-winning photojournalist Josh Sisk.

"What emerges," Tropea says, "is a vision of Baltimore that's open-hearted and raw, cosmopolitan and compassionate—and a portrait of a photographer who exposed his love for the city and all its variety in every shot."

Later during a phone interview, France says the show was strange for her to look at when she first saw it. "I know a lot of those photographs," the 54-year-old says. "I was there."

France adds that she was "warned" about Kohl when she started at Pizza Hut, that fellow employees told her Kohl took pictures of everything and often asked people to pose nude for him. "You have to realize," she says, "Joe was a teddy bear, but he was different. First, he was a big guy. And he wore these big, wire-rim glasses, had a longish, bowl haircut and giant muttonchops. Nobody had muttonchops then.

It's funny, too. He did ask a lot of people to pose nude for him but never me."

Although his illness came about unexpectedly and his life was cut short, Kohl left behind a substantial body of work—some 55,000 photographs now in the Maryland Historical Society collection.

"[Joe] called me one day and told me he was in the hospital and was in a pretty weakened state," France says of her old friend. "I asked him if he wanted me to come by, and he said, in his Joe way, 'That's why I'm calling, bitch.'

"I thought I'd better go," she says. "I went that weekend, and that was the last time I talked to him."

150. Rolling with It

"I've been coming here for a *long* time," says Shamia Howard, 9, smiling after skating off the freshly laid hardwood with a gaggle of 15 friends, cousins, and aunts at the grand reopening of Upton's legendary Shake and Bake Family Fun Center Friday night. "I like to come every weekend."

Last August, the iconic West Baltimore roller rink and bowling alley, founded by former Colts star Glenn "Shake & Bake" Doughty in 1982, closed for major repairs. But without a timetable for a new start, there were fears that the 36-year-old institution might not make a comeback.

Friday night proved otherwise, with lines stretching down Pennsylvania Avenue before the official 7 p.m. re-opening. During the shutdown, the center received a $300,000 overhaul from the city, including the current skating floor, plus heating, roof, and air conditioning upgrades, as well as a new paint job and flatscreen televisions (turned to CBS and the NCAA March Madness basketball tournament for an appreciative number of non-skating fathers on hand).

"When I shut it, down you would have thought I shut down heaven," Mayor Catherine Pugh said earlier Friday while standing next to Doughty, who sold the Shake & Bake, which has struggled financially over the years, to the city long ago. But "the roof was falling in, the floor was buckled, you were hard-pressed to find matching skates in here."

Doughty returned for the reopening wearing a vintage Colts warm-up jacket with his No. 35 emblazoned across the front and said that what he liked about Shake & Bake is that it is "an oasis in a neighborhood with some challenges."

"You've got the conscience of America saying, 'What are you all doing in urban areas?' Shake & Bake is it," Doughty told reporters. "This is a model for the country."

Doughty brought excitement and fun, on and off the field, to Baltimore when he arrived from the University of Michigan before the 1972 season. One of the game's most colorful downfield threats during his eight-year career, all in Baltimore, was when he helped lead the team's stunning worst-to-first AFC East turnaround in 1975, pacing wide receiver corps in catches, yards, and touchdowns.

The same year, he formed The Shake & Bake Band with teammates Ray Chester, Freddie Scott, and Lloyd Mumford.

No. 35 didn't forget Baltimore after his playing days ended in 1979. Three years later, after 60 months of fundraising efforts, the former Colt brought the $5 million Shake & Bake project to fruition. An emotion-filled Doughty, who grew up in Detroit's tough lower east side and recognized the lack of investment in Baltimore's Black neighborhoods, donned a white tuxedo for the ribbon-cutting with then Mayor William Donald Schaefer. He called the occasion "a dream come true."

According to the *Baltimore Afro-American*, the 70,000-square-foot structure, which also includes 40 bowling lanes, video games, and a snack bar, represented one of the first major Black-owned and -operated facilities of its kind in the country when it was built. In 1984, Doughty coaxed Muhammad Ali into paying a visit, filling not just the roller rink but quite a bit of Pennsylvania Avenue outside, too.

The Shake & Bake is estimated to have served more than a million visitors over its history, including 34-year-old Faunyette Brown. "I love to dance, and I love to skate, and I love the combination of the two," says Brown, a public relations manager at the Maryland Jockey Club who was at the reopening Friday evening.

"I wanted to be an ice skater, a figure skater, when I was 5 years old, but there was nowhere close by to go, and so my babysitter started to bring me here," continues the Upton native. "I've been coming to the Shake & Bake since 1988. I'll be back Sunday, too."

151. Outside Help

A cold and steady, wind-blown rain falls outside the Baltimore Central Booking and Intake Center, where a half-dozen volunteers, staying dry beneath a small canopy, wait for men and women getting released this evening. Hot coffee and tea sit on a folding table, as well as cookies, oatmeal cream pies, and bottled water. Extra sweaters and coats are packed in a box.

A sandwich board says that everything is free, including cigarettes, first aid, phone calls, phone charging, even rides—whether that means to a home, to a family member or friend's sofa, or to a shelter.

"People get arrested in their home at night or in the morning, and they might only be wearing pajamas," explains Zach Zwagil, 31, an artist and activist and one of the group's founding organizers. "One woman had been arrested in her underwear, and all she'd been given was a pair of shear cotton—I can't even call them pants—before she was released. It was in the 40s that night. She would have frozen."

Known simply as Baltimore Jail Support, the informal network has gathered here for nearly three years, beginning not long after the death of Freddie Gray and the ensuing unrest, protests, and arrests.

"Thank you for looking out for these people," says a man walking past the jail. "I've been to jail, and I appreciate you all being out here for these folks. Folks you don't even know."

Just before 6 p.m., a group of about a dozen men walk out of Central Booking together. A few walk to friends or family in nearby cars. Others head toward the nearest bus stop. A couple stop by the table for cigarettes. "You got a light?"

The jail support group is here every Sunday evening, as well as a few other notable days of the year. On New Year's Eve, they bang pots and pans to let those incarcerated know that someone is thinking about them. On Mother's Day, they coordinate with local legal aid groups to raise bail money for moms who can't pay to be released.

"Some people, who are doing weekends in jail, you see almost every week," says Molly, 30, a dental hygienist, who asked that her last name not be published because of an arrest at a recent political protest in Washington, D.C. "We don't ask, but you'll hear people's story when you give them a ride. Sometimes they live in Glen Burnie or Catonsville and have no money and no way to get home," she continues. "There was a young guy whose family wouldn't take him back in [when we got there]. Mostly, they are upset and mad at themselves."

152. Learning to Fly

"What are they doing?"

"Flying drones. Racing drones."

"Shut up."

The curious, Friday night Light City crowd standing outside the massive caged "playing field" can barely follow the action—mad, miniature UFOs zipping through and around tightly spaced obstacles while hurtling through a specifically designed course at upwards of 100 miles per hour. Until they crash. Which seems inevitable.

"I caught the netting," says Cody Wright, 31, a videogame designer at the Hunt Valley-based ZeniMax Online Studios, as he untangles his lightweight, 1-square-foot, four-propeller aircraft. Wright's competitor, meanwhile, clanged into a metal post moments earlier, sending its owner back to the repair tent for soldering work.

After his heat, Wright, who has been racing drones for about three years, pulls down his virtual-reality goggles, explaining how provide a cockpit view from his aircraft—and a genuinely intense, pilot-like experience. "It's as if you are in *Star Wars*. That's the best analogy I know," he says, offering a nod to the famous pod-racing scene out of *Episode I – The Phantom Menace*. "It's mesmerizing. You're not thinking about anything else in the world."

Described as a never-seen-before mix of art, sport, and technology, The DronePrix at Light City is a second-year partnership between festival organizers; McCormack and Figg, a Baltimore-based artist collaborative commissioned to build the lighted sculptural obstacles and course; and Global Air Media, a Baltimore-based company that, among other services, supplies drone mapping and photography services. Founded by former Gilman School classmates Eno Umoh and Austin Brown, Global Air Media works largely with real estate, commercial development, and construction companies but also the U.S. State Department, most recently helping to surveil the damage in Puerto Rica after Hurricane Maria.

"The drone racing is a fun component of what we do," says the 31-year-old Brown, adding that they've been working with a youth drone racing team from the Greenmount Community Center that entered the amateur division. "It's a good way to attract kids to get involved with our STEM education programs and summer camp."

Most of the competitors this week, such as Wright, who took seventh out of 19 competitors in the professional class (first place garnered $1,200 in prize money), start as aerial photography enthusiasts, branching out later into the fast-growing sport.

"I started out with photography, which I love, but this is totally different," says Gabriel Dorsch, a 26-year-old software engineer from Columbia whose wife has come to watch him race this evening, "You kind of don't know about it until you know about it, and then you want to know all about it.

"There are smaller drones, too, ones you can fly in your house," Dorsch continues, lifting a tiny, four-inch, four-propeller device from a box. "Haven't knocked over any lamps yet. There have been a few close calls with the cat."

153. Ramblin' Man

When Bob Wagner was a kid, he'd jump on his Dad's Schwinn bike in his 1970s tube socks, short shorts, and sneakers and take off by himself all day. "I was the youngest of three," Wagner recalls. "We lived in Towson, and by the time I came around, Mom had her hands full. She'd say, 'Be home for dinner.' Later, she'd ask what I did, and I'd tell her, 'I went to Pennsylvania, I ate a sandwich, and then rode back.' Mom would be like, 'Great.'"

When Wagner, 53 and a picture framer by trade who majored in folklore at Indiana University and does not own a cell phone, started the long distance Rando Rambles bicycling series a decade ago, he wanted to re-experience that childhood feeling of adventure. Rando is shorthand for randonneuring, a form of all-day, non-competitive, bicycle trekking from city to city, popular in Europe.

He dubbed the first "ramble"—a 97-mile down and back from the Washington monument in Baltimore to the Washington monument in the nation's capital—the Monument to Monument ride, and it unexpectedly has become a must-do event, if you can call it an event, for local cyclists. There are no entry forms, no fees, no support vehicles, no commemorative T-shirts or rules. Wagner simply posts the date on his WordPress blog with the route—always a surprisingly scenic run through the back roads of Anne Arundel, Howard, and Prince George's counties—and photos from previous years. He encourages people who join him to prepare themselves and their bike.

The jaunt attracts as many as 100 cyclists in sunny years—college students, semi-professional riders, and Medicare-eligible participants—and as a few as a half-dozen when forecasts call for showers. For the 10th anniversary Monument to Monument ride this year, about 40 riders meet on the cobblestones of Mount Vernon on the first weekend in June, departing for Washington at 8:30 a.m. Inevitably breaking into smaller groups by the time they twirl around the towering obelisk on The Mall, most grab lunch at Union Station. Others join Wagner for a beer and a sandwich at a nearby Irish bar before heading back to Baltimore. For about half, the mileage was no great feat; for others, more than a few inspired by Wagner's bike travelogue, it was their first century ride.

Vinny DeMarco, the state's irrepressible grassroots lobbyist, practically smiled the whole way, occasionally singing verses of "Volare" ("To Fly"), Dean Martin's Italian-English hit, which he calls the official song of the Monument to Monument ride.

All apparently made it home for dinner.

"The thing is, suddenly D.C., which you're used to being snarled in traffic trying to get to, becomes a place that you can reach on your bike," says Lars Peterson, a mechanic at Race Pace bicycles in Federal Hill who has done the ride a couple of times. "A weird shift in perspective takes place."

Until recently, Wagner tackled a 100-mile or longer route every month. Other Rando Rambles over the years have included undertakings to Havre de Grace, Gettysburg, Chesapeake Beach, and the Conowingo Dam. Most have particular, sometimes unique, destinations in mind. The Pancake Intercept ride, which rolls through the old farms and craggy woods of Carroll County, just happens to include a rest stop at an all-you-can-eat breakfast at a Union Bridge firehouse.

The toughest ride, coined The Northern Chesapeake Circumnavigation, was a 180-mile loop from Baltimore to Elkton to Delaware, past Chestertown, across the bay aboard the Kent Island

Express to Annapolis, and then back to Charm City. Eight riders, including Wagner, leaving from Middle Branch Park at 5 a.m., survived.

When he started the Rambles, Wagner, who sets a moderate pace and generally keeps an eye out for those in the back of the pack, says he was just thinking about creating personal challenges. In the early years, he biked 5,000, 7,000, and even 10,000 miles a year, meticulously documenting the best off-the-main-thoroughfare routes for his maps. That's more mileage than he annually puts on his 1964 Chevy station wagon, which remains in his Hampden garage most of the week while he bike commutes to work in Timonium.

And if no one came to his party, that was fine. If 100 came, that was fine, too. He was excited either way.

"Usually at least two or three people always showed up," he says over a drink later at the Golden West Cafe. "The time commitment is kind of crazy. You have to say to anyone who loves you, 'I'm going to be gone all day long. I may be even be in some danger today.' There is the chance you could fall, get in a collision, suffer dehydration, or have a mechanical breakdown. Or get lost. But it's that feeling [of] 'I don't know' that I'm after. Can I do it? 'I don't know.' What will the roads look like today? 'I don't know.' Will it be dark when I get back? 'I don't know.'"

154. Survival Skills

For decades, pediatrician Ralph Brown noticed a difference between the white and Black children he saw. Nearly all the white kids in his Sinai Hospital practice learned to swim by age 7 or 8. "Not the case with African-American families," says Brown. "I'm embarrassed to admit, it did not register what that meant until I saw a CDC report, maybe a half-dozen years ago, that Black children are five times more likely to drown than white kids."

It also wasn't until then, adds Brown, who recently retired, that he understood the statistic's relationship to segregation and Jim Crow.

"There were limited opportunities for their grandparents and great-grandparents to swim, and that legacy has been passed down," Brown says. He began asking the parents of Black children who did know how to swim how they had learned. "And I kept hearing, 'Mr. Thorpe.'"

The Mr. Thorpe to whom his patients' families were referring is a tall, soft-spoken 50-year-old who was taught to swim by his father, Marvin Thorpe Sr., in their cozy backyard pool just off the Beltway in Baltimore County. The elder Thorpe, who once said he dreamt "of a day where there are no reports of a child drowning," began offering swimming lessons to the public behind their Windsor Mill bungalow in 1972. He had managed to learn to swim in segregated Lynchburg, Virginia, by hounding local lifeguards and developed a lifelong passion for the water. He died in 2004, at which point, Marvin II took over the annual Memorial Day to Labor Day enterprise.

Together and separately, Thorpe and his father have taught an estimated 15,000 people to swim over the past 46 seasons. Mostly, that's been Black kids, but not all, by any means. They've introduced three generations, in some cases, to swimming, including parents and grandparents who decided to learn after their children and grandchildren became swimmers. Former mayors Kurt Schmoke and Stephanie Rawlings-Blake brought their children to the Thorpes. So have the Mosbys—Marilyn and Nick, the city state's attorney and state delegate, respectively—Ravens linebacker Terrell Suggs, and former Harlem Globetrotter Choo Smith.

"Word of mouth," says Thorpe, getting the tidy 16-yard pool ready on a recent morning. "We've never done any advertising."

His father's first pupil, in fact, was his son, who nearly drowned in the family's then-above-ground pool as a 4-year-old. "My father was a physical education teacher in the city school system and coached swimming and tennis at Southwestern High for four years," Thorpe says. "He taught me to swim the next day. He started teaching swimming in our backyard that summer, built an inground pool a few years later, and I was a part of it, helping him from day one."

The popularity of the program did not manifest because of his father's fun teaching style or teddy bear nature. The elder Thorpe was a taskmaster who did not allow parents to stay during lessons and was generally unmoved by children's tears. "Dad could be very tough, even mean, I thought sometimes, but you did what he wanted. He didn't think it should take longer than two weeks, two hours a day, to learn to swim," says Thorpe. "But, at the end of those two weeks, he'd invite the parents to come afterward, and there'd be a Saturday barbecue, and the kids could jump off the diving board and slide if they were ready. He called them 'closing exercises,' but they were more like a party. He loved those barbecues."

Thorpe says he was "programmed" by his dad to take over. (His mother, who always handled the admin work, was also a schoolteacher.) He has several siblings, but it was clear his father always intended for him to inherit the job.

At 6-foot-4, Thorpe possesses some of the imposing physical qualities of his father but also a gentler manner. Still, he went through a prodigal son period. "I moved out when I was a teenager," he says. "I didn't want to do this with my life, do the same thing as him. I quit for three years. Then I realized I loved to teach like he did. He never said a word about it when I came back. I didn't have to work my way back up the ranks or into his good graces. It was just like I never left."

155. Moving Images

Siobhan Hagan digs Elvis and Polaroid photos. She has a metal Scooby-Doo lunch box. She wears 1950s dresses and vintage sweaters, and when the 33-year-old's grandmother passed away, "I moved everything from her house into mine," she says with a self-deprecating laugh. The confessed "old-stuff nerd" was born in the city and earned a graduate degree in Moving Image Archiving and Preservation from NYU's Tisch School of the Arts. Her thesis there was built around the archives of WJZ-TV, which proved a fortuitous decision. The station hit the airwaves in 1948, and 70 years is a long time, enough for film to deteriorate and oxide particles to fall off magnetic television tape.

Hagan had grown up watching WJZ. "My mom turned on *Rise and Shine* every morning," she says. "It was my alarm clock as a kid." She founded the nonprofit Mid-Atlantic Regional Moving Image Archive (MARMIA) two years ago and, in the process, acquired WJZ's archives, then being stored at the University of Baltimore but with no plan to preserve the collection.

Hagan is in the process of digitizing as much of the 25,000-piece acquisition as she can before the early footage and videotapes disintegrate.

On a recent night in Hampden, Hagan screened some WJZ throwback tapes as part of a fundraising effort. Highlights included *Eyewitness News* coverage of Hurricane Agnes in 1972, Richard Sher and Oprah Winfrey hosting *People Are Talking*, Chuck Thompson recapping the O's stunning World Series sweep in 1966, irrepressible weatherman Marty

Bass ditching an embarrassing hairpiece, behind-the-scenes clips of *The Buddy Deane Show* (the inspiration for John Waters' *Hairspray*), and *Romper Room* with Nancy Rogers Claster. Plus Jerry Turner burying his head into the anchor desk in uncontrollable laughter after a rabbi's son made funny faces, unbeknownst to his father, to the camera throughout an entire Chanukah segment.

Beside the time-capsule clips of life in Charm City, which also include WJZ's disco-era *Evening Magazine*, is footage from the '68 riots, investigative pieces on racial issues and public housing, and coverage of the colorful 44th mayor of Baltimore, William Donald Schaefer.

"People's memories are sensitive to time, and these [tapes and films] are, too. They don't last forever. They're endangered," says Rob Schoeberlein, who oversees the cavernous Baltimore City Archives in Better Waverly, which houses MARMIA's office and the WJZ collection. "Normally, when we think of archiving material, it's manuscripts, letters, legal documents, and photographs. This is now important material, too."

Beyond MARMIA's WJZ-TV collection, the nonprofit gathers other local films, found VHS tapes, mixtapes, and home movies in an effort to document the arts, history, and culture of the Mid-Atlantic region. Hagan will even digitize old wedding films—as long as MARMIA gets to keep a copy.

One couple, in their 80s, Hagan recalls, had never seen their wedding film—shot by the bride's father and essentially lost for six decades—until their daughter rediscovered it and asked Hagan to digitize it. They all watched it for the first time last fall on a pop-up screen at the City Archives building.

"My parents had been bickering during the ride down. Over what, who knows? Just the way old couples do," Susan Hebble says. "They were married in 1956, and the reception had been at the Casablanca, a jazz club in Liberty Heights that later became the Sportsman's Lounge when former Colt Lenny Moore bought it. Zim Zemarel's swing band played. You could see the name on the drum kit."

Hebble says her family watched the film again over Christmas, and then again during her mother's funeral this spring. "My mother had begun having some memory issues by the time we went [to the City Archives], but she had none while looking at their wedding. Everything came back, and she became her normal, bubbly self again. The whole way home, my parents were very romantic toward each other. My dad told my mother he had forgotten how beautiful she was."

156. Lost and Found

The first old photograph Chris Whitaker reunited with its family, he discovered in a Montana antique shop. The black-and-white picture is a portrait of a boy attired in a wool suit, tie, and a pressed, white, short-collared shirt in the style of the day—about 1890. His hair is parted, there's a hint of a smile above his dimpled chin, and on the back of the photo, someone long ago scrawled the boy's name and hometown: Samuel Reynolds, Kingman, Kansas.

The few words on the back also described young Samuel as "my cousin." The vacationing Whitaker decided to track down the boy's family, searching census records and ancestry databases. A grateful descendant on Samuel's family tree came across his research and blog, which included the picture of Samuel, and later drove across the country to the same store and unearthed more than 40 other lost family photographs. Whitaker was elated.

"I just thought if someone found a photograph of my great-grandfather, I'd be thrilled," says Whitaker in his north Baltimore home office. "It was really that simple."

Over the past three years, the retired Whitaker has fleshed out the identities of hundreds of wayward vintage portraits, most of which he has stumbled across in the dustbins of Hampden's antique, book, and curio shops. Placing these mysteriously adrift portraits with their loved ones, at times, has proven difficult for unexpected reasons.

Shortly after his initial success with Samuel's portrait, for example, Whitaker contacted the West Virginia daughter of a woman in a lovely

1940s portrait via Facebook. Not only did the woman not respond, she blocked him. "I think it creeped out the woman when I messaged her and I told her I had a picture of her mother," Whitaker recalls with a laugh. Ever since, he just scans the photographs and posts them on his blog, including the subjects' names and the location where he found the photo, encouraging people to email him if they discover an ancestor.

"It's rewarding," he says. "And I like the detective work."

In one case, Whitaker provided a woman in her 80s with the last photograph of her dad, taken four days before he was killed in a plane crash when she was a girl. He connected Reed Young to a youthful portrait of his grandfather, who died before the Johns Hopkins University Applied Physics Laboratory program manager was born.

Whitaker's found photos have taken him through time to the blocks of what was once "Little Bohemia" in East Baltimore to the former stoop of former big-leaguer Edwin Americas Rommel, reportedly the first pitcher to deploy the knuckleball after the spitball's banning in 1920. And to Fells Point, where a young wife named Ruth Collier sent photos of herself to her husband while he served in the South Pacific during World War II. (He returned home and the couple raised a family here.)

A Tennessee native, Whitaker became interested in genealogy in the mid-1980s when he found only scant information about his maternal great-great-grandfather and absolutely no pictures. He did, however, eventually locate his ancestor's Civil War pension records at the National Archives. There, Whitaker read the firsthand account of the shot—from a Confederate rifle—that killed his great-great-grandfather at the Battle of Stones River.

Whitaker learned that his great-great-grandfather and both of his brothers had fled Tennessee after its secession to join Kentucky's 9th Volunteers Infantry. All three gave their lives to the Union cause. "I don't know if I fully absorbed their actions when I first came across that," Whitaker says. "My appreciation and pride in what they did has continued to grow over the years.

"My younger brother, who is now deceased, and I grew up in Tennessee in the 1970s, when Confederate flags and Southern rock were all the rage," Whitaker continues. "He gave me a lot of grief when I married my first wife because she was a Yankee from Philadelphia. [Learning about our great-great-grandfather] turned everything he believed on its head, which I thought was great."

157. Corner Petaler

"Mr. Van feeds 'em chili peppers," an older gentleman, chatting up a pair of two-and-a-half-foot-tall macaws, informs a buddy as they wait for a bus outside Pearson's Florist on the corner of North Charles and North Avenue. "Makes them talk more."

"It does," Vander Pearson, the longtime shop owner, confirms later, adding that friends "Shiloh" and "Partner" have served as his sidewalk welcoming committee for five and 10 years, respectively. "I got them to keep me company. I take them out of the cage when I bring them inside so they can stretch their wings." Every few days or so, Pearson likes to hold the big birds on his lap, careful to mind their beaks as he strokes their bellies.

The soft-spoken but steadfast Pearson, 59, opened his storefront at the crosshair intersection that divides East and West Baltimore almost four decades ago. A Rite-Aid and a Payless shoe store, a men's clothing store, and a bank were all were across the street back then. The clothing store burned to the ground and is now the site of the repurposed Ynot Lot. The shuttered building where Gov. Larry Hogan stuck his temporary Baltimore reelection office after pasting over a rooftop billboard that read "Whoever Died From a Rough Ride?"—a reminder of Freddie Gray's death in police custody.

O'Dell's, a popular, if notorious, disco (one owner was involved in a major heroin ring, and shootings outside the club were not uncommon) let loose a few doors down before closing in 1992. In fact, the cozy flower shop earned its 15 minutes of fame during season two of *The Wire*, essentially standing in for itself when Bodie came in to buy a funeral arrangement after "co-worker" D'Angelo Barksdale was killed. (On cue, as we're discussing *The Wire* filming, a young man enters right before closing and asks for a dozen roses, which he pays for after pulling a baseball-sized roll of $20 and $100 bills from his jacket.) "There was foot traffic the first five years, but it was a little chaotic, especially with O'Dells," says Pearson, who has witnessed the blossoming of Station North, including the renovation of the historic Parkway Theatre directly out his window, from the best possible perch. "Between 1987 and 1992, everything left. But no, never thought of leaving. People kept coming to see me. A scared man can't win anyhow."

When the Maryland Institute College of Art bought the old Jos. A. Bank building and transformed it into a graduate center, Pearson noticed a turn. College kids with drawing assignments began showing up to buy day-old flowers, which he gladly gave away.

Pearson got his start in the flower trade at 12, unloading deliveries at Crip's Family Florist in West Baltimore. After moving to the east side, he began working at wholesale florist Claymore C. Sieck. In 1981, with Easter and Mother's Day falling close together, he scraped together as much cash as he could, bought as many roses as he could from his employer, and sold them himself at the corner of North Avenue and Harford Road. He netted $6,000 those holiday Sundays and spotted a "for rent" sign in the window of what is now his back room.

For years, he pulled his early shift at Sieck's before opening his own shop in the afternoon. A lifelong bachelor, he still arranges every order personally and occasionally spends nights at the shop when orders keep him swamped.

"I learned from Mr. Crip. I'd add a flower or two to an arrangement he'd been working on," Pearson says, referring to the late Clarence Crip, a well-respected West Baltimore flower man. "He let me know if he didn't like it, which hurt my feelings, but I learned. He told me to think of a bouquet as a canvas and you're making a painting. That stuck with me."

Recently, with his 60th birthday upcoming this March, Pearson got his first passport. Having seen it all, he wants to see something else.

"I watch the Travel Channel," he says. "I've put a little money aside. After prom season, I plan to take a cruise to see the Alaskan glaciers. Then, I want to hike the Alps and visit Rome."

Working late hours and living alone all these years (dinner has often meant a sandwich or bowl of cereal before bed), he also intends to visit Paris. "I watch the Food Channel, too."

158. Bootleg Bunch

Inside the sprawling metal shop that bears the family name, Joe Kavanagh's nephews, Paul and Patrick Kavanagh, huddle after hoisting a 12-foot steel beam—assisted by an overhead electric lift—onto an 18,000-pound, medieval wheel-like device for bending. (When you see buildings with cool, curved walls or arches, this is the place where their support architecture takes its final shape.) "Sometimes you've got to let them figure it out for themselves," says Joe, glancing over his shoulder.

Thirty-one and 28, respectively, the younger Kavanaghs represent the sixth generation to work in the business, a century-and-a-half-old institution that's struggling to stay afloat as President Trump's tariffs wreak havoc on the cost of steel and aluminum.

It's hardly the first time national politics have threatened the company's bottom line. Their ancestors made their first real money building and servicing distilleries in hard-drinking, post-Civil War Baltimore. In fact, the original Joe Kavanagh—great-great-grandfather of the 54-year-old Joe now in charge—socked away enough dough to rebuild after his first plant (and most of the city) burned to the ground in 1904. (The name—Joseph Kavanagh Co. Practical Coppersmith—remains legible in huge, if weathered, block lettering at the former Pratt Street and Central Avenue location where they plied their trade for more than eight decades before moving to Dundalk.)

But the Great Baltimore Fire proved a minor setback compared to Prohibition, which took effect 100 years ago this month. "Half of their business was in distilleries," recounts Joe, as his nephews ready the steel girder for a second pass. "They were afraid they were going to lose everything with Prohibition."

Enter Jimmy Connolly, aka "Jack Hart," who had married into the family a year earlier, wedding Kitty Kavanagh following his release from Sing Sing. Hart let it be known to Kitty's male cousins, then running the operation, he had the connections to wholesale some whiskey if they wanted, or needed, to stay in the distillery business. And so, the Catholic, previously pious and upstanding Kavanaghs became bootleggers, with Jack and Kitty eventually earning infamy as Baltimore's Bonnie and Clyde. It's all documented in taped, family oral histories and news accounts, which the current Joe has spent years poring over.

"We've had our share of 'colorful' characters in the family," acknowledges Joe, a talkative and colorful character himself, who has owned the business with his sister since his father retired and brother passed, both of whom he spent decades working alongside. "Kitty's father shot a Baltimore bartender in the neck and ran off for Chicago after a prison stretch." The Kavanaghs have also seen their share of tragedy. One ancestor who worked in the business died in a train accident coming back from a job in Connecticut. Another quit the business and took to Panama to work on the canal after his son and wife died. He succumbed to malaria in the Canal Zone.

Not content with mere bootlegging, Hart later became the subject of one of the biggest manhunts in the city's history in the summer of 1922 after he and an accomplice robbed $7,263 in payroll from a local company, shooting and killing the company's treasurer in the process.

Apprehended at a Washington, D.C., hideout a month later, Hart attempted a half-dozen prison escapes, succeeding twice—first in 1924 by bending a pair of metal bars with an iron rod, and then again in 1929 after cutting his way through three locks of his solitary confinement cell. "Using tools of *his* trade, not ours," Kavanagh notes.

The FBI kept Kitty under constant surveillance each time Hart went on the lam, but she never wavered in support of her beloved husband and never tipped off police to Hart's whereabouts. Although the press reported that she fainted once after being informed he'd been captured.

Meanwhile, the rest of the Kavanaghs kept making clandestine distilleries, secretly shipping them out to clients, likely via the Baltimore harbor, while also mixing their own rye whiskey.

Through Prohibition, the Depression, two World Wars, and too many recessions and crises to remember, the Kavanaghs—more than two-dozen have worked here in the company's history—kept at their legal work as well, of course. They have contributed railings, piping, and fittings to everything from the Statue of Liberty to the Hippodrome, Oriole Park at Camden Yards, and the rehabbed Parkway Theatre. They built the track for the famous 360-degree shot of Robin Williams being killed on the TV show *Homicide*.

Later, as Joe pulls out some company artifacts in a spare room, including a throwback beer bucket and "whiskey thief"—a short pole used to sample a batch in distilling—he says he hopes to hand the family kit and caboodle off to Paul and Patrick one day. He's unsure about the company's future, however.

"Look, we're okay right now, but after this winter when everything slows, who knows?" he says. "I don't want to lose this business. Not on my watch," he continues. "I started working on Saturdays with Dad when I was 12. You know, I studied classical guitar for two years at Peabody. Everyone in the family is a musician. Patrick plays clarinet, Paul plays the trumpet and tuba, my uncle played the piano, and my dad sang. And nobody asked me to quit college and come full-time. It was my decision. This place just gets under your skin and there wasn't any reason to put it off any longer. This place was my destiny."

159. World Cafe

When Iman Alshehab arrived at JFK Airport in 2016, she did not have anyone she knew to meet her. A caseworker from the International Rescue Committee picked up the widowed Syrian grandmother, emigrating to the U.S. alone, and dropped her off at her new, temporary home in Dundalk. "It was getting dark on the four-and-a-half hour drive," Alshebab recalls. "I kept crying."

"My second full day in Merry-land was Thanksgiving, and I decided I am going to make my neighbors dinner," she recounts in Arabic and some English. "I used Google Translate and knocked on everyone's door to invite them. I was very brave. I was worried people would say no." A former chef at the Four Seasons Hotel in Damascus, she made hummus, rice, chicken, and tabbouleh pasta salad. More than 20 neighbors, including several refugee women from other countries, came over, plus her caseworker. Each departed, hands full, with leftovers.

Fast-forward two years. Just before this past Christmas, Alshehab—today a founding member of the Mera Kitchen Collective, a worker-owned initiative supporting refugee and immigrant women—helped cook for more than 500 people as part of an arts feast at the historic St. John's United Methodist Church, also known as the 2640 Space, in Charles Village. "I sold out everything," she says. So did women from Afghanistan, Burkina Faso, El Salvador, Eritrea, Nigeria, and Sudan.

The name Mera, explains Aishah AlFadhala, another founding member and a Kuwaiti immigrant, is derived from the Greek word *meraki*, which means to "to do something so passionately that you leave some of yourself in it." In addition to Alshehab and AlFadhala, the collective was founded by Liliane Makole, who owned a cafe in her native Cameroon, Brittany DeNovellis, a program coordinator for Baltimore City Community College's Refugee Youth Project, and Emily Lerner, who has worked in the field with Doctors Without Borders.

Years ago, before she began cooking at the Four Seasons, Alshehab mopped the floors at the luxury Syrian hotel to support her three children. Police had already killed her husband by that point. After bringing her stuffed grape leaves and kibbeh meatballs with spiced yogurt to work one day, she was promoted to the kitchen.

"They told me to focus on grape leaves and meatballs after that," she recalls.

Later, she lost her 6-month-old granddaughter to the war when a bomb struck her son's home, and she eventually fled to the Jordanian border after a bomb destroyed her house. Her children, now adults, and seven surviving grandchildren, all of whom she hasn't seen since immigrating, have not received word on their applications for visas.

The mission of the collective is to empower immigrant and refugee women in the city through food entrepreneurship. All of Mera's chefs are experienced cooks who had to leave their home countries and start their professional and personal lives from scratch [in America or here in Baltimore]. Alshehab worked at Blind Industries and Services of Maryland, teaching sewing to the sight impaired—taking two buses each way—before being able to redirect her energies to Mera. Mona Ahmed, who lives with her husband and five children in an apartment near Alshehab, will soon complete a food handling certification course. She spent 11 years in a refugee camp after fleeing violence in Sudan.

After first hosting fundraising dinners in their homes, the women organized pop-ups at Alma Cocina Latina, Clavel, and Hersh's Pizza—immigrant owned, co-owned, or immigrant friendly in the case of Hersh's. All have children, all struggle with English, and none own a car. Together, says AlFadhala, who came to the U.S. to attend college

347

nine years ago and moved to Baltimore four years ago to work at the Kennedy Krieger Institute, they help each other cope with school, child care, medical, and transportation issues. And simply navigating life in Baltimore, which can be re-traumatizing in the low-resource, high-crime neighborhoods where the women and their families are typically placed.

Despite these obstacles, the Mera women opened a tent at the Baltimore Farmers' Market & Bazaar last spring, learning each other's specialties and sharing recipes. They've also ventured into catering, serving an event at the Baltimore Museum of Art, and have begun offering cooking classes. Ultimately, the goal is to open a permanent restaurant and community hub and employee 30-plus refugees, immigrants, and Baltimore women of color from underserved communities.

"Often, their children, who learn the language very quickly once they are in school, are like, 'Oh, my mom doesn't speak English and doesn't know anything,'" notes AlFadhala. "They view their mothers as people without education or value. But when they see people coming to pay to eat their mother's food, that turns everything around. You can see the image of their mom change right before your eyes."

Having survived so much, the Mera women did not come here to survive—or remain isolated. They want to thrive.

"Food has always been the source of bringing people around me," says Alshehab, placing a grilled falafel sandwich with tahini sauce, pickles, eggplant with red pepper, and freshly squeezed lemonade in front of two visitors to her small apartment on a recent afternoon.

160. Palace Intrigue

In the halcyon 1950s, Hutzler's department store employed 1,500 sales, office, and Colonial tea room dining staff. "Probably 2,000 during the holidays," says Michael Lisicky, author of *Hutzler's: Where Baltimore Shops.* "You went downtown to shop, lunch, see a show, go back and shop again," he says. "Lexington and Howard was the busiest intersection in the state."

In a twist of fate hardly fathomable when the 140-year-old family business shuttered in 1989, that corner—and specifically the former luncheonette basement of the old Hutzler Brothers Palace—is now home to one of the busiest "intersections" in the world. An estimated 25 percent of global internet traffic—including half of the emails, Amazon orders, Netflix streams, and iPhone downloads in the U.S.—pass through the stacks of underground AiNET servers there.

Many Baltimoreans know the backstory: In 1858, 23-year-old Abram Hutzler convinced his father, Moses, a German-Jewish peddler, to sign for credit so he could open a dry-goods store, which eventually set a record among American department stores for tenure at its original location.

Fewer know the current story: Deepak Jain, son of Indian immigrant parents, launched AiNET—originally a web-hosting company whose revenues now surpass $100 million—in his parents' basement while attending Glenelg High School. (When he was a restless 6-year-old in a rural community without a lot of children nearby to play with, his parents had gotten him a Texas Instruments TI-99/4A home

349

computer to keep him occupied.) By 1994, while in theory a sopho-more Johns Hopkins University pre-med student, Jain's business was growing fast enough that he could pay his own tuition.

Since then, AiNET, which employs two dozen workers on site, has expanded into a data center, cloud storage, IT services, and cyber-se-curity business. Clients include federal contractors Jain can't mention, as well as tenants at his telecom hotel, such as Comcast and Verizon. In 2014, Jain bought the five-story Hutzler Brothers Palace on Howard and the adjoining seven-story building on Lexington known as One Market Center—where the Hutzlers tried and failed to reinvent them-selves in 1985.

One of Jain's related missions is Future Cities, an effort to bridge Baltimore's digital divide by building a free Wi-Fi network across the city. Meanwhile, change has been percolating on the outskirts of the long-desolate block. The Everyman and Hippodrome theaters and Bromo Arts District have sparked activity. Historic Lexington Market is also due for a $30-million-plus redesign.

For his part, Lisicky would like to see more AiNET initiatives sim-ilar to its collaboration with The Contemporary art museum in 2017, which opened the Hutzler Brothers Palace's renowned Art Deco door-ways to the public for the first time in nearly three decades.

The irony that what was once such a social hub now channels our digital communication—even a local text or email sent via the inter-net inevitably bounces through AiNET servers—isn't lost on Lisicky. "There's still a heartbeat in that building. It's just digital and buried."

As far back as 1941, Albert Hutzler, then company president, saw the handwriting on the wall. Long before his beloved department store came to its end, he had alerted a city planning conference at Hopkins that urban blight, unchecked, would lead to falling downtown real-es-tate values and transform Baltimore into a "ring city" with a shrinking core surrounded by thriving suburbs.

He added that such flight is not so much a problem for a merchant. "They go to the outlying communities and go on to build there," said

Hutzler, who would build stores in Towson, Catonsville, Dundalk, Glen Burnie, Woodlawn, Bel Air, and White Marsh. "It is the city itself that goes to pieces."

161. Pop Goes the . . .

The first time Mahala Morefield met Weasel, aka Jonathan Gilbert, she was a law firm receptionist posing as a music writer from the Lone Star Dispatch. It was 1975. Morefield had relocated to Washington, D.C., from Austin and stumbled across a high-pitched nasal voice spinning records on an eclectic, midnight-to-6 a.m. show at a 3,000-watt station with the call letters "High-Fidelity Stereo." Little Feat, the Stones, Frank Zappa—an eight-fingered, Romani-French jazz guitarist named Django Reinhardt—somehow it all fit together each night. "I had a musical crush on Weasel," recalls Morefield. "I set up a phony 5 a.m. meeting and held onto the cassette tape of that 'interview' forever."

Fast-forward almost 45 years, and the WHFS days—including the later years when the station moved to Annapolis and blasted its new 50,000-watt signal toward Baltimore—are long past. The station's epic HFStival, of course, are gone, too. But Weasel, whose nickname was bestowed by an American University classmate who thought he resembled the creature on the cover of Zappa's 1970 album *Weasels Ripped My Flesh*, is still on the air, spinning now for Towson University's WTMD. Because Gilbert doesn't drive (he still lives in the same apartment in Bethesda's Triangle Towers where the old WHFS studio was located and where its ancient transmitter remains impaled on the roof), a revolving band of 50-plus volunteers, fondly referred to as Weasel's Wagon Train, takes turns transporting the unlikely D.C.-Baltimore cultural icon to Towson to record his once-again, organic, free-range shows on WTMD. (Passionate, engaging, witty at the microphone, Gilbert isn't quite a recluse off air, but he's not on Facebook or other social media either. "Why would I do that? I want to listen to music, and I want other people to listen to music.")

A Long Island-native, Gilbert's extraordinary curatorial gifts began with a great natural ear, followed by a deep curiosity and an impeccable memory. "It started with a transistor radio when I was 10 years old," he says. "I'd stay up all night, covers pulled over my head, not wanting to miss a thing. Sometimes that was one of the great jocks from WBAI in New York, sometimes it was a baseball game. On a good night, you could get Bob Prince from Pittsburgh. I listened to Chuck Thompson from WBAL long before I came to Baltimore."

An older brother introduced him to Chuck Berry and Little Richard. He heard the records his uncles, aunts, and parents played, their personal interests skipping from folk to jazz to Sinatra and big band. Singing in the school choir, playing clarinet through 12th grade, and graduating high school in 1967 when album-oriented rock was transforming radio, Gilbert absorbed everything. To this day, his play-lists pop with surprises and style as he juxtaposes songs in the same key and effortlessly raises and lowers the tempo. "You create a nar-rative, an emotional journey," he says, thumbing through a tattered notebook during a recent set that spanned gospel, early civil rights-era, and Black-power soundtracks on Martin Luther King Day. "Music is visceral."

In between, he provides the kind of nuggets and backstories that music lovers geek out over.

"When I hear something new that I like—and it could be some-thing that's old—I'm still that 10-year-old kid," he says. "I want to hear it 10 times. And, like a guitar player figuring out the chords, I want to slow it down and see how they did what they did."

By coincidence, Morefield, who moved back to Texas in the late '70s, returned to the area shortly before Gilbert joined WTMD nine years ago. After not conversing since her "interview" when both were in their mid-20s, she's now a friend and occasional Wagon Train driver. A whole lot—and nothing—has changed.

"He plays your soul, your heart," she says of his Weasel Wild Weekend shows. "A maestro of the radio. One song vibrating off the next."

162. Brush with Life

The first portrait Kimberly Sheridan painted was a close-up of James Smith III, smiling in a barber chair and holding, symbolically, a small lamb and lion cub in his lap. On his third birthday, in 1997, at a barbershop near Sheridan's Pigtown home, James had been shot in the head and killed as he waited with his mother to get his haircut.

That painting, made six years ago, was a reaction, Sheridan explains, "after Congress couldn't even pass a gun bill with background checks," following the massacre of 20 Sandy Hook kindergarten and first-grade students. "I had become enraged. The next morning, I stood outside the Plaza Art store on Cathedral before they opened to buy supplies."

A 58-year-old self-taught artist with impaired sight but genuine vision, Sheridan had never forgotten James. Nor had she forgotten local church custodian Ron Waggener, her best friend, killed around the corner from her home in 2004. Waggener became her second portrait a few days later. "It's healing to paint," she says. "It's my way of advocating for stricter gun control laws. It's the way I reach out to others who are grieving."

Taking her cue from Yoko Ono, who tweeted after Sandy Hook that more than one million people in the U.S. had been killed by guns since her husband's death, Sheridan pledged to paint a million victims of gun violence, starting with those in close proximity. "I wondered, who were these million people?" she says. "Especially the forgotten people. The ignored. What if we brought them into the light?" Today,

176 of her works fill a second-floor front room of her modest row-house. Colorful, joyous, and imaginative, they are informed by whatever pictures and biographical details Sheridan can cobble together.

They are, overwhelmingly, portraits of people cut down before their lives had fully formed. "For some, I have to draw from mug shots," Sheridan says. "But I paint everyone with the same sympathy. Picturing them at their best. When they were their true selves."

Subjects include a father and son, cousins killed months apart, a pair of girlfriends, a police officer, a young man killed by police, former Councilman Kenneth Harris, and Charmaine Wilson, a 37-year-old mother of eight who was targeted in 2017 after reporting to police that her son was being bullied. There's also Raquan Campbell, a 15-year-old football player and honor roll student, affectionately nicknamed Ra-Ra because of his ebullient personality, who was shot 10 times in 2010. "I met with Raquan's mother a week before Christmas this year at the Cherry Hill Shopping Center," Sheridan recalls. "She does an annual coat drive there. She saw me coming, holding the painting, and started to cry."

To date, Sheridan has exhibited at a Pigtown church, the former Liam's Pub in Station North, and a small business in Canton. She doesn't sell her work, instead offering her paintings to each victim's family for free. She has coordinated more than a dozen such "homecomings" as she calls them, with more on the way. In terms of painting a million portraits of victims of gun violence, she says the only thing required is more artists. "There's one in St. Louis and another in Miami doing something similar I know of," she says. "It's a start."

Meanwhile, she keeps a running list of everyone killed in Baltimore. "More than 5,000 this century," she says, shaking her head. "We are all witnesses to a slow-motion genocide of Black males in this city." Recently, Sheridan formed a nonprofit to partner with other anti-violence and family survivor organizations.

"It's a never-ending treadmill of pain and anger leading to murder," she continues. "We keep making little kids orphans when we kill their father, their mother, their brother and sister, and then they end up shooting someone else's father, mother, brother, and sister. Why aren't we seeing the whole picture? That's the question I ask myself when I paint."

163. The Bid and The Kid

Gerald Delp liked Ronnie Franklin from the start. "He was small, but he didn't take any shit from anybody, and he was funny," the 56-year-old Delp recalls. "He was from Dundalk, and I grew up in Laurel. We clicked. Just the way you do with some people."

As teenagers, they shared a mutual love of horse racing, girls, partying, and skipping school. Delp had known since he was 7 that he wanted to follow in the footsteps of his dad, legendary trainer Grover "Bud" Delp, and he quit school after the ninth grade. Franklin had no interest in school, either, or a Baltimore factory job (in the mid-'70s, when such things still existed), and he quit Patapsco High and went to Pimlico looking for a job, even though he'd never been near a horse in his life. "I was 13, and Ronnie was probably 15 when we first met," Delp says. "We began walking horses together."

A few years later, in the spring of 1979, Delp's father trusted the reins of a colt he called "the greatest horse ever to look through a bridle" to then 19-year-old Franklin, who rode the race of his life at the Kentucky Derby, rallying a slow-starting Spectacular Bid past six horses into the winner's circle. In front of 72,607 at Pimlico, The Bid, owned by Baltimore builder Harry Meyerhoff, and The Kid did it again at the Preakness, producing two of the biggest moments in local sports history in the span of two weeks.

Franklin, who passed away on March 8, 2018, at 58 from lung cancer, went on to win 1,403 races and $14 million in prize money during a 15-year career. "Horses liked to run for Ronnie," says Walter

Cullum, Franklin's nephew and a former jockey. "You have to be fearless, and Ronnie was, and he was strong, but his gift was in his hands and the way he communicated with them. God-given ability." Delp recalls a horse named Pioneer Patty, so tightly wound she'd climb the walls of her stall.

"We put rubber padding around to protect her from herself," he says. "She was Ronnie's first mount. He rode her to five straight wins."

Bud Delp had sent a green Franklin to the Middleburg Training Center for experience, and it was there that Franklin first developed a bond with Bid, a charcoal gray yearling. By that time, Franklin, the youngest of six, had moved in with Bud Delp, who was raising his two boys, Gerald and Doug, by himself.

The road to the Derby and Preakness was not easy for Franklin, however. With such little experience under his belt, he was pulled at one point off Bid, clearly a thoroughbred with the potential to be one of the sport's all-time greats. "He'd eat twice as much as a normal horse, a sign he wanted to work," Gerald Delp recalls. Franklin got the mount back when Bid didn't respond to seasoned Panamanian jockey Jorge Velásquez.

The road after the Derby and Preakness was not easy, either. Franklin and Bid missed their Triple Crown shot at the Belmont Stakes when Franklin took him out too fast. Shortly afterward, the young star was busted for cocaine, and addiction became an on-and-off struggle. "Ronnie loved people. He'd give you the shirt off his back," says Gerald Delp. "We all have our demons, including me."

Franklin was again working with horses in California when he was told he had Stage IV lung cancer in 2017. He returned Dundalk, which had welcomed him home after his Kentucky Derby victory with banners up and down Merritt Boulevard. Franklin, who told a reporter then, "I never had no dreams of being nothing until I came to a race track," had remained close to his family throughout.

"He lived the life he wanted to live," says Cullum, who was just 5 in 1979, when Franklin gave him his whip and dusty racing goggles from the Kentucky Derby as a keepsake. "He didn't have many regrets," Cullum continues. "The only thing he wanted was to live until May so he could go crabbing again. He didn't quite make it."

164. Eyes of the Law

"What does it profit a man to gain the whole world, yet forfeit his soul?"
—inscription above the altar at St. Elizabeth of Hungary

In 1971, Jim Cabezas's rookie year walking a Greenmount Avenue beat, there were 323 homicides in Baltimore. Twelve months later, a then-record 330. Heroin was sold openly on street corners, and he worked alongside more than a few, in his words, "brutal racists." (Cabezas once threw his body on top of a handcuffed Black citizen getting savagely kicked by fellow officers, only to be told if he tried anything like that again, he'd never receive backup.)

Less than two years on the job, a federal grand jury returned bribery indictments against six detectives and two former detectives. Other indictments soon came down against five lieutenants, six sergeants, and three patrolmen. The same year, former Baltimore County Executive and Governor Spiro Agnew resigned as Vice President over extortion and other charges while in office in Maryland. Agnew's successors as Baltimore County Executive and governor would face indictments for their own misdeeds.

Recently, an older woman approached Cabezas, who just wrote his autobiography with former *Sun* reporter Joan Jacobson, and asked the former Baltimore cop and state political corruption investigator if he thought things had improved since he became a police officer. It should be noted: Cabezas spent three years working undercover as a taxi driver on The Block in the mid-'70s, and later, after losing his eyesight to a degenerative condition, oversaw the investigations that ended the tenures of former City Comptroller Jacqueline McLean and former Mayor Sheila Dixon. He also won a pair of election law guilty pleas from a former Mayor Catherine Pugh campaign aide and, though newly retired, filed a formal complaint against Pugh with his old State Prosecutor's Office after the *Healthy Holly* children's book scandal broke, alleging that she deliberately failed to report the income in disclosure forms while she was a state senator.

"Probably the same," the good-natured, matter-of-fact 69-year-old Cabezas told the woman. "Maybe worse," he added, reflecting further.

The son of devout Latino immigrants, Cabezas grew up next to Patterson Park, attending St. Elizabeth of Hungary Catholic Church. His childhood was idyllic—baseball, football, and school—for a time. A near-fatal reaction to an antibiotic triggered a rare, progressive eye disease, which ultimately caused him to go blind in the middle of his career. Shortly afterward, while still a boy, he lost his mother to brain cancer. Then, as a cop, but still just 22, his father—"my best friend"— was robbed and murdered.

Much of Cabezas's 46-year career was spent in the chaotic Baltimore quadrant that by perfect quirk of fate includes The Block, City Hall, and police headquarters. Telling everyone he'd had enough and quit the department in 1975, he actually went deep undercover for three years, posing as a regular taxi driver even to his future fiancée, as he began frequenting The Block to determine if the Philadelphia mafia had infiltrated the prostitution, drug, gambling, and loan-sharking operations based there. He also followed up on FBI concerns that the New York mob had infiltrated the local docks and longshoreman's union. Neither, he would determine, had their hand in the Charm City underworld. "Baltimore had a reputation as a 'rat town,'" Cabezas says. "Nobody would keep an out-of-towner's secrets, and that made the Philly and New York mobs nervous. Instead, it became a town where the mafia exiled people who'd gone awry but [who they] didn't want to kill."

A likable chameleon with an unmistakable Highlandtown accent, he found corruption at each turn. "The culture on The Block is [drug] abuse and being abused and it's sad, but there is at least some honor among thieves, and a few people do look out for each other," Cabezas says. "With the police and with politicians, it's only greed and hubris."

After 15 eye surgeries, two well-timed minor miracles allowed Cabezas to maintain his near half-century pursuit of wrongdoers. The first was an offer to join the Maryland State Prosecutor's office in the mid-'80s when his vision had deteriorated to the point where he couldn't carry a gun any longer. The second was the arrival of new computer software for the blind that enabled him to stay on that job after a state doctor recommended his termination due to his disability.

At 69, enjoying newfound renown from his book, he says he is still surprised his corruption busts never served as a deterrent to others. He highlights, for example, not just the numerous politicians he has convicted but also the arrests of school principals and officials, including former Baltimore County Schools Superintendent Dallas Dance, who went to jail last year.

The other surprise was that his focus improved as he lost his eyesight over the course of his career. "I learned how to listen better," Cabezas says. "You can tell a lot from what's in a person's voice. I heard things with my heart that I never saw before."

165. Coming Clean

The light turns red at the intersection of President and Pratt in Harbor East, and a half dozen teenagers in T's, jeans, and unlaced high tops spring from the grassy median, holding up Windex spray bottles in one hand and gas station-style squeegees in the other. Two skinny, younger boys jump into the street first. A couple of older kids shout and laugh at each other over the idling traffic. It's a clear, bright, Sunday afternoon in May. The school year is almost over.

They try to make eye contact through rolled-up windows.

"I got you," says one of the teenagers, leaning over the hood of a Honda, spraying a dab on the windshield.

"How are you?" a kid says to another driver. "What's up?"

"I got you."

A second teenager sprays a shot of soapy water on another windshield, trying to drum up business. The woman behind the wheel simply continues to stare at her phone.

To still another driver: "You look good, bro. You look sharp. You wanna wash?"

A 40-ish white man in a Range Rover emphatically waves his hands behind his rolled up windows. "No, no, no! Don't touch my car."

Another woman in a Honda Accord smiles as she shakes her head toward James, the self-possessed 16-year-old high school student who serves as this group's informal crew chief. "I don't have any money," she says. But then she offers him her French fries, which he accepts.

Before the light changes, four drivers get quick windshield wipes. They appear happy, or at least content, to hand over a buck or two for a slightly better view of the world. An equal number of drivers appear annoyed. The rest look relieved they avoided the kids' face-to-face pitch.

It's such a familiar scene by now in Baltimore, the two-minute productions play out like a choreographed dance.

"The overall reaction? I'd say 50-50," James says as he steps back to the median as cars begin rolling again. "Some people definitely resent you. Hey, I get it. You're walkin' up on their car. Other people tell you they're glad you're out here making an honest dollar."

"Most of the time," James continues, "it's not even about us. Everybody's bringing their own stuff they got going on, and it gets directed at you."

Baltimore's "squeegee kids" have been a source of hot, racialized debate, law enforcement confusion, and political puzzlement for decades. In 1985, the City Council voted 11-7, splitting along white-Black lines, to ban the practice and called for arrests. Black council members saw the proposal as racist because the young entrepreneurs the legislation targeted were almost exclusively Black. Baltimore Congressman Parren Mitchell, the first African-American to represent Maryland, decried the hysteria around the squeegee kids in his regular column in *The Afro*. So did former *Sun* columnist Roger Simon, generating a maelstrom of pre-social media letters to the editor.

Then-police chief Bishop L. Robinson, coincidentally the City's first Black police commissioner, said he had sought the ban not just because some drivers had complained they felt threatened by the youth but because he was concerned about the squeegee kids' safety—and some drivers had complained that they had felt threatened by the youth. (Indeed, a 14-year-old was killed the next year by a tractor-trailer.) Facing a backlash, Mayor William Donald Schaefer sought time to appoint a commission to study the issue. Ultimately, the bill went into effect with a compromise—the removal of the threat of incarceration, a law that stands to this day. None of this flap and fury makes sense to Derrick, who is two years younger than James and has been working a spray bottle and squeegee alongside him since they were 10 and 12, respectively. He doesn't understand why any of this has been an issue.

He also says that after all this time, he still can't get his head around the gamut of responses he receives—and endures—on a daily basis from adult drivers.

"Honestly? It's confusing," the 14-year-old says. "Someone will give you a $10 bill and thank you, and the very next person will cuss at you." Both Derrick and James, like most of the teenagers hustling at this end of I-83, live in the Douglass Homes housing project near The Johns Hopkins Hospital. The urban highway was built in the 1960s to ferry suburbanites in and out of the city. "How do you make sense of that when you didn't do one thing different?"

"What do you want us to do for money?" James says. "Cut grass? That's a white people thing. There ain't no grass around here."

166. Writing on the Wall

Ernest Shaw heard the news that acclaimed author Toni Morrison had passed away while he was driving over to Station North Arts Cafe Gallery for breakfast. "It's a family atmosphere there and that's all everyone was talking about," Shaw says, noting cafe owner Kevin Brown had founded the James Baldwin Literary Society in Baltimore decades earlier. "As I was listening to the conversation, I started searching images on my phone."

By afternoon, following a quick stop for spray paint at nearby Artist & Craftsman Supply, the muralist and longtime city school arts teacher found himself in North Howard Street's Graffiti Alley, putting the finishing touches on a large-scale, pop-up work of Morrison, who won a Pulitzer for her novel *Beloved* in 1988. By evening, the soulful portrait had gone viral, and Shaw spent the next two days, including his 50th birthday, in the alley-turned-tourist-attraction doing television and newspaper interviews.

"I'd found some photos of her when she was younger, one of which I liked initially, but I wanted something instantly recognizable, from the period when she became known to the world," Shaw says. "I consider [her death] the acquiring of an ancestor. She earned that status. The portrait was my way of asking for permission to move forward."

Situated directly behind Motor House, the nonprofit arts hub, gallery, and performance venue where Shaw maintains a studio, Graffiti Alley, has, as one might anticipate, a colorful history. Not visible from the street, the L-shaped alley had long been a receptacle for trash, spent needles, used condoms, and, occasionally, graffiti before artist Sherwin Mark bought the abandoned Lombard Office Furniture building and transformed it into the Load of Fun studio complex in 2005. (Burlesque star and then-tenant Trixie Little suggested the Load of Fun moniker to Mark, pointing out that he only needed to remove some of the Lombard Office Furniture letters from the building to make it work.) Motor House moved into the location in 2015, and its name pays homage to Baltimore's first Ford dealership, which predated the furniture store.

Almost immediately after Load of Fun opened, more stylized graffiti began appearing in the alley. Mark appreciated the artwork; City officials did not. He was cited for refusing to cover over the graffiti, and eventually a City anti-graffiti crew took matters into their own hands, erasing all the work with white primer. When racist slogans and gang symbols went up on the suddenly stark canvass, Mark, with the support of nearby business owners, convinced officials to allow the graffiti writers to return. Today, while the penalty in Maryland for graffiti can include a sentence of up to three years in prison and a $2,500 fine, Graffiti Alley remains the one place in the state where the practice is legal. Attracting artists on a daily basis, the work in the alley remains almost constantly in flux. In recent years, the space has hosted a chamber music concert by Baltimore Symphony Orchestra musicians, an aerial arts festival, and too many weekend dance parties to count.

It's just by coincidence that Shaw's recent portrait of Morrison also serves as an outdoor extension of his current show inside Motor House, *Testify! A Life's Time of Emerging Blackness*, which includes paintings of Baldwin, Nina Simone, and Thelonius Monk, among other African-American artists and figures.

"I'm not used to spraying paint. When I do a mural, it's with brushes and rollers, but this is a space where I can practice," Shaw says, gesturing to the Morrison portrait, adding that he's gotten tips on different techniques and nozzles from accomplished Baltimore street artists Nether and Gaia. He notes that graffiti writers don't typically appreciate the type of realistic portraiture work he does—particularly in a space like Graffiti Alley that they've claimed for themselves. "I did a Pablo Picasso that got covered right away," he says. "Same with a blue-on-black John Coltrane portrait that was framed in a nice spot. Same with a [Grammy-winning jazz trumpeter] Roy Hargrove that I did right after he died. That one meant a lot to me because we were the same age and I'd followed his career. The next day, my signature was crossed out and someone had taken my Roy Hargrove portrait and put a different portrait right on top of it.

"What can you do? You get used to it because you have to. Everything in life is changing all the time," Shaw says, taking a long pause. "But yeah, truth is, I've been peeking out of my studio and checking every morning to see if the Toni Morrison portrait is still up."

167. Time Machine

Trudy Morgal doesn't remember anyone taking her photograph at Woodstock. She does remember sitting on top of her band's VW bus with Ricky Peters, a singer and drummer in their Baltimore group Light. A wisecracking pistol who also sang and played the drums—imagine a multitasking Hampden-esque Janis Joplin—Morgal can also recall the white umbrella she held up in defense against the pouring rain during the three-day deluge of peace, love, music, and mud.

The picture of two youthful, barefoot musicians atop the wild art bus, slightly grim in the face of the gray weather—in other words, an indelible representation of the festival, and just maybe an entire generation—had gone viral afterward, appearing in *Rolling Stone*, *Life* magazine, and newspapers across the country. Not that Morgal knew it.

"I wasn't aware that photograph existed until two decades later," Morgal recounts with a laugh. "I'd been helping a friend put wallpaper up in her kitchen when the 20th anniversary was coming up in 1989. We stopped for lunch and I grabbed *The Baltimore Sun*, and the picture was staring back at me on the front page of the Metro section. All those years, I'd been looking at movies and photos from Woodstock, squinting to see if I recognized anyone. Suddenly there *I* am. On top of the bus with Ricky. I almost fell off my chair."

Slowly at first, and then over time as the anniversary celebrations piled up, the image of Morgal and Peters, who died in 1998 ("Such a sweet guy"), sitting on the roof of the Light Bus, emerged as an iconic portrait of Woodstock and the counterculture. It even appeared on the cover of a textbook about the '60s. Interest in the whereabouts of the colorful minibus—hand-painted with religious and esoteric symbols by renowned Baltimore artist Bob Hieronimus—began percolating as Woodstock's half-century anniversary approached. (In somewhat related news, the German automaker announced new plans to remake the hippie-throwback VW Bus as a next-gen, all-electric vehicle.)

Several years ahead of the tentatively scheduled 50th reunion concert in upstate New York, Canadian documentarian John Wesley Chisholm approached Hieronimus about recovering and refurbishing the legendary van. Ultimately, after a six-month search came up empty, a Kickstarter campaign landed them an authentic 1963 VW Bus, which Hieronimus and five other artists painted by hand, recreating the art bus' original Egyptian, Indian, Hebrew, and astrological blessings. (Those unfamiliar with Hieronimus's work should check his mural *Historic Views of Baltimore 1752-1857*, inside the new jury room at the Clarence M. Mitchell Courthouse. It depicts Lord Calvert standing beneath Federal Hill, as George Washington and the Beatles' Yellow Submarine cross the Inner Harbor.)

The VW origin story actually began a year before Woodstock in Judges, a circus-themed Greenmount Avenue bar, complete with trapeze. That was where Hieronimus met kindred spirit Bob Grimm, Light's guitarist, who owned the soon-to-be-famous van. By then, Hieronimus had already been introduced to Jimi Hendrix, whose label wanted him to illustrate an album cover for $100. Grimm countered with an offer of $1,000 for Hieronimus to paint and turn his VW into a "magic bus," and the pony-tailed, oft-broke Hieronimus obliged.

Ironically, Hieronimus had purchased a ticket to Woodstock, but then begged off because he had no interest in being surrounded by the anticipated crowd of 50,000, let alone the near half-million people who ultimately showed up. Meanwhile, the band (which went to spectate not perform) had arrived later than anticipated following a detour to the Jersey Shore. Stopped at the gates, Grimm convinced security that the Light Bus was part of a planned art exhibition, which got them waved through and planted stage right, near the food vendors, port-o-potties, and aid station. "You heard all kinds of announcements—like 'Don't eat the brown acid,'" Grimm recalls. A year or so after Woodstock, Light broke up over record label squabbles, and Grimm donated the van to Hieronimus, who had started a commune on the site of the old Ruscombe Mansion in Northwest Baltimore.

"We went to Woodstock for the music, we had a good time despite the rain, and I'm glad we went," Grimm says. "It didn't seem like the big moment it became in hindsight. I've learned more looking back on Woodstock than I did being there," he adds. "I learned the years fly by."

168. Heavy Metal

It was a 52-foot, 10-ton object of controversy, curiosity, and, for the most part, derision, when it was installed in front of Penn Station in 2004. A *Baltimore Sun* editorial described the aluminum, five-story Male/Female statue as "oversized, underdressed, and woefully out of place." Columnist Dan Rodricks wrote that artist Jonathan Borofy's intersecting male and female silhouettes resembled the robot Gort from the sci-fi horror movie *The Day the Earth Stood Still*. A cab driver called it "an abomination" in one story. Several times, *City Paper* readers voted the massive sculpture—a $750,000 donation from the Municipal Arts Society—Baltimore's "Best Eyesore."

Almost immediately, it prompted calls for removal from its prominent juxtaposition outside the 1911-built Beaux-Arts style station. Now, oddly enough, just as the city seems to be developing some affection for the gender-inclusive giant with the outstretched arms and phosphorescent heart, its fate may be in doubt.

In order to handle new high-speed Acela trains and an expected passenger boom in coming years, Amtrak has pledged a $90-million Penn Station makeover. Those plans include the transformation of the historic station into a more pedestrian-, bicycle-, bus-, and taxi-friendly transit hub—and a proposal to turn the south station plaza into a venue with the potential for events and cultural programming. No official has said the sculpture needs to be moved to overhaul the Penn Station area. No one has indicated it will stay, either. There is simply no sight of the towering statue in current renderings and maps.

Bill Struever, CEO of Cross Street Partners, one of the developers on the Amtrak project, says he's "staying agnostic." Ultimately, he expects a resolution on the development of the south station plaza, and thus on the statue, will grow out of a community planning process.

Baltimore architect and artist Jerome Gray, one of the statue's defenders, believes the scale of the sculpture simply overwhelmed city viewers at first. Gray, who maintains a watercolor "sketchbook" practice, recently did a portrait of the sculpture. "I got off the train coming back from D.C. right after the sun went down the other night and there it was," he says. "I thought, 'Just enough light.'" The sculpture's provocative intersection of the male and female forms—and its colorful, single, pulsating heart, widely visible at night—personally appeals. "I love weird things," he says. "And I like anything that challenges you. In that way, it's great. It makes you think."

Discussing the sculpture and its potential upheaval after a recent Baltimore City Historical Society board meeting, Kathleen Kotarba noted that moving a large public sculpture is not unprecedented. Far from it.

The statue of Maj. General Samuel Smith, hero of the defense of Baltimore during the War of 1812, was moved three times before finally finding a home atop Federal Hill. The seated Edgar Allan Poe homage, dedicated in Wyman Park in 1921, was removed for its own safety and adopted by the University of Baltimore, where it's become an unofficial campus mascot. The statue of the legendary Greek poet Orpheus at the entrance of Fort McHenry, a monument to Francis Scott Key, was relocated from the spot it was first unveiled by President Warren Harding. The pink marbled *Good Shepherd* work, originally at Eastern High School, was disassembled and moved to Lake Clifton High after the school closed and then disassembled and moved back when the school building was repurposed into an office complex. The bronze and granite Union Soldiers and Sailors Monument, dedicated in Druid Hill Park, was relocated to Wyman Park in 1959 to accommodate the Jones Falls Expressway. Others, too, have been moved.

Most recently, the city's four Confederate monuments were pulled down from public view. (Ryan Patterson of the Baltimore Office of Promotion & the Arts notes any relocation or decommission of the Male/Female statue would involve a process that includes the artist, who in this unique case, is alive and well.)

"The thing about city life is everything is always on the move," says Kotarba, who served as president of the Commission of Historical and Architectural Preservation when it signed off, unanimously, on the placement of the Male/Female statue at Penn Station. "Even the statues."

169. The Last Autoworker in Baltimore

Guy White's alarm goes off at 4:40 a.m., the same time it has for the past decade for the UAW Local 239 shop steward. It's early, but it beats the years working nights and crazy swing shifts. He tries not to disturb his wife (the kids are grown and gone) and starts a pot of coffee. He grabs a couple of hard-boiled eggs, packs a sandwich for his lunchbox, and attempts to keep his thoughts on his daily routine. Most of the coffee, as usual, ends up in his thermos for the 20-minute commute to White Marsh and the General Motors plant there, which has been sitting idle, as quiet as his kitchen at 4 in the morning, since mid-May. It is now the third Friday in September, and the United Automobile Workers' existing contract with GM is set to expire over the weekend. He's scheduled to fly to Detroit the next the day to vote on GM's offer and whether the UAW should strike over wages for new hires and recent plant closings.

For White, however, and the 250 White Marsh union autoworkers, the die has been cast. Late last year, GM informed them that the plant's beloved-by-gearheads, six-speed, heavy-duty Allison transmission—the kind that powers the Silverado and Sierra pickups—was being replaced by a newly designed 10-speed transmission. That new transmission, management added, would be made in Ohio.

For the past few months, White had kept going to his office to facilitate relocations and retirements for his fellow UAW members. In fact, White was so sure that Friday morning in September would be his last that he had cleaned out his desk and booked a Delaware shore vacation. He put in 19 years at White Marsh and, before that, 15 at the old GM facility on Broening Highway. When he clocks out at 2 p.m., it punctuates the end of GM's epic 85-year relationship with this city.

At its peak here, the Big Three automaker produced American classics, such as the Pontiac Grand Prix and GTO, the Chevelle and Monte Carlo, the Oldsmobile Cutlass and Buick sedans—not to mention Chevy pickups, station wagons, and, later, three million Astro and Safari minivans. Even during the stagflation of the 1970s, the Broening plant hummed along, employing 7,000 autoworkers in Southeast Baltimore. In those days, Western Electric and Lever Brothers were still down the street; Bethlehem Steel was a stone's throw away.

"General Motors announced after everyone returned from the Thanksgiving holiday the plant would become 'unallocated,' meaning we wouldn't have a product," White explains, standing outside the UAW union hall in Greektown on a recent morning. He's still trying to understand management's decision to close the factory, which had also produced Chevy Spark electric motors, and to grasp the end of the automobile manufacturer's near-century history in his hometown.

"I'm 62. My wife wants me to retire, but I was hoping to work a few more years," White says. "We were still busy, working seven days a week a week to fill orders."

Two weeks later, walking a picket line outside the empty, 600,000-square-foot facility in support of the national strike that was eventually called by UAW, White continued to push the case for his plant. "We have experience in electric motors. We have experience in transmissions," he tells a reporter from *The Sun*. "This is a good-sized building. I don't care what we build. Scooters? Bicycles? Just give us something to build." Instead, the union hall itself is for sale.

The story began in the fall of 1934. With the automobile industry exploding, representatives from the Chevrolet Motor Company, a division of GM, came to town to put shovels in the dirt alongside then-Mayor Howard Jackson for the groundbreaking of a massive assembly and body plant at Broening Highway. A dozen years earlier, there had been one automobile on the road for every 11.5 Americans. By the time the plant opened, there was already one car for every four people. To keep pace, Chevrolet said the factory would be operational in record time, produce 80,000 vehicles a year, and, with the nation in the throes of the Great Depression, deliver 1,500-2,000 jobs. It was a godsend. City officials promised only Baltimoreans would be hired, and Chevy executives were fêted with a downtown parade.

Covering the equivalent of 40 football fields, the original GM plant consisted of five buildings, rail lines, driveways, walkways, test roads, and a parking lot for employees' cars. (At a recent UAW retirees meeting, 100 percent of the vehicles in the packed Oldham Street lot were American-made, 95 percent GM brands.) The first trucks and cars rolled off in March 1935. That May, the United Automobile Workers was founded in Detroit.

In Baltimore, the auto industry, GM, and the UAW would come of age together.

"It was a time of a huge organizing movement, in large part because New Deal policies and court decisions made it possible," Baltimore labor historian Bill Barry explains. "There were marches and tough sit-down strikes in the '30s, including a two-month strike in Flint [settled when Michigan Governor Frank Murphy negotiated GM's recognition of the UAW in 1937], and the creation of the National Labor Relations Board." Ford, which had set up a security and espionage unit within the company and was not reluctant to use violence against union organizers and sympathizers, didn't recognize the UAW until 1941. "By the 1950s, an era many people say they want to return to, more than a third of the U.S. workforce was represented by a union," Barry adds. "Today, it's 11 percent." Those union jobs at GM, as well as Bethlehem Steel, once the world's largest steel plant, became the bedrock of Southeast and East Baltimore neighborhoods in the city, and Dundalk, Turner Station, Rosedale, Parkville, Essex, and Middle River in the county.

"Half of Dundalk worked at Beth Steel, the other half at GM," says Fred Swanner, a past UAW Local 239 president, who graduated from Dundalk High School in 1968 and started at Broening Highway a few days later. "You didn't turn down a job that good. [Economists] say each job at a GM plant generates or affects five to seven other jobs, and someone in every household worked at one of those two places, or the Port, or a job that supported those industries." The Broening site, which over time tripled in size to 180 acres, sat inside the city line, with Dundalk on the other side. By 1960, with a population topping 85,000, Dundalk was the second-largest city in the state. But like Baltimore, it shed 30 percent of its population over the next few decades—the result of the city's and nation's deindustrialization—and long ago became a symbol of changing economic conditions. Jimmy's Famous Seafood remains on Holabird Avenue, but nearly every other GM post-shift bar and restaurant, like the Chevrolet Inn and Poncabird Pub, to name two, have disappeared.

Looking for a real-time bellwether? A one-million-square-foot Amazon fulfillment center sprang up on the exact site of the demolished Broening Highway plant in 2015. It was no small coincidence that at Sparrows Point, atop the same grounds where Baltimore steelworkers smelted the iron ore that built the Golden Gate Bridge and the Empire State Building—and the muscle cars down the road at GM—a second, 855,000-square-foot Amazon fulfillment center popped up last year. Needless to say, the thousands of packaging jobs at Amazon—the highest-valued company in the world, owned by the wealthiest man in the world—pay half the wages of a union steel or automobile job. And they don't include the health, pension, vacation, sick, and family leave benefits, nor the job protections that typically come with a collective bargaining agreement. From August 2017 to September 2018, for example, 300 workers were fired from the Amazon fulfillment center at Broening Highway, according to documents from a recent wrongful termination suit. "It's a sign of the times," Barry laments. "But it's up to them to organize," he says of Amazon workers.

Meanwhile, GM's decision to close its modernized White Marsh plant remains frustrating, to say the least, for UAW members and the elected officials who fought for $115 million in local, state, and federal grants to build its electric motors operation in 2012. That money came on top of a federal, $50-billion bailout loan (cost to taxpayers: $11.2 billion) during GM's 2009 bankruptcy.

Worth highlighting: GM earned $35 billion in North America profits over the past three years. Barra, whose father was a UAW tool-and-die maker for 39 years, makes 295 times the average employee and took home nearly $22 million last year.

At 18, White, the future UAW shop steward, had enrolled at then-Towson State University after graduating from Perry Hall High School in 1975. But he quickly realized he didn't want to sit in a class-room for another four years. He liked working with his hands and figuring out how things functioned and took a job in a motorcycle shop. Riding was a hobby. He realized soon enough, however, the pay wasn't going to cut it. He tried driving a truck. Again, he didn't see a future in it for himself. "I couldn't take staring at the road all day," he says. Eventually, an acquaintance, and good math scores, landed him a steamfitter apprenticeship. It was a path to earning a genuine living, and he asked his girlfriend, now-wife Clare, to marry him. Following assignments at the former Hawkins Point Glidden Paint factory and toxic Allied Chemical plant in Harbor East ("You could see the vapors rising toward the skylight windows"), he was relieved when he got switched to the Broening plant. He quit the steamfitters local to join the UAW just after GM awarded the plant a major minivan contract. For the next two decades, sturdy, no-frills Astros and Safaris were the plant's lifeline. When sales slipped in the early 2000s, GM pulled the plug on the facility without ever bothering to upgrade the minivan's design or retool for another product.

White, fortunately, had already moved to the White Marsh transmission plant. As the Broening facility wound down, 2,100 UAW members were forced to other plants, mostly in Michigan and Texas. "I was lucky," he says.

He and Clare had bought a brick, Cape Cod-style home in Parkville. Four bedrooms, two upstairs and two downstairs. They raised three kids there and sent them to college. They vacationed at Ocean City. "Do you get rich working in a union? No. Was it easy? No," says White, who, at 6-foot-1, remains solidly built. "Working in an auto plant isn't for everyone. But being part of a union meant my wife could be with the kids. It meant we worked with a sense of purpose and dignity, which was important to me, personally. Even before I was hired there, my father drove Chevrolets because that's where people who lived in our neighborhood worked. You know, there still isn't anything out of Germany or Japan that's better than the Allison transmissions we made.

"I got 30 years in and can retire with a pension," he says. "I joined the UAW in 1985, the beginning of the end for manufacturing and union jobs in this country. I tell people I feel like a surfer who caught the last wave."

170. The Life of Reilly

Mary Carol Reilly refused to drop her drawers in a room full of men. Even at gunpoint. "I thought, 'This is it, I will just have to die right here,'" the 77-year-old former nun-in-training, one-time Romper Room teacher, erstwhile actress, ex-cabbie, and still-serious poker player recalls with a blue-eyed twinkle.

Armed robbers had busted into the illegal backroom poker game in Greektown where she had a seat at one of the playing tables—the only woman there—and told everyone to stand, face the wall, and pull down their pants to their ankles. "They broke in yelling, 'Mother-effer this, Mother-effer that' and pistol-whipped one guy because he wouldn't, or couldn't, open the safe. The guy next to me was shaking like a leaf. I put my hand on his shoulder to steady him."

Known in local poker lore as "The Hold'em Hold up," the 2006 stick-up gained real notoriety because of what happened next. A player who had stepped out moments before to call his girlfriend heard the commotion and flagged down a patrol car. Police broke up the heist—the bandits had been tipped off about the high-stakes game— and recovered almost $24,000.

Such games, often moving from site to site, were common around the city before the Horseshoe Casino opened, Reilly notes, and high-profile attorneys and cops themselves sometimes got busted for taking part. How a former Catholic postulant, who became Chicago television's *Romper Room* teacher in the late 1960s—and later acted in national commercials with Jodie Foster, the Pillsbury Doughboy, and

Folger's Mrs. Olsen—ended up in Greektown is a circuitous story. Among other highlights from her Zelig-like journey: Reilly was in the courtroom galley during the Manson trial and nearly got tossed out after she began sobbing when the details of Sharon Tate's death were presented. She landed a bit part in the groundbreaking '70s TV series *All in Family*, from which she still receives the occasional 17-cent royalty check, she drove a cab in Hollywood, hosted a talk show on WJZ (Phil Donahue was once a guest), volunteered in New Orleans after Katrina, and taught English in China. In between, she taught literature to Archdiocese of Baltimore middle-schoolers for 25 years.

"If you want to understand my life," she volunteers before, yes, a lively poker game including several political types at a secret backroom location in Southeast Baltimore, "you've got to understand I was always running away from three things: my mother, the Catholic Church, and Baltimore."

But always running back, too.

Reilly grew up in a multi-generation household near Pimlico (she snuck in to pet the horses as a girl), the daughter of a depressive alcoholic father, who ran the family's downtown leather shop, and an overworked, neurotic, repressed, loving, and kind mother.

After attending the Catholic, all-girls Seton High, Reilly started at what is now Frostburg University before quitting to join the Sisters of St. Cyril and Methodius convent in rural Pennsylvania. "A girl I had a crush on left school to get married, and that had broken my heart," recalls Reilly, who was still coming to terms with her own sexuality.

However, after learning of her parents' mental health issues (her father had undergone electroshock therapy), the convent asked her to leave. A few years later, her beloved younger brother's suicide sent her into a half-decade alcoholic tailspin. She's been sober for 44 years.

In the early 1970s, Reilly finally told her mother she was gay (by then, Reilly was sharing an apartment in New York with a prominent women's rights leader). She and her mother were driving to Sunday Mass at St. Patrick's. Initially, her mother appeared more flummoxed than shocked or angry. "We were in the car, just me and her, and I'll never forget it, she said, 'What do you do?' I said, 'Mother! I don't ask what you and Daddy do.'

"We didn't talk the rest of the way. Then, as we were walking up the steps to St. Patrick's, she slipped her arm underneath my arm. The sweetest gesture. Said more than any words."

The poker, she explains, is social and competitive, which she likes, but also soothing, keeping her mind focused on the game and people around her. She's competed twice in World Series of Poker tournaments in Las Vegas, never winning, nor losing, outrageous money.

At Delaware Park, she's known as "Sister Mary," which she doesn't mind. On occasion, she'll hear, "Nice hand, Granny," which she does. "I told one guy, 'F--- you,' and they threw me out."

171. Picture This

Monica Bland isn't sure what made her veer from her usual route. She was picking up her godchildren one afternoon last year when she mistakenly took a different turn and suddenly found herself staring up at a two-story image of a family of nine shopping for Easter shoes. It was a mural recreated from a 1956 photograph in the *Baltimore Afro-American* newspaper. "And I realized, as the faces in the mural are looking back at me, that I know this family," recounts Bland, who runs a small local business. "It's my grandparents, all my aunts, my uncle, and my mother."

Michael Owen, of Baltimore Love Project renown, painted the larger-than-life black-and-white image as it appeared in print on Holy Saturday. It's not quite photorealism, but it's close enough given the rough-concrete sidewall of the Midtown rowhouse where the work towers over an otherwise empty lot.

In fact, the mural is a collaboration between Owen and photographer Webster Phillips, whose grandfather, Henry Phillips, shot the picture for the *Afro-American*. The plaque next to the mural implored viewers to reach out to the younger Phillips if they could ID the people featured: "Help us save Baltimore history." Startled, and moved, Bland called.

"I was blown away," Phillips says. "You hope you get a call like that. You don't really expect it."

Phillips has spent the past several years digitizing his grandfather's work—some 10,000 images to date, mostly shot between 1945 and

1965—organizing gallery shows, posting photographs across social media, and now venturing to senior centers in hopes of identifying more folks in the photos.

Fortunately, the elder Phillips, who died in 1993, stored all his negatives, allowing for the creation of new, authentic, hi-resolution reproductions. (There's actually three generations of Phillips photographers. Henry Phillips's son and Webster Phillips's father, Irving Phillips, became *The Sun*'s first Black photographer.) There was simply no one else documenting mid-century Black Baltimore life like Henry Phillips did at a time when new flash and film technology enabled photographers to ditch their tripods, become mobile, and capture moments as they happened.

To date, the cache includes photos of Louis Armstrong blowing his horn backstage at the Royal Theatre, Billie Holiday shopping on Pennsylvania Avenue, Ella Fitzgerald playing ping-pong in a fur coat, Duke Ellington performing in Baltimore, Joe Louis boxing *and golfing* in Baltimore, Jackie Robinson at spring training, and a singularly poignant photo of former First Lady Jacqueline Kennedy comforting Coretta Scott King in a private moment at her husband's funeral in 1968.

Equally compelling, significant, and gorgeous are the portraits that Henry Phillips took of everyday Baltimoreans: a child eating cotton candy, students roller-skating at recess, the first Black graduate in a sea of white faces and white uniforms at the Naval Academy, women on their way to church in their Sunday best, and *Afro-American* cartoonist Thomas Stockett at his drafting table.

"I thought Henry Phillips was a very quiet, understated man on a mission," Leslie King-Hammond, founding director of the Center for Race and Culture at the Maryland Institute College of Art, once said. "He told the other side of the story—that, in spite of the hardships of being an African American in this country, we still made a life of substance and meaning, and dignity and elegance."

Webster Phillips says, for him, the best thing about working with his grandfather's collection isn't actually the photographs themselves but the feeling of walking in his grandfather's shoes.

"He took pictures everywhere he went," Phillips says. "He'd come home from work, stop, and take a portrait of someone he met outside a corner store, develop it, and give to him. And then, I'm also with him at the 1963 March on Washington. I've looked at more than 10,000 of his photographs. Think about it. It's like going through your grandfather's Instagram or Facebook. Wouldn't you like to do that?"

Acknowledgements

This book owes an enormous debt to *Baltimore* magazine editor-in-chief Max Weiss, who trusts me (most of the time) to come back with a story as I chase my curiosity down the alleyways of this city. And also to my other colleagues at the magazine, most notably Jane Marion, Ken Iglehart, and Lydia Woolever, who along with Max, have served as trusted first-readers and editors of these stories over the years. Former arts and culture editor Lauren LaRocca, a great friend and collaborator, gave the entire re-worked collection an initial round of invaluable editing, for which I am extremely grateful. Of my wonderful and supportive partner, Helen Yuen, all I can say is thank you for everything, including your willingness to share your kitchen table with my laptop. More than anyone else, however, this collection owes its existence to Dick Basoco, who led *Baltimore* magazine for two decades before "retiring" (he remained an indispensable sounding board) at the end of 2017. Dick passed away after a long illness as this book was going to print. His encouragement, subtle and otherwise, integrity, intelligence, and deep commitment to the magazine, storytelling, and the staff, made not just the publication better but the people at *Baltimore* magazine better, including myself.

About the Author

Ron Cassie is a senior editor at *Baltimore* magazine, where he's won national awards for his coverage of the death of Freddie Gray, sea-level rise on the Eastern Shore, and the opioid epidemic in Hagerstown. He reported from Haiti in the days following the tragic earthquake, New Orleans in the aftermath of Hurricane Katrina, and from Uganda as part of a humanitarian relief effort. His work has appeared as a notable selection in *The Best of American Sports Writing*, in partnership with the Pulitzer Center, at *CityLab*, in *Newsweek, Huffington Post, Grist, The New York Daily News, The Baltimore Sun*, several alternative weeklies, including *Baltimore City Paper*, and *Urbanite*, where he served as editor-in-chief before coming to *Baltimore*. He has been a finalist for the Folio and City and Regional Magazine Association Writer of the Year awards. He is a two-time Religion Writer of the Year runner-up. He holds master's degrees from Georgetown University and The Johns Hopkins University, and teaches feature writing at Towson University. Prior to becoming a full-time journalist, he spent almost two decades swinging a hammer, riding a bike, and pouring drinks for a living.

CPSIA information can be obtained
at www.ICGtesting.com
Printed in the USA
BVHW090351071220
594776BV00002B/95